Promoting Wellness and Resiliency in Correctional Officers

Correctional officers face considerable stress, risk, and danger that lead to poor physical and mental health outcomes. In fact, their life expectancy is 15 years shorter than the national average. Public perception and media portrayals of correctional officers tend to reinforce stereotypes of brutish, improper, and uncontrolled behavior. Yet the reality is that correctional officers are operating a default public and mental health system for a sizeable portion of our society, a responsibility that exposes them to considerable risk. These negative effects have been compounded by an international staffing crisis that has made our jails and prisons far less safe for working officers. To address this situation, this book features an examination of a combined 11,313 correctional officers and 42 of their family members in the United States, Canada, and Europe. It explores proactive strategies that can reduce rates of posttraumatic stress disorder (PTSD) in correctional officers, which currently surpasses those found in returning military veterans who experienced combat. It then delves into the dynamics of correctional officer suicide, featuring the perspectives of their families. This book highlights innovative approaches that can build on existing strengths including the role of international exchange programs. It presents universal themes that impact the safety, wellbeing, and resiliency of correctional officers, along with positive outcomes related to evidence-based programs that maximize health in the correctional workplace. This book will be of interest to researchers and advanced students of criminology, mental health, public policy, social work, and sociology.

The chapters in this book were originally published as a special issue of the journal *Criminal Justice Studies*.

Hayden P. Smith is Professor of Criminology and Criminal Justice at the University of South Carolina. His principal focus of study is the intersection of the criminal justice and public health systems. This includes self-injurious and suicide behaviors in incarcerated populations, the physical and mental health needs of incarcerated populations, best practices for inmate reentry and reintegration, jail diversion, and supporting safety, wellbeing, and resiliency in correctional staff. Dr. Smith has expertise in program evaluation and policy analysis, and he has worked with numerous correctional and health systems. Dr. Smith's previous publications have appeared in *Justice Quarterly, Crime & Delinquency*, and *Criminal Justice & Behavior*.

Promoting Wellness and Resiliency in Correctional Officers

Edited by
Hayden P. Smith

Routledge
Taylor & Francis Group
LONDON AND NEW YORK

First published 2023
by Routledge
4 Park Square, Milton Park, Abingdon, Oxon OX14 4RN

and by Routledge
605 Third Avenue, New York, NY 10158

Routledge is an imprint of the Taylor & Francis Group, an informa business

British Library Cataloguing in Publication Data
A catalogue record for this book is available from the British Library

ISBN13: 978-1-032-40702-9 (hbk)
ISBN13: 978-1-032-40709-8 (pbk)
ISBN13: 978-1-003-35439-0 (ebk)

DOI: 10.4324/9781003354390

Typeset in Myriad Pro
by Newgen Publishing UK

Publisher's Note
The publisher accepts responsibility for any inconsistencies that may have arisen during the conversion of this book from journal articles to book chapters, namely the inclusion of journal terminology.

This book is dedicated to Xosé Cristian Flores
Gracias a ti, este mundo es un mejor lugar para muchos.
Te recordaremos siempre por tu luz, amor, alegría
y por enseñarnos a vivir en el presente.

Contents

Citation Information

The chapters in this book were originally published in the journal *Criminal Justice Studies*, volume 34, issue 4 (2021). When citing this material, please use the original page numbering for each article, as follows:

Chapter 1

Introduction
Hayden P. Smith
Criminal Justice Studies, volume 34, issue 4 (2021), pp. 353–360

Chapter 2

Exploring organizational risk factors for health & wellness problems in correctional officers
Logan Lavender and Natalie Todak
Criminal Justice Studies, volume 34, issue 4 (2021), pp. 361–379

Chapter 3

Stress doesn't kill us, it's our reaction: exploring the relationship between coping mechanisms and correctional officer PTSD
Katie Hughes Taylor and Kristin Swartz
Criminal Justice Studies, volume 34, issue 4 (2021), pp. 380–396

Chapter 4

Clarifying the role of officer coping on turnover in corrections
Jessie Harney and Amy E. Lerman
Criminal Justice Studies, volume 34, issue 4 (2021), pp. 397–422

Chapter 5

Barriers to help-seeking among correction officers: examining the influence of institutional culture and structure
Candence Wills, Kayla Bates, Natasha A. Frost and Carlos. E. Monteiro
Criminal Justice Studies, volume 34, issue 4 (2021), pp. 423–440

Chapter 6

Job demands, organizational justice, and emotional exhaustion in prison officers
Andrew James Clements and Gail Kinman
Criminal Justice Studies, volume 34, issue 4 (2021), pp. 441–458

Chapter 7

AMStrength program in Canadian federal correctional services: correctional officers' views and interpretations
Rosemary Ricciardelli, Marcella Siqueira Cassiano, Michael Adorjan and Meghan M. Mitchell
Criminal Justice Studies, volume 34, issue 4 (2021), pp. 459–476

Chapter 8

A comparative perspective on officer wellness: american reflections from norwegian prisons
Veronica L. Horowitz, Emily R. Greberman, Patrick E. Nolan, Jordan M. Hyatt, Chris Uggen, Synøve N. Andersen and Steven L. Chanenson
Criminal Justice Studies, volume 34, issue 4 (2021), pp. 477–497

Notes on Contributors

Michael Adorjan is Associate Professor in the Department of Sociology at the University of Calgary, Canada and Fellow with the Centre for Criminology, University of Hong Kong. His recent research and teaching focus on youth and cyber-risk, privacy, and surveillance.

Synøve N. Andersen is Postdoctoral Fellow at the Department of Sociology and Human Geography, University of Oslo, Norway. Broadly speaking Andersen's work has focused on the ways in which public policy affects individual behavior, and in particular in the ways in which correctional policy and programming affect employment, family relations and recidivism. She also works on co-offending networks and is especially interested in the processes that precede co-offending and the effect of co-offending on subsequent criminal behavior.

Kayla Bates is Doctoral Student at the College of Social Sciences and Humanities Northeastern University, USA. Kayla's research interests focus on the impact of trauma among various populations within correctional environments, specifically the impact of adverse childhood experiences.

Steven L. Chanenson is Professor of Law and Faculty Director of the David F. and Constance B. Girard-diCarlo Center for Ethics, Integrity and Compliance, at the Villanova University, USA. He writes primarily in the areas of sentencing and criminal procedure. Professor Chanenson has frequently spoken on sentencing before groups of judges, lawyers, and policy makers, including the U.S. Sentencing Commission, the Pennsylvania Conference of State Trial Judges, the annual Judicial Conference for the U.S. Court of Appeals for the Ninth Circuit, and the Federal Judicial Center.

Andrew James Clements is an occupational psychologist registered with the Health and Care Professions Council, and an Associate Fellow of the British Psychological Society. Andrew's research interests include wellbeing at work, and participatory approaches to organisational development.

Natasha A. Frost is Professor of Criminology and Criminal Justice at the College of Social Sciences and Humanities, Northeastern University, USA. Her research involves collaborating with criminal justice agencies to evaluate practices, increase effectiveness, improve employee safety and wellness, and strengthen community perceptions of the criminal justice system.

Emily R. Greberman is Masters Student at the Department of Criminology, University of Pennsylvania, USA. Her research interests include prison reform, juvenile justice, and using social media as a criminological tool.

Jessie Harney is PhD Student at the Goldman School of Public Policy, University of California, Berkeley, USA. Her research interests are in criminal justice system reform with a specific focus on mental health and improving outcomes for those whose lives are impacted by the carceral system.

Veronica L. Horowitz is Assistant Professor at the Department of Sociology, University at Buffalo, The State University of New York, USA. Broadly, her research focuses on American criminal punishment with subfoci on mercy, gender, and social stratification.

Jordan M. Hyatt is Associate Professor at the Department of Criminology and Justice Studies, Drexel University, USA. Hyatt works to develop effective and actionable criminal justice policies. Hyatt's work is relevant for agencies with policy agendas focused on improving reintegration, public safety, and implementing evidence-based policies.

Gail Kinman is a chartered psychologist and Fellow of the BPS and the ASS. She is Visiting Professor of Occupational Health Psychology at Birkbeck, University of London, UK. Gail has published widely in the field of occupational health psychology, with a particular interest in the wellbeing of people working in emotionally demanding jobs such as health and social care and the emergency and security services.

Logan Lavender is Graduate Research Assistant at the Department of Criminal Justice, University of Alabama at Birmingham, USA.

Amy E. Lerman is the Michelle Schwartz Endowed Professor of Public Policy and Political Science and Director of the Possibility Lab at the University of California, Berkeley, USA. Her research focuses on issues of race, public opinion, and political behavior, especially as they relate to punishment and social inequality in America.

Meghan M. Mitchell is Assistant Professor at the Department of Criminal Justice, University of North Dakota. Her current research examines the areas of corrections, subcultures, re-entry, and research methodologies.

Carlos. E. Monteiro is Assistant Professor at the Sociology Department, Suffolk University, USA. His research focuses largely on corrections and punishment with a specific focus on recidivism and re-entry.

Patrick E. Nolan is Senior Undergraduate Student at the University of Minnesota, Twin Cities, USA, majoring in Sociology of Law, Criminology, and Deviance. His research interests include incarceration, penology, and recidivism.

Rosemary Ricciardelli is Research Chair in Safety, Security, and Wellness, Professor of Maritime Studies, at the Fisheries and Marine Institute at Memorial University of Newfoundland. Her research centers on evolving understandings of gender, vulnerabilities, risk, and experiences and issues within different facets of the criminal justice system.

Marcella Siqueira Cassiano is Postdoctoral Research Fellow at the Sociology Department, Memorial University, Newfoundland, Canada. Her research focuses on surveillance, correctional services, and mental health.

Hayden P. Smith is Professor of Criminology and Criminal Justice at the University of South Carolina, USA. His principal focus of study is the intersection of the criminal justice and public health systems. This includes self-injurious and suicide behaviors in incarcerated populations, the physical and mental health needs of incarcerated populations, best practices for inmate reentry and reintegration, jail diversion, and supporting safety, well-being, and resiliency in correctional staff.

Kristin Swartz is Associate Professor at the Criminal Justice Department, University of Louisville, USA. Her research interests tend to center on how offending and victimization are shaped by context, with a special focus on the role of cultural effects in the contexts of schools, neighborhoods, and social networks.

Katie Hughes Taylor is Assistant Professor at the Criminal Justice Department, Central State University in Ohio, USA. Her research interests include jails, prisons, and correctional officer health and wellness.

Natalie Todak is Associate Professor at the Department of Criminal Justice, University of Alabama at Birmingham, USA. She studies policing using mixed and qualitative research methods. Dr Todak's research involves collaborating with criminal justice agencies to evaluate practices, increase effectiveness, improve employee safety and wellness, and strengthen community perceptions of the criminal justice system.

Chris Uggen is Regents Professor and Martindale Chair in Sociology and Law at the University of Minnesota, USA. His current projects include a comparative study of reentry from different types of institutions, sexual harassment and employment discrimination, crime and justice after genocide, monetary sanctions, and the health effects of incarceration

Candence Wills is Doctoral Candidate at the College of Social Sciences and Humanities, Northeastern University, USA. Her research focus is primarily on trafficking in persons and institutional responses to marginalized populations, including racial/ethnic minorities, gender, sexual minorities in domestic and international context.

Introduction

Hayden P. Smith

During 2021 the National Institute of Corrections (NIC) approached me to conduct a webinar on the topic of 'Promoting Wellness and Resiliency in Correctional Staff'. My approach when conducting and presenting research on the health of correctional staff centers on maximizing partnerships between academics and practitioners, with the goal of providing conceptual frameworks that can drive real-world programs and policies (Smith, 2021; Smith, Power, Usher, Sitren, & Slade, 2019; Smith & Ferdik, 2016). As such, it was an easy decision to build on an existing partnership between me (an academic) and a very experienced and knowledgeable practitioner: Ms. Karin Ho (Division Director, Victim Services & CISM Program: Critical Incident Stress Management, South Carolina Department of Corrections). This webinar was initiated and developed by Mr. Scott Richards, Correctional Program Specialist, Prisons Division, and his team at the National Institute of Corrections (NIC). As the webinar date approached the National Institute of Corrections contacted the presenters to inform us that the audience response was unprecedented, and they could not add more participants due to a bandwidth limitations. The webinar was a success, and the day of live broadcast there were over 1,200 participants, from all US states and ranging from academics to practitioners from institutional and community corrections of all ranks and working in diverse settings. Participants continue to view the recorded video posted at the National Institute of Corrections (NIC) and email the team with follow-up questions, comments, and seeking more information (Smith & Ho, 2021). The webinar can be found here: https://nicic.gov/promoting-wellness-and-resiliency-correctional-staff

The experience was very gratifying but also sobering. These practitioners working in our jails, prisons, probation, parole, juvenile detention, and other community settings expressed a strong need for any guidance or information on how to support the wellness and resiliency of correctional staff. While I was honored to provide conceptual and research-based suggestions and Ms. Karin Ho detailed real-world programs for staff wellness, it was clear that we were communicating with an audience who were seeking practical solutions while struggling to work in the midst of a staffing-health crisis. The NIC webinar was the impetus for this special edition on correctional officer wellness and resiliency.

The conversation about the health and wellbeing of correctional officers is reflective of recent social changes. While antiquated textbooks focus on the punitive 'get tough on crime' incarceration policies that led to overcrowded jails and prisons, a more contemporary perspective recognizes that this narrative is no longer accurate. Two factors in particular, incarceration rates and unemployment, have created a new reality for the criminal justice system. With regard to the former, the United States has experienced declining incarceration rates for decades, from 980 per 100,000 adult U.S. residents held in state or federal prisons or local jails at year-end 2009, to 810 per 100,000 at year-end 2019 (Minton, Beatty, & Zeng, 2021). The U.S. incarceration rate is the lowest it's been since 1995 (Minton et al., 2021). With regard to the later, in 2019 the national unemployment rate dropped 0.3 percentage points to 3.5%, leading to the lowest jobless rate in 50 years (Edwards & Smith, 2020). Reduced incarceration rates and low unemployment are a blessing for mainstream society, though a curse for corrections.

Correctional agencies faced the challenge of attracting and retaining correctional officers, in many cases to fill large gaps of retiring baby boomers and a thriving job market. This created a staffing crisis whereby correctional agencies would attempt to mass-hire new correctional officers, along with new incentives like signing bonuses, and improved health care and retirement packages, only to have these new employees' 'ghost' when they found a more preferable job. This destructive cycle was already established prior to the impact of the COVID-19 pandemic which has produced the most significant decarceration of jails and prisons in modern history. Minton, Zeng, and Maruschak (2021) found that in the month of March 2020 there was an 18% reduction in the jail population, followed by an 11% reduction in April, producing the lowest U.S. jail population since 1996. At mid-year 2019, the total occupied bed space in all U.S. jails was 81% and by midyear 2020 occupied bed space had fallen to 60% (Minton et al., 2021). These data do not indicate an overabundance of inmates but rather they are an indication of an absence of correctional officers.

For the correctional officers who remain employed in jails and prisons the research documenting their working experience is disheartening. Exposure to a range of dangers, risks, and stressors lead to correctional officer's disproportionately experiencing poor physical and mental health outcomes (Ferdik & Smith, 2017). The list of potential risks is so overwhelming that researchers use categories as a means of grouping them by common features. For example, Ferdik and Smith (2017) used work-related dangers (e.g. exposure to infectious disease, violence, etc.), institutional-related dangers (e.g. role ambiguity, role conflict, understaffing, etc.), psycho-social dangers (e.g. work and family conflict, media scrutiny, etc.), mental health risks (e.g. stress, burnout, substance abuse disorders, etc.), and physical health risks (e.g. injuries and death) to understand these risks. Correctional officers perceive that working in a jail or prison is a direct threat to their health and these perceptions are accurate. Correctional officers have lower rates of physical and mental health compared to their counterparts working elsewhere in criminal justice, first responders, and security occupations (Clements & Kinman, 2020). In fact, when researchers from other disciplines study correctional officers they are surprised by the chronically low levels of mental and physical health (Clements & Kinman, 2020). Correctional officers also die earlier, at an average of 59 years of age, some 15 years less than the average age of death of the general public (Cheek, 1984; New Jersey Police Suicide Task Force, 2009). This early mortality includes increased risk of suicide, with correctional officers dying by suicide at rates of 39% higher than the general working-age population, and double that of law enforcement officers (New Jersey Police Suicide Task Force, 2009; Stack & Tsoudis, 1997).

The paramilitary structure of correctional agencies can create a work culture where emotions are suppressed and seeking help is viewed as a weakness. Correctional officers are often unable and/or unwilling to share their traumatic experiences with family, friends, or the general public (who are often already biased due to negative media portrayals). A natural response to such stress is to attack or withdraw. Attack is the most common emotional response, as correctional officers experience high rates of work conflict with supervisors and administrators (much more than conflict with inmates). Correctional officers often battle ineffective leadership, vacillating and nonsensical policies, and apathetic support for their needs. This produces cynicism, burnout, and a reduction in the quality and enjoyment of work. These officers become hypervigilant to the risks that surround them and without pro-social outlets or support this stress manifests in the body. As van der Kolk states, 'trauma comes back as a reaction not a memory' (see van der Kolk, 2014). For correctional officers who withdraw, their family and friends become concerned about their isolation and detachment, they may engage in alcohol and/or substance abuse, and develop self-harming and other dangerous behaviors. Over time absenteeism increases, and so does staff turnover. Between 2000–2008, approximately 16% of all correctional officers left their job after only three years (Management and Training Corporation, 2011). In the United States, some state prison agencies experience 35% of correctional officers voluntarily resigning in a single year (Ferdik & Smith, 2017). As mentioned, correctional agencies attempt to increase signing bonuses and incentive health benefits and retirement packages, though the institutional factors remain the same, therefore the negative health outcomes in staff continue. This destructive cycle is not only inefficient and ineffective, but it is also unsustainable.

Correctional officers have been labeled, 'A Forgotten Profession,' due to the lack of research that documents their health, resiliency, and overall wellbeing (see Clements & Kinman, 2020). However, 'forgotten' implies that correctional officers were noticed in the first place. A more apt expression is that correctional officers are an 'Invisible Population'. If one examines pro-social interventions that demonstrated efficacy for front-line workers exposed to trauma, correctional officers are noticeably absent. For example, evidence-based yoga and mindfulness program occurring in correctional settings are frequently published in criminological journals. The effectiveness of yoga and mindfulness on inmate health is reinforced by randomized controlled studies (Kerekes, Fielding, & Apelqvist, 2017) and multiple systematic reviews and meta-analyses (see Auty, Cope, & Leibling, 2015). In contrast, empirical assessments of yoga and mindfulness programs on correctional officers are so rare and/or new, that they tend to be published as pilot studies in occupational health journals, with few examples in criminology or criminal justice journals. This does not reflect a reluctance of researchers to engage in work on correctional officers, but rather a bias towards inmates who tend to capture scholarly attention when compared to a largely 'invisible' work group of officers. This preference may also reflect available funding opportunities. However, with correctional systems now serving as default mental health facilities, there is value in an ecological approach where the health of all working groups is reinforced. The current approach requires the sick to treat the sick, and expect positive outcomes, which are unlikely and have not been forthcoming.

Invisibility may be preferable to the unfavorable media portrayals and public perceptions of correctional officers. Ray Surette (2015) writes that correctional officers are routinely portrayed as 'caricatures of brutality, incompetence, low intelligence, and indifference to human suffering' (p. 274). Such media stereotypes were evident during the Stanford Prison Experiment, which remains one of the most well-known psychological studies of correctional officer behavior. Despite being 50 years old, the legacy of the Stanford Prison Experiment has been solidified in movies, television shows, and college classrooms. However, the Stanford Prison Experiment is a textbook example of non-generalizability; it is based on a small convenience sample of privileged, white students enrolled at a prestigious university who had little experience or exposure to corrections, and it relies entirely on anecdotal evidence. Prior to the experiment Zimbardo coached students who were playing the correctional officer role to act in 'negative, hostile, affrontive and dehumanizing' ways (Haney, Banks, & Zimbardo, 1973, p. 80). Zimbardo did not include any correctional officers to provide insight or guidance, though he did consult with Carlo Prescott a former prison inmate, prior to the experiment. Prescott (2005) later said, 'At the time, I had hoped that I would help create a valid, intellectually honest indictment of the prison system. In hindsight, I blew it. I became an unwitting accomplice to a theatrical exercise that conveniently absolves all comers of personal responsibility for their abominable moral choices.' (2005, p. 5).

Such portrayals do a disservice to correctional officers, as well to science, as they begin with the conclusion and work backwards. There is no doubt that power of authority, aggression, cognitive dissonance, role ambiguity, and a host of other negative concepts are a feature of corrections. Yet studying these dynamics requires theoretical frameworks coupled with empirical data that can guide real-world policy solutions. This begins with researchers having an open and respectful approach to studying correctional officers and the milieus they work in. In an article titled 'Why Zimbardo's Prison Experiment Isn't in My Textbook' Peter Gray (2013) poses the following thoughtful question: 'What would have happened if Zimbardo had said to the guards, at the outset, that the purpose of the experiment was to prove that it is possible to be both a guard and a decent human being, or in some way implied that the goal was to prove that guards can be kind? I bet the results would have been entirely different. The "situation" would have been the same, but the "demand" would have been different and the results would have been different.' Instead, students were asked to 'act out their stereotyped views of what prisoners and guards do' (Gray, 2013), with participant Dave Eshelman becoming 'John Wayne' and mimicking a sadistic (though fictitious) correctional officer from the 1967 film Cool Hand Luke. Eshelman's total reliance on media portrayals of correctional officers was clear, as he later stated, 'I consciously created this persona. I was in all kinds of drama productions in high school and college. It was something I was very familiar with: to take on another personality before you step out on the stage' (Ratnesar, 2011). Without experience or contact with a correctional officer as part of the experiment, Eshelman deferred to theater, media portrayals, and public perceptions to construct his role.

Correctional officers have become one of the most invisible, misunderstood, and maligned working groups in our society. Additionally, prisons and jails remains the most secure and remote components of the criminal justice system and without direct experience, people are apt to rely on stereotypical media portrayals of correctional officers which are not only offensive but harmful. That's what makes this special edition so exceptional. It features a combined sample of 11,313 correctional officers and 42 of their family members, as well as, *a complete absence of secondary data*. Work such as this simply cannot be conducted from the confines of the Ivory Tower. Correctional officers are experts at recognizing authenticity, in fact their health, wellbeing, and lives depend on it. Effective correctional officers have an intuitive way of calculating honesty, openness, and integrity, and the data in the following studies suggest that these researchers passed the test. It is one thing to calculate a regression analysis using secondary data while sitting in a university office; it is another thing entirely to interact with a correctional officer who is weighing fear of ridicule or weakness from coworkers while trusting the ethics of a researcher and completing a survey that clearly reflects symptoms of mental distress, to taking American correctional officers on an intense experience in Norwegian prisons, and when conducting face-to-face interviews with family members of correctional officers who died by suicide. These are just some of the research foci that are in this special edition. That is not to say that this special edition does not contain theoretical approaches that use cutting edge quantitative and qualitative methods, but rather the very nature of the problem requires that researchers experience the field. There is no substitute for the quality surveys, interviews, and audio recordings, in this special edition.

The ethos of the special edition is such that a reader can select one article of interest or follow a sequence. This begins with three studies that employ theoretical approaches and statistical methods to assess the crisis of Post-Traumatic Stress Disorder (PTSD) that is chronically high in correctional officer populations within the United States. Lavender and Todak surveyed jail and prison officers in Washington State and report 'astronomical rates of PTSD' that not only surpass rates in law enforcement, but also war veterans. These researchers carefully articulate how this crisis is worsening and add policy implications to address the problem. This neatly transitions into Hughes-Taylor and Swartz's study of 245 correctional officers across seven adult state institutions engaged in a mindfulness program designed to reduce stress. What emerged was the important finding that coping styles can determine risk of PTSD, particularly the concepts of planning and denial. Researchers from UC Berkeley, Harney and Lerman, provide further insight on PTSD by drawing on the Stress Process Paradigm to model the relationship between exposure to violence and mental health. This sample of 8,334 correctional officers from every state prison in California is analyzed using structural equation modeling and highlights the divergent pathways of problem-focused coping versus avoidant coping. While I cannot do these articles justice in this introduction, they indicate that something positive happens when correctional officers are provided prosocial interventions that allow them to talk with someone they trust.

A natural fit for this special edition is a study from a research team out of Northeastern University, and Suffolk University, both located in Massachusetts. Wills, Bates, Frost and Monteiro examine the barriers that inhibit correctional officers from seeking help. This includes a content analysis of 42 semi-structured interviews with family members and friends of correction officers who died by suicide and 395 interviews with officers working for a state department of corrections. This work requires one to look into the darkness to find the light, and these researchers should be praised for engaging in such potentially traumatizing work. These data are rich, and they are presented as subthemes around institutional culture and structure, particularly the role of power hierarchies, mental illness stigma, patient confidentiality, and the need for supportive working environments in corrections.

The three remaining studies are compatible as they occur in international contexts, with findings clearly generalizable to numerous correctional settings. Clements and Kinman are occupational health experts in the UK who surveyed 1,792 correctional officers working in prison. They employed the Jobs Demands-Resources Model in order to test a number of occupational and organizational stressors that lead to burnout. Clements and Kinman present the policy implications of these risks with a particular focus on the need to manage the workload of correctional officers. In Canada, the team of Ricciardelli, Cassiano, Adorjan, and Mitchell use semi-structured interviews to examine the effectiveness of the Advanced Mental Strength and Conditioning (AMStrength) program on 70 correctional officers. This study provides support for programs like AMStrength improving the mental health of correctional officers. Another innovative study is provided by Horowitz, Greberman, Nolan, Hyatt, Uggen, Andersen, and Chanenson as they assess the experiences of twelve correctional officers from Pennsylvania who travelled to Norway as part of a correctional exchange program. Data collection occurred daily via audio recordings and surveys that fully document the reactions of these correctional officers. American officers were paired with mentors working in Norwegian prison, and the results demonstrate the remarkable power of experiential learning. These studies highlight the universal themes that impact the wellbeing and resiliency of correctional officers, along with positive outcomes related to programs that maximize health in the workplace.

I am very proud of the academic studies in this special edition. They represent a range of academic disciplines, theoretical approaches, methodological techniques, and most of all, real-world policy implications. These articles meet the challenge that is best articulated by Horowitz and colleagues in this special edition, namely that the 'extant literature on CO experiences focuses almost exclusively on CO *unwellness*'. It is no longer an acceptable practice to publish studies of risk factors, dangers, stressors, and poor health outcomes for correctional officers only to offer a conclusion of 'more research needed'. This approach does not help address the current crisis in correctional officers. Instead, research must offer support for this vulnerable population in order that they can balance public safety with supporting the needs of other vulnerable populations, that is, other correctional staff, correctional administrators, and of course, offenders and inmates.

While the challenge may be daunting, there are recent efforts beyond this special edition worth mentioning. The National Institute of Corrections (NIC) and National Institute of Justice (NIJ) increasingly recognized the need for funding, resources and scholarly attention to promote Correctional Officer Wellness and Resiliency. Researchers are becoming more involved in studying the dilemma of correctional officer health, often with expertise and partnerships from external health care agencies. Correctional agencies are increasingly creating 'Employee Wellness Centers' with dedicated and trained staff who provide a holistic approach to improving health. I hope this continues. For people reading this special edition I hope you find it enjoyable, thought provoking, and optimistic. It is important to note that this special edition would not be possible without the support and kindness of Editors Richard Tewksbury and David Baker, both very experienced researchers who support the need to improve the health of correctional officers. Thank you both for allowing me the opportunity to serve as guest editor on this topic.

As a final mention, this special edition is dedicated to the men and women who work in our corrections system. These correctional officers face a concentration of complex problems that society has placed in the 'too hard' basket and tried to forget. These officers experience exposure to a range of psychological and physical dangers, and some don't come home from work. They are often invisible, disparaged, and powerless. Yet they serve a fundamental role in the modern-day criminal justice system. The uniqueness of the working life of correctional officers is captured by the reflection that law enforcement often see people at their worst, courts often see people at their best, but corrections tends to see people as they truly are. I hope this special edition provides one small step towards honoring the work that correctional officers perform.

Disclosure statement

No potential conflict of interest was reported by the author(s).

References

Auty, K.M., Cope, A., & Liebling, A. (2015). A systematic review and meta-analysis of yoga and mindfulness meditation in prison: Effects on psychological well-being and behavioural functioning. *International Journal of Offender Therapy and Comparative Criminology, 61*(6), 689–710.

Cheek, F.E. (1984). *Stress management for correctional officers and their families*. Alexandria, VA: American Correctional Association.

Clements, A.J., & Kinman, G. (2020). A forgotten profession: The need to invest in the wellbeing of prison officers. In P. Birth, and L.A. Sicard (Eds.), *Prisons and community corrections: Critical issues and emerging controversies* (1st ed.). London: Routledge .

Edwards, R., & Smith, S.M. (2020, April). *Job market remains tight in 2019, as the unemployment rate falls to its lowest level since 1969*. Monthly Labor Review, U.S. Bureau of Labor Statistics. Retrieved from https://www.bls.gov/opub/mlr/2020/article/job-market-remains-tight-in-2019-as-the-unemployment-rate-falls-to-its-lowest-level-since-1969.htm#_edn4

Ferdik, F., & Smith, H.P. (2017). *Correctional Officer Safety and Wellness Literature Synthesis*. U.S. Department of Justice, Office of Justice Programs, National Institute of Justice . Retrieved from https://www.ncjrs.gov/pdffiles1/nij/250484.pdf

Ferdik, F.V., & Smith, H.P. (2016). Maximum security correctional officers: An exploratory investigation into their social bases of power. *American Journal of Criminal Justice, 41*(3), 498–521.

Gray, P. (2013). Why Zimbardo's prison experiment isn't in my textbook. Retrieved from https://www.psychologytoday.com/us/blog/freedom-learn/201310/why-zimbardo-s-prison-experiment-isn-t-in-my-textbook

Haney, C., Banks, C., & Zimbardo, P. (1973). Interpersonal dynamics in a simulated prison. *International Journal of Criminology & Penology, 1*(1), 69–97.

Kerekes, N., Fielding, C., & Apelqvist, S. (2017). Yoga in correctional settings: A randomized controlled study. *Frontiers in Psychiatry, 8*, 204.

Management and Training Corporation. (2011). *Correctional officers: Strategies to improve retention*. Centerville, UT: Author.

Minton, T.D., Beatty, L.G., & Zeng, Z. (2021, July). Correctional populations in the United States, 2019 – statistical tables. BJS Statistician. NCJ 300655. Retrieved from https://bjs.ojp.gov/sites/g/files/xyckuh236/files/media/document/cpus19st.pdf

Minton, T.D., Zeng, Z., & Maruschak, L.M. (2021, March). Impact of COVID-19 on the local jail population, January-June 2020. BJS Statistician. NCJ 255888. Retrieved from https://bjs.ojp.gov/content/pub/pdf/icljpjj20.pdf

New Jersey Police Suicide Task Force. (2009). *New Jersey police suicide task force report*. Trenton, NJ: Author. Retrieved from https://dspace.njstatelib.org/xmlui/handle/10929/25070

Prescott, C. (2005, April 28). *The lie of the Stanford prison experiment*. Stanford Daily, in News section.

Ratnesar, R. (2011). Stanford Magazine – Article. [online] Alumni.stanford.edu. Available at: http://alumni.stanford.edu/get/page/magazine/article/?article_id=40741

Smith, H.P., & Ho, K. (2021, February 2). *Promoting wellness and resiliency in correctional staff.* Webinar for 1,200 correctional staff and administrators on the topic of officer wellness and resiliency. National Institute of Corrections (NIC). Retrieved from https://nicic.gov/promoting-wellness-and-resiliency-correctional-staff.

Smith, H.P., Power, J., Usher, A.M., Sitren, A.H., & Slade, K. (2019). Working with prisoners who self-harm: A qualitative study on stress, denial of weakness, and encouraging resilience in a sample of correctional staff. *Criminal Justice and Mental Health*, *19*(1), 7–17.

Smith, H.P. (2021, May 27). *Solving the dilemma of self-injurious behavior in the incarcerated population. Webinar for 700 correctional staff and administrators on the topic of inmate self-injurious behavior.* National Institute of Corrections (NIC). Retrieved from, https://nicic.gov/solving-dilemma-self-injurious-behavior-incarcerated-population .

Stack, S.J., & Tsoudis, O. (1997). Suicide risk among correctional officers: A logistic regression analysis. *Archives of Suicide Research*, *3*(3), 183–186.

Surette, R. (2015). *Media, crime, and criminal justice: Images, realities, and policies*. Stamford, CT: Cengage Learning.

Van der Kolk, B. (2014). *The body keeps the score: Brain, mind, and body in the healing of trauma.* New York: Viking/Penguin.

Hayden P. Smith

Exploring organizational risk factors for health & wellness problems in correctional officers

Logan Lavender and Natalie Todak

ABSTRACT

Previous research has documented high rates of stress, PTSD, and other health and wellness problems in U.S. correctional officers (COs). In some studies, rates of mental health issues among COs surpassed those observed in combat-experienced veteran and police officer samples. Unfortunately, this crisis has not received much empirical attention. Drawing on a survey of COs working in Washington state (*N* = 420), we test whether facility and shift variables are related to CO stress, PTSD, and quality of life across four domains: physical health, mental health, social relationships, and physical environment. Few organizational factors were significantly related to health and wellness problems in COs. However, PTSD and stress levels were much higher in our sample than has been reported in past studies (e.g. 27% of our sample met the criteria for diagnosable PTSD). Thus, we find that the mental health crisis among COs is both worsening and unaffected by organizational variables like shift, weekly hours, and facility type. Additional research investigating this crisis is needed.

Introduction

As a result of the unique nature of corrections work, health and wellness problems are highly problematic in the correctional officer (CO) population (Vanltallie, 2002). For example, James and Todak (2018) found that post-traumatic stress disorder (PTSD) was prevalent in 19% of a large sample of Washington state COs – rates equivalent to military veterans who served in combat in Iraq and Afghanistan (Tanielian & Jaycox, 2008). In a summary of their findings, one newspaper article described PTSD rates afflicting COs to be at 'warzone level' (Remsberg, 2019). The stressors of corrections work are also connected to higher rates of insomnia, anxiety, depression, and physical pain or injury (James & Todak, 2018; James, Todak, & Best, 2017; Armstrong, Atkin-Plunk, & Wells, 2015; Bierie, 2010; Lambert, Hogan, Camp, & Ventura, 2006; Şenol-Durak, Durak, & Gençöz, 2006; Perrewe & Ganster, 1989). Research has also found increasingly problematic rates of stress, burnout, absenteeism, poor health, and psychological distress in this population (Gould et al., 2013; Armstrong & Griffin, 2004; Brough & Williams, 2007; Griffin, Hogan, Lambert, Tucker-Gail, & Baker, 2010; Härenstam, Palm, & Theorell, 1988).

There are many organizational aspects of corrections work that could be contributing to this crisis. Generally, COs work nontraditional shifts, including rotating and night shifts, which are linked with poor health and sleep quality (Wickwire, Geiger-Brown, Scharf, & Drake, 2017; Caruso et al., 2006; Pilcher & Coplen, 2000). Also, while working in a high demand, high risk, and potentially fatal environment, COs face threats from a variety of sources, such as physical assault, exposure to contaminated fluid, being threatened or having one's family threatened, seeing someone get hurt or killed, and managing a riot, to name a few (James et al., 2017). Research suggests the risky correctional environment is a major contributor to mental health issues for COs. For example, a few studies (e.g. James & Todak, 2018; Regehr et al., 2021) have found that exposure to critical incidents was significantly related to PTSD symptomology, while other studies have found extended work hours, perceptions of danger/risk, role conflict, and role ambiguity contribute to higher stress rates and other health and wellness problems (Lambert et al., 2014; Armstrong & Griffin, 2004; Castle & Martin, 2006; Garcia, 2008; Keinan & Malach-Pines, 2007). Certainly, all of these problems are exacerbated in facilities with overcrowding and limited staffing (Lahm, 2009; Lambert, Hogan & Griffin, 2007; Steiner & Wooldredge, 2015). However, there is limited evidence available to dictate whether specific policies or structural changes could be adopted to reduce these problems and their corollary effects on COs.

Further investigation into how the correctional environment and the structuring of corrections work affect CO health and wellness would be useful for understanding this crisis and identifying avenues for rectifying it. In the current study, we examine whether facility type (prison or jail), population served (men, women, or mixed), security level (maximum security or not), time of shift (night, day, or swing), shift length, overtime, and/or moonlighting are related to CO stress, PTSD, and quality of life. We analyze these questions using survey data from 420 COs who were working in Washington state in 2019 and 2020. Based on our findings, we investigate whether correctional facilities can be restructured in ways that improve health and wellness outcomes in COs.

The correctional work environment

COs face countless unique risks and dangers in the workplace, including the risk of death or serious injury, that can have significant effects on their overall health and wellness (Ferdik & Smith, 2017). COs run the risk of being bitten, spit on, beaten, or injured, contributing to the overall perception of danger on the job (James & Todak, 2018). The constant contact with persons in custody (PICs) means COs are susceptible to life threatening diseases as they may encounter sharp objects or contaminated bodily fluids (Alarid & Marquart, 2009). Prison gangs are also prevalent in the corrections system, increasing the threat to security and violence against COs (Fleisher & Decker,2001).

More generally, violent conduct from PICs is common and can include physical and/or sexual assault, murder, suicide, and rape (Byrne, Hummer, & Taxman, 2008; Rocheleau, 2014). On average, COs are exposed to approximately 28 acts of violence in their careers (Spinaris et al., 2012). Expanded definitions in the DSM-5 have drawn more focus to indirect, or vicarious, trauma and its connection to PTSD (American Psychiatric Association, 2013). While research has not explored how vicarious trauma affects COs, it is important to note the potential consequences as corrections work involves some of the highest exposure rates to violence, direct or indirect (Denhof, Spinaris, & Morton, 2014; Spinaris et al., 2012). Further, the rise in the number of incarcerated persons with mental illness continues to be a prevalent issue as many facilities and COs are ill-prepared to address their complex needs and behaviors (McLearen & Ryba, 2003). Finally, riots are a rare but concerning element to the corrections environment with even the threat of a riot posing harmful health and wellness consequences (Carrabine, 2005). Overall, corrections work comes with the risk of being exposed to various traumatic events that threaten the health and safety of COs.

COs also face institutional and administrative problems (Finn & Kuck, 2006). Financial issues have resulted in limited resources, causing COs to be responsible for more tasks, to work with old equipment, and have limited training (Brower, 2013; Summerlin, Oehme, Stern, & Valentine, 2010). These budgetary limitations are an added strain on COs and lead to increased burnout (Brower, 2013). Additionally, COs face problems with the administration such as unclear goals and policies, inability to make timely and effective decisions, and an overall lack of support (Finney, Stergiopoulos, Hensel, Bonato, & Dewa, 2013). Brough and Williams (2007) found that friction between COs and administration lead to decreased job satisfaction and psychological well-being. According to Brower (2013), these frictions can also lead to problems with distrust and disengagement from their jobs.

Shiftwork and correctional officer health

Research on the effects of shiftwork for COs is very limited (Finn, 2000; Swenson, Waseleski, & Hartl, 2008), though shiftwork in general has been linked to many physical and psychological consequences. Rotating and night shifts in particular can be damaging and result in declines in cognitive abilities, emotion management, and the ability to make rational decisions (Vila, 2000). Further, as Finn (2000) discussed, rotating shiftwork can cause family issues and affect overall quality of work due to fatigue, irritability, or worse. Shiftwork is also a contributing factor to poor sleep quantity and quality (James et al., 2017).

Fatigue and sleep loss can have dangerous and even deadly consequences in a correctional environment (Akerstedt, 2003; Swenson et al., 2008). Konda, Reichard, and Tiesman (2012) found fatigue was a primary contributor to transportation accidents – a common cause of work-related deaths for COs. Sleep loss related fatigue can also have a dramatic effect on cognition, alertness, quality of decision making, mood, and affect (Swenson et al., 2008). Each of these factors could result in a CO not responding appropriately to a potentially violent situation or emergency, increasing the chances of harm to themselves and the people under their care and supervision.

Excessive work hours and mandatory overtime policies have also been identified as crisis level problems in corrections. Shortages of COs often result in excessive overtime hours, contributing to an increased rate of burnout among remaining staff (Finn, 2000). As Caruso and colleagues (2006) observed, long, unpredictable hours can cause physical and social problems for employees including cardiovascular disease, insomnia, family dysfunction, and mental health issues. Staff shortages can pose further consequences as staff-to-PIC ratios shrink. While there is a general lack of research on staff-to-PIC ratios, Lahm (2009) connected a rise in the number of PICs a CO must supervise with increased risk of being assaulted. Increased responsibilities and diminishing support on the job may also lead to increased fear, stress, potential for harm, and other corollary effects.

Other health and wellness problems in correctional officers

Stress

COs face a variety of stressors that contribute to poor health and wellness outcomes. Occupational stress stems from work-related factors such as job demands, job satisfaction, perception of danger, role problems, and supervisory support (Brough & Williams, 2007; Dowden & Tellier, 2004). Research suggests that perceived dangerousness is a more significant factor predicting occupational stress than objective role difficulties (Dowden & Tellier, 2004). Role conflicts, defined as contradictory or conflicting expectations of a job, are also stressors that significantly impact COs (Castle & Martin, 2006). These role problems include unclear goals and policies, a lack of ability to make timely and effective decisions, and a lack of support from the organization (Finney et al., 2013). The stress and strain that COs face can also negatively affect home life, which adds to job stress levels and a decrease in job satisfaction (Lambert et al., 2006).

While the last couple of decades have witnessed an increase in research on the prevalence, causes, and effects of CO stress, recent research suggests that working in correctional facilities, as compared with police officers and veterans, is still among the most stressful jobs in American society (James & Todak, 2018; Keinan & Malach-Pines, 2007; Castle & Martin, 2006; Şenol-Durak et al., 2006; Dowden & Tellier, 2004; ;Cheek & Miller, 1983). The uniquely stressful nature of this work, largely a function of exposure to violence and threat of harm, poses significant risks for CO mental illness. For example, research has found a positive correlation between stress and depression, anxiety, hopelessness, PTSD, and suicide in COs (James & Todak, 2018; James et al., 2017; Şenol-Durak et al., 2006). Stress experienced by COs also significantly impacts sleep quality and physical health. For example, CO stress has been linked with chronic pain (Bierie, 2010; VanItallie, 2002).

Finally, suicide among COs is a particularly critical area of concern (Frost & Monteiro, 2020). After examining a cluster of at least 20 CO suicides in Massachusetts between 2010 and 2015, Frost and Monteiro found that a combination of personal (life and mental health struggles) and organizational (violence exposure, cultural expectations that officers 'suck it up') risk factors explained the string of suicides. The authors concluded that CO suicides cannot be understood as individual cases but as a product of their workplace environments and cultures.

Mental health and PTSD

As noted, COs are regularly exposed to incidents that involve violence, injury, or death, which can have a cumulative, traumatic effect on their health and wellbeing (Konda et al., 2013; Spinaris et al., 2012). Work-related injuries and fatalities are some of the main concerns as COs experience some of the highest rates of each when compared to all US workers (see, e.g. Carleton et al., 2020; Konda et al., 2013). These events put COs at significant risk for long-term, stress-related conditions such as depression and anxiety.

While depression and other mental health issues among COs have been well studied and documented, PTSD has not been a common area of focus. James and Todak (2018) found COs are significantly at risk for PTSD as they experience rates six times higher than the general population and equivalent to police officers and veterans who have served in Iraq and Afghanistan (Tanielian & Jaycox, 2008). PTSD was, in part, a result of exposure to critical incidents, such as being threatened, witnessing traumatic events, and being put in dangerous situations (see also McCaslin et al., 2006; Robinson, Sigman, & Wilson, 1997).

Quality of Life

Scholars typically evaluate quality of life as a product of four domains: physical health, mental health, social relationships, and physical environment. In the current body of research, there is considerable evidence that COs suffer from problems in all four of these domains. As previously discussed, COs face risks to their physical health on a daily basis from threats by PICs. However, the nature of corrections work, particularly critical incidents, can also have a prolonged, negative effect on the physical health of COs. Critical incidents have been shown to increase insomnia levels and stress levels, which often are then related to other physical issues such as chronic pain (James et al., 2017; Bierie, 2010). Obidoa and colleagues (Obidoa, Reeves, Warren, Reisine, & Cherniack, 2011) found 31% of correctional officers met the criteria for serious psychological distress. Furthermore, strains felt by COs as part of their jobs often spill over into their home life, causing work-family conflict (Armstrong et al., 2015; Lambert et al., 2006; Triplett, Mullings, & Scarborough, 1999). COs experience a high rate of work-family conflict that often adversely affects their access to social support (Obidoa et al., 2011) and increases the strain they face at work (Lambert et al., 2006). Overall, these issues would be expected to have a significant negative impact on one's quality of life.

Methods

Within the body of research on CO health and wellness, there has not been sufficient focus on facility-level or shift-level factors that may be contributing to the severe health and wellness crisis documented thus far. In the current study, we examine relationships between organizational and shift-level factors and CO stress, PTSD, and quality of life. Data were collected through an online Qualtrics survey distributed to prison and jail COs in Washington state in Fall 2020 and Spring 2021 (N = 420). All procedures were approved by the Office of the Institutional Review Board at the authors' university.

Sampling and data collection

Participants were recruited through the King County Corrections Guild (KCCG) and South Correctional Entity (SCORE) jail. KCCG serves as the collective bargaining representative for all COs and sergeants of the King County (Seattle) Department of Adult and Juvenile Detention, representing approximately 1,200 employees. SCORE jail is a regionally owned jail in Des Moines, WA that serves confinement needs of six member cities and several contract agencies. To recruit individuals for our study, contacts at KCCG and SCORE jail sent emails to COs represented by these organizations via their work email addresses. The content of these emails included the information required for informed consent and a link to complete the survey in Qualtrics. Given that recruitment was done by agency contacts, it is unknown how many COs received the emails, and we are unable to calculate and report a response rate.

Survey instrument and analysis

The full survey questionnaire included six sections: 1) demographics, 2) work history, assignment, and organization, 3) health and wellness, 4) sleep, 5) stress, and 6) trauma and critical incidents. The survey is modified from past research (James et al.,2017; James & Todak, 2018). Using all valid cases, we first report descriptive statistics for each study variable. Percent missing data ranged from 0–1% for work variables, 11–16% for demographic variables, and 0–14% for dependent variables. Using descriptive statistics, we compare rates of stress, PTSD, and overall wellbeing observed in our sample with those reported in previous research with analogous populations (i.e. police officers, military veterans, and correctional employees). We then use ordinary least squares (OLS) regression to examine relationships between organizational and shift-level factors and CO stress, PTSD, and quality of life. OLS estimates the strength of a relationship between two or more explanatory (or independent) variables and one continuous dependent variable. Here, OLS is used to calculate the strength of the relationships between organizational and shift factors on perceived stress, PTSD, and quality of life.

Dependent variables

The perceived stress scale (PSS) is our measure of CO *stress* (Cohen & Williamson, 1988). The PSS score is a numerical measure of the perceived level of predictability and control each person feels they have over their life. Using a 5-point Likert-type scale (from 'Never' to 'Very Often'), items ask respondents questions such as, 'In the last month, how often have you been upset because of something that happened unexpectedly?' (see Appendix A for full set of questions). The PSS score was calculated by summing responses to all 10 items. Scores range from 0–40, with those ranging from 0–13 considered low stress, scores ranging from 14–26 considered moderate stress, and scores ranging from 27–40 considered high stress (Bhat, Sameer, & Ganaraja, 2011).

The PTSD Checklist for DSM-V (PCL-5) is a 20-item questionnaire where participants rate their experiences with various PTSD symptoms (such as vivid flashbacks, nightmares, and/or strong physical reactions to reminders of trauma) on a scale from 'Not at All' to 'Extremely' (Weathers et al., 2013; Weathers, Marx, Friedman, & Schnurr, 2014; see Appendix A for a full set of questions). Scores on the PCL-5 range from 0–80 when all items are summed, where higher scores indicate higher *PTSD* symptomology. The cutoff score that has been clinically determined to meet the criteria for diagnosable PTSD is 38 (Weathers et al., 2013).

The World Health Organization's Quality of Life Brief Assessment (WHOQOL-BREF) is an abbreviated version of the WHOQOL-100 that provides a cross-culturally applicable, detailed assessment of an individual's perception of their quality of life (World Health Organization, 1996). The 26-item questionnaire assesses quality of life on four domains (*physical health, psychological health, social relationships*, and *environment*). Using a 5-point Likert scale from 'Not at All' to 'Extremely,' respondents answer questions such as, 'To what extent do you feel that physical pain prevents you from doing what you need to do?'

including 3 positively worded items that were reverse coded (see Appendix A for a full set of questions). Each of the 4 domain scores are calculated separately. The average response is calculated in each domain and then multiplied by 4. Scores in all domains range from 4–20 where lower scores indicate lower quality of life.

Independent variables

Facility variables included *facility type* (dummy coded: prison, jail, other), *population served* at the facility (dummy coded: men, women, mixed), and overall percent of *time spent with persons in custody (PICs)*. Time spent with PICs was initially measured continuously and then, because of its skewed distribution, recoded into a dummy variable indicating 75% or less (coded as 1) and 76% or more (coded as 2). A dummy variable indicating whether the individual worked at a *maximum security facility* (1 = yes; 0 = no) was also included.

Shift variables included regular *shift length*, total *monthly work hours*, and total *monthly overtime hours*, which were all measured continuously to the nearest hour. *Shift* was measured as a series of four dummy variables indicating that the person worked days, swing, nights, or other. *Moonlighting* is a dummy variable indicating whether the person worked a second job. Based on low variation on this variable (only 11 individuals reported moonlighting), it was excluded from regression models.

Demographic variables

Demographic variables included participants' *years of experience* in corrections and *age*, both measured continuously in years. Gender is reported as a dummy variable where 1 = man and 2 = woman (*woman officer*). Race is a categorical variable indicating whether an individual was *White, Black, Asian, American Indian, Pacific Islander, Mixed* (where an individual indicated more than one race), or *other*. Ethnicity was measured as a dummy variable indicating whether the individual reported being *Hispanic*. Finally, our measure of education is a dummy variable indicating whether the individual had a *college degree* (1 = Bachelor's degree or higher; 0 = Associates degree or less).

Findings

As Table 1 shows, most of the sample was between 30 and 60 years old (84%), White (58%), and male (82%). More than half had over 10 years of correctional experience. As shown in Table 2, the majority worked in a men's facility (57%), though mixed gender facility was also well represented (40%). Most worked in a prison (59%) during the day shift (59%) and spent a significant amount of time with PICs in the course of their work. As noted, moonlighting was very uncommon in our sample. According to the Bureau of Labor Statistics, the average age of a CO in the United States in 2018 was 40 years or more, while 62.3% were White, 19.6% were Black, and 73.9% were men. Thus, our sample closely matches the national averages based on race, gender, and age, as well as samples used in past research with COs in the United States (e.g. Lambert, 2006). Years of experience appears to be slightly skewed towards COs with more work experience. This may be because we worked with the King County Corrections Guild to recruit participants rather than directly with facilities in King County. It may be that officers with established careers are more likely to join the Guild.

Table 1. Participant demographics (N = 420).

Demographics	N	Valid %
Sex		
Male	304	82
Female	67	18
Age		
24–30	14	4
31–40	71	18
41–50	118	36
51–60	106	30
61+	43	12
Race		
White	244	58
Black	22	5
Asian	14	3
American Indian	8	2
Pacific Islander	7	2
Mixed	26	6
Other	45	11
Ethnicity		
Hispanic	88	21
Education		
≤ Associate's	280	75
≥ Bachelor's	92	25
Years of Experience		
1–10 years	129	31
11–20 years	165	39
21–30 years	111	27
30–40 years	14	3

Table 2. Study variable descriptive statistics – Categorical (N = 420).

Assignment	N	Valid %
Population Served		
Men	239	57
Women	15	3
Mixed	166	40
Facility Type		
Prison	247	59
Jail	155	37
Other	17	4
Security Level		
Maximum	269	64
Medium	266	63
Minimum	218	52
Other	97	23
Shift		
Day	245	59
Night	58	14
Swing	98	23
Other	18	4
Moonlighting	11	2.7
Time Spent w/ PICs		
≤ 75%	203	48
≥ 76%	216	52

Table 3 shows that our sample worked an average of 8.5 hours per shift, 129.5 hours per month, and 30.6 monthly hours of overtime. In other words, almost 20% of total monthly hours worked by our sample are overtime. The average PSS score for our sample was 21.5, which, on a scale of 0–40, falls on the high end of moderate stress. Over 12% of

Table 3. Study variable descriptive statistics – Continuous (N = 420).

Variables	Mean	SD	Min	Max
Shift Length Hours	8.5	1.5	4	18
Monthly Work Hours	129.5	63	1	360
Monthly Overtime Hours	30.6	32.8	0	250
PSS	21.5	4.4	6	40
PCL-5	26.7	18.3	0	78
WHOQOL-BREF				
Physical Domain	13.3	2.8	4	20
Psychological Domain	13.2	2.9	4	20
Social Domain	12.9	3.6	4	20
Environmental Domain	13.6	2.7	5.5	20

our sample met the criteria for 'high stress' (score of 27 or higher). PCL-5 scores range from 0–80 with 38 being a clinically determined cutoff score for diagnosable PTSD. In our sample, the average PCL-5 score was 26.7 and 27.2% of the sample met the criteria for diagnosable PTSD (scored 38 or higher). Each of the four domains in the WHOQOL-BREF produces a score ranging from 4–20. The average scores in our sample were 13.3 (physical), 13.2 (psychological), 12.9 (social relationships), and 13.6 (environmental).

Tables 4 and 5 report the results of the OLS regression models estimating PTSD, stress, and the four aspects of quality of life. Our data did not show problems with multicollinearity as all variance inflation factors (VIFs) were below 10. Out of the 6 models,

Table 4. OLS regression model estimating PTSD and stress (N = 420).

	PTSD (PCL-5 Score)			Stress (PSS Score)		
Variables	*b*	SE	β	*b*	SE	β
Independent Variables						
Facility Type						
Jail	11.127†	5.857	0.310	2.498†	1.466	0.279
Other	10.854†	5.623	0.123	−0.587	1.387	−0.028
Population Served						
Women	−3.526	6.629	−0.033	−0.986	1.668	−0.037
Mixed	−11.821*	5.649	−0.331	−2.422†	1.406	−0.272
Time Spent w/ PICs	7.120***	2.212	0.200	0.363	0.554	0.041
Maximum Security	−0.578	2.286	−0.016	0.588	0.564	0.064
Shift Length	0.576	0.942	0.044	0.299	0.220	0.098
Monthly Work Hours	−0.028	0.018	−0.100	0.002	0.005	0.023
Monthly Overtime	0.058†	0.035	0.105	0.004	0.009	0.030
Shift						
Night	−0.756	3.089	−0.016	−0.569	0.773	−0.047
Swing	−4.281	2.808	0.098	−0.232	0.703	−0.021
Other	−8.063	6.278	−0.080	−1.472	1.512	−0.061
Demographic Variables						
Years of Experience	0.108	0.187	0.050	0.088†	0.046	0.164
Age	−0.068	0.149	−0.038	−0.070†	0.037	−0.159
Woman Officer	−5.273†	2.809	−0.115	−0.676	0.700	−0.059
Race						
Black	−1.503	5.146	−0.018	0.922	1.295	0.043
Asian	4.930	6.065	0.049	0.852	1.336	0.038
American Indian	−7.209	7.025	−0.063	−1.752	1.766	−0.061
Pacific Islander	−1.410	6.951	−0.012	−3.166†	1.747	−0.110
Mixed	−1.067	4.202	−0.015	0.277	1.058	0.016
Other	−6.936†	3.771	−0.127	−0.675	0.929	−0.050
Hispanic	1.658	3.023	0.040	−1.103	0.755	−0.106
College Degree	−1.488	2.552	−0.037	−0.121	0.638	−0.012
Intercept		1.620**			29.261***	
F		1.620*			1.351	
R^2		0.049			0.028	

Note. Prison excluded as facility reference group. Men excluded as population served reference group. Day shift excluded as shift reference group. White excluded as racial reference group.
b = coefficient; SE = standard error; β = standardized coefficient.
*** $p < 0.001$; ** $p < 0.01$; * $p < 0.05$; † $p < 0.10$.

Table 5. OLS regression models estimating quality of life in correctional officers ($N = 420$).

	Physical Domain			Psychological Domain			Social Domain			Environment Domain		
Variables	*b*	SE	β	*b*	SE	β	*b*	SE	β	*b*	SE	β
Independent Variables												
Facility Type												
Jail	0.135	0.903	0.025	−0.176	0.962	−0.030	1.398	1.211	0.193	0.252	0.847	0.050
Other	0.299	0.854	0.023	−0.179	0.910	−0.013	−0.041	1.146	−0.002	−0.323	0.801	−0.027
Population Served												
Women	0.837	1.030	0.051	0.534	1.095	0.031	−0.249	1.379	−0.11	0.099	0.963	0.006
Mixed	−0.143	0.866	−0.026	0.571	0.922	0.099	−0.717	1.162	−0.100	−0.046	0.812	−0.009
Time Spent w/ PICs	0.916*	0.343	−0.167	−0.088	0.364	−0.015	−0.669	0.459	−0.093	−0.192	0.321	−0.038
Maximum Security	−0.279	0.351	−0.050	−0.169	0.371	−0.029	−0.380	0.467	−0.051	−0.265	0.327	−0.051
Shift Length	−0.151	0.137	−0.080	−0.099	0.144	−0.050	−0.032	0.182	−0.013	0.135	0.127	0.078
Monthly Work Hours	0.005†	0.003	0.120	0.003	0.003	0.069	−0.001	0.004	−0.010	0.002	0.003	0.047
Monthly Overtime	0.010†	0.005	−0.112	0.011†	0.006	−0.119	−0.003	0.007	−0.024	−0.003	0.005	−0.038
Shift												
Night	−0.003	0.481	0.000	0.328	0.512	0.042	0.800	0.638	0.082	0.049	0.446	0.007
Swing	0.286	0.435	0.043	0.570	0.463	0.080	0.892	0.581	0.101	0.428	0.406	0.069
Other	1.264	0.987	0.081	−0.179	0.910	−0.013	1.992	1.249	0.102	2.156*	0.873	0.157
Demographic Variables												
Years of Experience	0.065*	0.029	−0.197	0.055†	0.030	−0.161	−0.024	0.038	−0.055	0.002	0.027	0.007
Age	−0.008	0.023	−0.029	0.037	0.024	0.124	0.004	0.031	0.012	0.011	0.021	0.045
Woman Officer	0.386	0.438	0.054	0.192	0.461	0.026	0.228	0.578	0.025	0.799*	0.404	0.123
Race												
Black	−0.125	0.826	−0.009	1.443†	0.849	0.105	0.421	1.070	0.024	1.093	0.743	0.090
Asian	0.328	0.823	0.024	−0.091	0.921	−0.006	−0.139	1.104	−0.008	−0.053	0.771	−0.004
American Indian	1.515	1.087	0.086	2.722*	1.158	0.147	3.067*	1.459	0.132	1.397	1.020	0.086
Pacific Islander	−1.144	1.077	−0.065	−0.561	1.146	−0.030	0.109	1.443	0.005	0.030	1.009	0.002
Mixed	0.003	0.652	0.000	0.545	0.694	0.049	1.610†	0.874	0.114	0.520	0.611	0.053
Other	0.458	0.575	0.055	0.943	0.610	0.108	0.711	0.768	0.065	0.360	0.537	0.047
Non-Hispanic	−0.407	0.437	−0.063	−0.165	0.495	−0.025	−0.308	0.624	−0.037	0.023	0.436	0.004
College Degree	−0.217	0.399	−0.035	0.403	0.420	0.062	−0.552	0.527	−0.068	0.013	0.370	0.002
Intercept	15.629***			12.283***			12.401***			10.803***		
F	1.374			0.995			0.809			0.926		
R^2	0.030			0.000			−0.016			−0.006		

Note. Prison excluded as facility reference group. Men excluded as population served reference group. Day shift excluded as shift reference group. White excluded as racial reference group.
b = coefficient; SE = standard error; β = standardized coefficient.
$^{***}p < 0.001$; $^{**}p < 0.01$; $^{*}p < 0.05$; $^{†}p < 0.10$.

only the model estimating PTSD using the PCL-5 had an F value that showed significance. This model indicated that time spent with PICs significantly predicted higher PTSD symptomology ($b = 7.120$). The PTSD model also indicated that COs working in mixed facilities, compared to men's only facilities, experienced less PTSD symptoms ($b = -11.821$). Although not significant at the $p < 0.05$ level, a few variables in the PTSD model had p values of less than .10 and are potentially still meaningful for the study of CO mental health. These were women COs (negative), COs that worked in jails compared to prisons (positive), those who worked more overtime hours (positive), and those who reported their race as 'other' (negative). Given that F tests for the models estimating the PSS score and quality of life domains were not significant, we do not report findings from those. We take this to suggest that organizational and shift factors do not significantly predict CO stress or quality of life.

Discussion

The goal of this study was to investigate relationships between organizational factors and CO health and wellness outcomes (i.e. stress, PTSD, and quality of life). Given that previous research has consistently documented poor health and wellness outcomes in CO populations, we sought to generate evidence that could help identify whether specific shift schedules and/or organizational policies could be implemented or reformed to improve these problems. In this way, adverse events, such as mistakes, uses of force, and death, could be reduced within prison environments, thereby increasing health and wellness outcomes for employees and for those in custody. While we did not find many significant relationships between organizational factors and our dependent variables, we did observe extremely high rates of mental health problems in our population of COs, above and beyond those observed in previous studies. Both sets of findings have meaningful implications and we discuss each of them in more detail below.

The findings from our regression models indicate that organizational factors had a limited impact on our variables of interest. The only regression model that showed overall significance was the one predicting PTSD, while the remaining models predicting CO stress and the four quality of life domains were not. Within the PTSD model, we found that COs who reported more time with PICs in the course of their work activities reported more PTSD symptoms compared to COs who spent less time with PICs, as did COs working in men-only facilities. The fact that very few of our organizational variables were directly related to CO health and wellness suggests that factors like facility type or shift length may not be responsible for these problems. Instead, our findings suggest that something about the custodial responsibility of COs and their face-to-face interactions with PICs (and men in particular) may be more strongly connected to the crisis of mental health among employees in this field. Nevertheless, more research is needed to understand the mechanisms driving this significant relationship.

Despite the nonsignificant relationships between our study variables, we did observe unusually high rates of PTSD and stress in our sample. To illustrate, the overall rate of PTSD in the general adult population is about 3.5% (Kessler, et al., 2005). In comparison, veterans who served in Iraq and Afghanistan show PTSD rates between 11–20%, while those who served in Vietnam show rates of about 30% (Kulka, Schlenger, & Fairbank et al.,

1990; Tanielian & Jaycox, 2008). Police officers are also at-risk for PTSD at a rate of 18% (Kilpatrick et al., 2013). Previously, James and Todak (2018) found COs reported PTSD rates of 19%, which is equivalent to, and in some cases higher than, those of veterans who served in Iraq and Afghanistan and police officers. By comparison, in the current study, approximately 27% of the sample met the criteria for diagnosable PTSD – a rate almost 50% higher than the findings of James and Todak (2018) and only slightly lower than the rates seen in veterans who served in Vietnam (Kulka et al., 1990). Thus, not only is PTSD a prevalent, critical issue among COs, the problem may be getting worse.

Likewise, the average PSS-10 score (measuring perceived stress) of the general adult population in the U.S. typically ranges from 12–14 (Cohen et al., 1994). Past studies have shown veterans who served in Iraq and Afghanistan have average PSS-10 scores from 10–17, which indicates low to moderate perceived stress (Garner, 2010). Police officers typically score on the high end of 'low stress' or the low end of 'moderate stress,' with average scores ranging from 12–15 on the PSS-10 and 18–19 on the PSS-14 (Gutshall, Hampton, Sebetan, Stein, & Broxtermann, 2017; Ramey et al., 2012). In the current study, the average PSS-10 score was 21, falling on the higher end of the moderate stress category. Therefore, we find that COs experience higher levels of stress than has been observed in general populations, police officers, and veterans who have served in Iraq and Afghanistan.

The general adult population experiences a moderate quality of life with average scores from the physical health, psychological health, social relationships, and environmental domains being approximately 15, 14, 13, and 12, respectively (Skevington, Lotfy, & O'Connell, 2004). Meanwhile, veterans with a history of depression report a low to moderate quality of life with average domain scores 11–12, 10–12, 9–10, and 13–14, respectively (Karlin et al., 2013). The average scores from veterans who served in the Korean war, including those with histories of depression, PTSD, or both, range from low to moderate quality of life, with scores being approximately 8–14 (physical), 10–15 (psychological), 10–15 (social relationships), and 12–16 (environmental; Ikin, Creamer, Sim, & McKenzie, 2010). Comparatively, our findings show that COs experience a moderate quality of life with average scores being 13 in the physical, psychological, and social relationship domains and 14 in the environmental domain. These findings indicate that COs generally experience a slightly lower quality of life, particularly as it pertains to physical and psychological health, than the general population. However, quality of life scores in this study were higher than those of veterans who had a history of depression and those who served in the Korean War (Ikin et al., 2010).

Our study is accompanied by several limitations. First, our use of a non-random sample of COs from two facilities in Washington state limits the generalizability of our findings. Importantly, our sample appears to be on the more experienced end of the spectrum and largely excludes COs with less time on the job. It is possible that the high rates of stress and PTSD we observed are somehow related to the non-probability sample used in our study and further research using larger, randomly selected samples is warranted.

These data were also collected immediately prior to the global COVID-19 pandemic, which began to afflict the United States in March 2020. Given the detrimental impact of the pandemic on jails and prisons nationwide (see, e.g. Novisky, Narvey, & Semenza, 2020), it is unknown how our findings may have changed since the data were collected. Further, given limitations with the survey, we are not able to examine the impact of staff-to-PIC ratio; specifically, whether more crowded facilities may be related to greater problems with mental health and wellness in COs. As noted, correctional facilities often experience staffing shortages, which increase the number of PICs that COs directly supervise. While this problem has generally lacked empirical attention, a few studies have found that a higher ratio is related to more CO stress (Lahm, 2009; Lambert, Hogan, & Griffin, 2007; Steiner & Wooldredge, 2015). Future research should investigate this possibility. Relatedly, we are unable to assess the relationship between working in a juvenile facility, as opposed to an adult facility, with our data. This is also an important research question for future studies.

Our research echoes the existing body of work finding that corrections is associated with very poor health and wellness outcomes. Outcomes like PTSD appear to be growing worse in the absence of research and targeted interventions working to understand and improve these problems. Unfortunately, organizational factors (like facility type and shift schedule) do not seem to be related to these outcomes. It appears that, regardless of where you work, what your shift is, or how many hours you clock in per week, corrections work is significantly detrimental to health and wellness.

Based on our findings indicating higher PTSD symptomology in COs who spend more time with PICs and those who work in men's facilities, further investigation into the overall time spent with PICs and the nature of work in men's facilities may be a good place to start. Research should examine the nature of corrections work, PIC-CO interactions, and whether working in a men's facility presents more trauma or other challenges. In sum, we find that there is a critical need for further research to continue investigating the crisis of PTSD and other health and wellness problems in COs, looking beyond organizational factors. The lives of COs, and the lives of those being guarded by them, depend on it.

Disclosure statement

No potential conflict of interest was reported by the author(s).

References

Akerstedt, T. (2003). Shift work and disturbed sleep/wakefulness. *Occupational Medicine, 53*(2), 89–94.

Alarid, L.F., & Marquart, J.W. (2009). Officer perceptions of risk of contracting HIV/AIDS in prison: A two-state comparison. *The Prison Journal, 89*(4), 440–459.

Armstrong, G.S., Atkin-Plunk, C.A., & Wells, J. (2015). the relationship between work–family conflict, correctional officer job stress, and job satisfaction. *Criminal Justice and Behavior, 42*(10), 1066–1082.

Armstrong, G.S., & Griffin, M.L. (2004). Does the job matter? Comparing correlates of stress among treatment and correctional staff in prisons. *Journal of Criminal Justice, 32*(6), 577–592.

Association, A.P. (2013). *Diagnostic and statistical manual of mental disorders (DSM-5)* (Fifth ed.). Washington D.C: American Psychiatric Association.

Bhat, R.M., Sameer, M.K., & Ganaraja, B. (2011). Eustress in education: Analysis of the perceived stress score (PSS) and blood pressure (BP) during examinations in medical students. *Journal of Clinical and Diagnostic Research, 5*(7), 331–1335.

Bierie, D.M. (2010). the impact of prison conditions on staff well-being. *International Journal of Offender Therapy and Comparative Criminology, 56*(1), 81–95.

Brough, P., & Williams, J. (2007). Managing occupational stress in a high-risk industry. *Criminal Justice and Behavior, 34*(4), 555–567.

Brower, J. (2013). "Review and input of correctional officer wellness and safety literature review." OJP Diagnostic Center. Office of Justice Programs.

Byrne, J.M., Hummer, D., & Taxman, F.S. (2008). *The culture of prison violence*. Boston, MA: Pearson Education.

Carleton, R.N., Ricciardelli, R., Taillieu, T., Mitchell, M.M., Andres, E., & Afifi, T.O. (2020). Provincial correctional service workers: the prevalence of mental disorders. *International Journal of Environmental Research and Public Health, 17*(7) MDPI AG. Retrieved from, 2203.

Carrabine, E. (2005). Prison Riots, Social Order and the Problem of Legitimacy. *The British Journal of Criminology, 45*(6), 896–913.

Caruso, C. C.,Bushnell, T., Eggerth, D., Heitmann, A., Kojola, B., Newman, K., . . . & Vila, B. (2006). Long working hours, safety, and health: toward a National Research Agenda. *American journal of industrial medicine, 49*(11), 930–942.

Castle, T.L., & Martin, J.S. (2006). Occupational hazard: Predictors of stress among jail correctional officers. *American Journal of Criminal Justice, 31*(1), 65–80.

Cheek, F.E., & Miller, M.D. (1983). The experience of stress for correction officers: A double-bind theory of correctional stress. *Journal of Criminal Justice, 11*(2), 105–120.

Cohen, S., Kamarck, T., & Mermelstein, R. (1994). Perceived stress scale. Measuring stress: A guide for health and social scientists, *10*(2), 1–2.

Cohen, S., & Williamson, G. (1988). Perceived stress in a probability sample of the United States. In S. Spacapan & S. Oskamp (Eds.),*The Social Psychology of Health* (pp. 31–67). Sage Publications, Inc.

Denhof, M.D., Spinaris, C.G., & Morton, G.R. (2014). Occupational stressors in corrections organizations: Types, effects and solutions. *US Department of Justice, National Institute of Corrections, 54,* 71–82.

Dowden, C., & Tellier, C. (2004). Predicting work-related stress in correctional officers: A meta-analysis. *Journal of Criminal Justice, 32*(1), 31–47.

Ferdik, F., & Smith, H. (2017). Correctional Officer Safety and Wellness Literature Synthesis. Office of Justice Programs, Accessed May 2021. https://www.ojp.gov/pdffiles1/nij/250484.pdf

Finn, P., & Kuck, S. Stress among probation and parole officers and what can be done about it. (2006). National Institute of Justice. Available at: https://www.ncjrs.gov/pdffiles1/nij/205620.pdf

Finn, P. (2000). Addressing Correctional Officer Stress: Programs and Strategies. *PsycEXTRA Dataset.* doi:10.1037/e507462006-001

Finney, C., Stergiopoulos, E., Hensel, J., Bonato, S., & Dewa, C.S. (2013). Organizational stressors associated with job stress and burnout in correctional officers: A systematic review. *BMC Public Health, 13*(1), 1.

Fleisher, M., & Decker, S. (2001). An overview of the challenge of prison gangs. *Corrections Management Quarterly, 5,* 1-9.

Frost, N.A., & Monteiro, C.E. (2020). The interaction of personal and occupational factors in the suicide deaths of correction officers. *Justice Quarterly, 37*(7), 1277–1302.

Garcia, R.M. (2008). Individual and institutional demographic and organizational climate correlates of perceived danger among federal correctional officers. *PsycEXTRA Dataset* 10.1037/e457282008-001

Garner, B. (2010). Sleep Disturbances in US Soldiers after Deployment to Afghanistan or Iraq.

Gould, D.D., Watson, S.L., Price, S.R., & Valliant, P.M. (2013). The relationship between burnout and coping in adult and young offender center correctional officers: An exploratory investigation. *Psychological Services, 10*(1), 37–47.

Griffin, M.L., Hogan, N.L., Lambert, E.G. Tucker-Gail, K.A., & Baker, D.N. (2009). Job involvement, job stress, job satisfaction, and organizational commitment and the burnout of correctional staff. *Criminal Justice and Behavior, 37*(2), 239–255.

Gutshall, C.L., Hampton, D.P., Sebetan, I.M., Stein, P.C., & Broxtermann, T.J. (2017). The effects of occupational stress on cognitive performance in police officers. *Police Practice and Research, 18*(5), 463–477.

Härenstam, A., Palm, U.-B., & Theorell, T. (1988). Stress, health and the working environment of Swedish prison staff. *Work & Stress, 2*(4), 281–290.

Ikin, J.F., Creamer, M.C., Sim, M.R., & McKenzie, D.P. (2010). Comorbidity of PTSD and depression in Korean War veterans: Prevalence, predictors, and impairment. *Journal of Affective Disorders, 125* (1–3), 279–286.

James, L., Todak, N., & Best, S. (2017). The negative impact of prison work on sleep health. *American Journal of Industrial Medicine, 60*(5), 449–456.

James, L., & Todak, N. (2018). Prison employment and post-traumatic stress disorder: Risk and protective factors. *American Journal of Industrial Medicine, 61*(9), 725–732.

Karlin, B.E., Walser, R.D., Yesavage, J., Zhang, A., Trockel, M., & Taylor, C.B. (2013). Effectiveness of acceptance and commitment therapy for depression: Comparison among older and younger veterans. *Aging & Mental Health, 17*(5), 555–563.

Keinan, G., & Malach-Pines, A. (2007). Stress and Burnout Among Prison Personnel. *Criminal Justice and Behavior, 34*(3), 380–398.

Kessler R C, Chiu W Tat, Demler O and Walters E E. (2005). Prevalence, Severity, and Comorbidity of 12-Month DSM-IV Disorders in the National Comorbidity Survey Replication. Arch Gen Psychiatry, 62(6), 617 10.1001/archpsyc.62.6.617

Kilpatrick, D.G., Resnick, H.S., Milanak, M.E., Miller, M.W., Keyes, K.M., & Friedman, M.J. (2013). National Estimates of Exposure to Traumatic Events and PTSD Prevalence Using DSM-IV and DSM-5 Criteria. *Journal of Traumatic Stress, 26*(5), 537–547.

Konda, S., Reichard, A.A., & Tiesman, H.M. (2012). Occupational Injuries among U.S. Correctional Officers, 1999-2008. *Journal of Safety Research, 43*(3), 181–186.

Konda, S., Tiesman, H., Reichard, A., and Hartley, D., (2013). US correctional officers killed or injured on the job. *Corrections Today, 75*(5), 122.

Kulka, R.A., Schlenger, W.E., Fairbank, J.A., Hough, R.L., Jordan, B.K., Marmar, C.R., and Weiss, D.S., (1990). *Trauma and the Vietnam War Generation: Report of Findings From the National Vietnam Veterans Readjustment Study*. New York: Brunner/Mazel.

Lahm, K.F. (2009). Inmate assaults on prison staff: A multilevel examination of an overlooked form of prison violence. *The Prison Journal, 89*(2), 131–150.

Lambert, E.G. Hogan, N.L., Camp, S.D., & Ventura, L.A. (2006). The impact of work–family conflict on correctional staff. *Criminology & Criminal Justice, 6*(4), 371–387.

Lambert, E.G. Hogan, N.L., & Griffin, M.L. (2007). The impact of distributive and procedural justice on correctional staff job stress, job satisfaction, and organizational commitment. *Journal of Criminal Justice, 35*(6), 644–656.

Lambert, E.G. Minor, K.I., Wells, J.B., & Hogan, N.L. (2014). Leave Your Job at Work. *The Prison Journal, 95*(1), 114–134.

Lambert, E.G. (2006). I want to leave: A test of a model of turnover intent among correctional staff. *Applied Psychology in Criminal Justice, 2*(1), 57–83.

McCaslin, S.E., Metzler, T.J., Best, S.R., Liberman, A., Weiss, D.S., Fagan, J., & Marmar, C.R. (2006). Alexithymia and PTSD symptoms in urban police officers: Cross-sectional and prospective findings. *Journal of Traumatic Stress*, *19*(3), 361–373.

McLearen, A.M., & Ryba, N.L. (2003). Identifying Severely Mentally Ill Inmates: Can Small Jails Comply with Detection Standards? *Journal of Offender Rehabilitation*, *37*(1), 25–34.

Novisky, M.A., Narvey, C.S., & Semenza, D.C. (2020). Institutional responses to the COVID-19 pandemic in American prisons. *Victims & Offenders*, *15*(7–8), 1244–1261.

Obidoa, C., Reeves, D., Warren, N., Reisine, S., & Cherniack, M. (2011). Depression and work family conflict among corrections officers. *Journal of Occupational & Environmental Medicine*, *53*(11), 1294–1301.

Organization, W.H. (1996). *WHOQOL-BREF: Introduction, administration, scoring and generic version of the assessment: Field trial version*. January 1 Geneva, Switzerland: World Health Organization.

Perrewe, P.L., & Ganster, D.C. (1989). The impact of job demands and behavioral control on experienced job stress. *Journal of Organizational Behavior*, *10*(3), 213–229.

Pilcher, J. J, & Coplen, M. K.(2000). Work/rest cycles in railroad operations: effects of shorter than 24-h shift work schedules and on-call schedules on sleep. *Ergonomics*, *43*(5), 573–588.

Ramey, S.L., Perkhounkova, Y., Moon, M., Budde, L., Tseng, H.-C., & Clark, M.K. (2012). The effect of work shift and sleep duration on various aspects of police officers' health. *Workplace Health & Safety*, *60*(5), 215–222.

Regehr, C., Carey, M., Shannon Wagner, Lynn E, Alden, Nicholas, Buys, Corneil, Wayne, ... White, M. (2021). Prevalence of PTSD, depression and anxiety disorders in correctional officers. *A Systematic Review, Corrections*, *6*(3), 229–241.

Remsberg, C. (2019). *New study: Prison workers have PTSD symptoms at war-zone level*. Des Plaines, IL: Force Science Institute. Accessed Aug 2021. January 19 https://www.forcescience.org/2018/07/new-study-prison-workers-have-ptsd-symptoms-at-war-zone-level/

Robinson, H.M., Sigman, M.R., & Wilson, J.P. (1997). Duty-Related stressors and PTSD symptoms in suburban police officers. *Psychological Reports*, *81*(3), 835–845.

Rocheleau, A.M. (2014). Prisoners' coping skills and involvement in serious prison misconduct and violence. *Victims & Offenders*, *9*(2), 149–177.

Şenol-Durak, E., Durak, M., & Gençöz, T. (2006). Development of work stress scale for correctional officers. *Journal of Occupational Rehabilitation*, *16*(1), 153–164.

Skevington, S.M., Lotfy, M., & O'Connell, K.A. (2004). The World Health Organization's WHOQOL-BREF quality of life assessment: Psychometric properties and results of the international field trial. A Report from the WHOQOL Group. *Quality of Life Research*, *13*(2), 299–310.

Spinaris, C., G., Denhof, M. D., & Kellaway, J. A. (2012). posttraumatic stress disorder in United States corrections professionals: prevalence and impact on health and functioning. In *Desert Waters Correctional Outreach*, 1-32. .

Steiner, B., & Wooldredge, J. (2015). Individual and environmental sources of work stress among prison officers. *Criminal Justice and Behavior*, *42*(8), 800–818.

Summerlin, Z., Oehme, K., Stern, N., & Valentine, C. (2010). Disparate levels of stress in police and correctional officers: Preliminary evidence from a pilot study on domestic violence. *Journal of Human Behavior in the Social Environment*, *20*(6), 762–777.

Swenson, D.X., Waseleski, D., & Hartl, R. (2008). Shift work and correctional officers: Effects and strategies for adjustment. *Journal of Correctional Health Care*, *14*(4), 299–310.

Tanielian, T., & Jaycox, L. (eds). (2008). *Invisible wounds of war: Recommendations for addressing psychological and cognitive injuries*. Santa Monica, CA: Rand.

Triplett, R., Mullings, J.L., & Scarborough, K.E. (1999). Examining the effect of work-home conflict on work-related stress among correctional officers. *Journal of Criminal Justice*, *27*(4), 371–385.

VanItallie, T.B. (2002). Stress: A risk factor for serious illness. *Metabolism*, *51*(6), 40–45.

Vila, B., Kenney, D. J., Morrison, G. B., & Reuland, M., (2000). Evaluating the effects of fatigue on police patrol officers. Washington, DC: Police Executive Research Forum.

Weathers, F.W., Litz, B.T., Keane, T.M., Palmieri, P.A., Marx, B.P., & Schnurr, P.P. (2013). *The PTSD Checklist for DSM5 (PCL5)*. National Center for PTSD. at www.ptsd.va.gov, 10.

Weathers, F.W., Marx, B.P., Friedman, M.J., & Schnurr, P.P. (2014). Posttraumatic Stress Disorder in DSM-5: New Criteria, New Measures, and Implications for Assessment. *Psychological Injury and Law*, *7*(2), 93–107.

Wickwire, E.M., Geiger-Brown, J., Scharf, S.M., & Drake, C.L. (2017). Shift work and shift work sleep disorder. *Chest*, *151*(5), 1156–1172.

Appendix A. Dependent variables scales

Perceived Stress Scale (PSS)

Response options: 0 = Never; 1 = Almost Never; 2 = Sometimes; 3 = Fairly Often; 4 = Very Often

(1) In the past month, how often have you been upset because of something that happened unexpectedly?
(2) In the past month, how often have you felt that you were unable to control the important things in your life?
(3) In the past month, how often have you felt nervous and stressed?
(4) In the past month, how often have you felt confident about your ability to handle your personal problems? (reverse coded)
(5) In the past month, how often have you felt that things were going your way? (reverse coded)
(6) In the past month, how often have you felt that you could not cope with all the things you had to do?
(7) In the past month, how often have you been able to control irritations in your life? (reverse coded)
(8) In the past month, how often have you felt that you were on top of things? (reverse coded)
(9) In the past month, how often have you been angered because of things that were outside of your control?
(10) In the past month, how often have you felt difficulties were piling up so high that you could not overcome them?

Posttraumatic Stress Disorder Checklist (PCL-5)

Response options: 0 = Not at all; 1 = A little bit; 2 = Moderately; 3 = Quite a bit; 4 = Extremely
In the past month, how much were you bothered by:

(1) Repeated, disturbing, and unwanted memories of the stressful experience?
(2) Repeated, disturbing dreams of the stressful experience?
(3) Suddenly feeling or acting as if the stressful experience were actually happening again (as if you were actually back there reliving it)?
(4) Feeling very upset when something reminded you of the stressful experience?
(5) Having strong physical reactions when something reminded you of the stressful experience (for example, heart pounding, trouble breathing, sweating)?
(6) Avoiding memories, thoughts, or feelings related to the stressful experience?
(7) Avoiding external reminders of the stressful experience (for example, people, places, conversations, activities, objects, or situations)?
(8) Trouble remembering important parts of the stressful experience?
(9) Having strong negative beliefs about yourself, other people, or the world (for example, having thoughts such as: I am bad, there is something seriously wrong with me, no one can be trusted, the world is completely dangerous)?
(10) Blaming yourself or someone else for the stressful experience or what happened after it?
(11) Having strong negative feelings such as fear, horror, anger, guilt, or shame?

(12) Loss of interest in activities that you used to enjoy?
(13) Feeling distant or cut off from other people?
(14) Trouble experiencing positive feelings (for example, being unable to feel happiness or have loving feelings for people close to you)?
(15) Irritable behavior, angry outbursts, or acting aggressively?
(16) Taking too many risks or doing things that could cause you harm?
(17) Being 'superalert' or watchful or on guard?
(18) Feeling jumpy or easily startled?
(19) Having difficulty concentrating?
(20) Trouble falling or staying asleep?

World Health Organization Quality of Life-Brief (WHOWOLF-BREF)

(1) How would you rate your quality of life?

Response Options: 1 = Very poor; 2 = Poor; 3 = Neither good nor poor; 4 = Good; 5 = Very good

(1) How satisfied are you with your health?

Response Options: 1 = Very dissatisfied; 2 = Dissatisfied; 3 = Neither satisfied nor dissatisfied; 4 = Satisfied; 5 = Very satisfied

The following questions ask about **how much** you have experienced certain things in the last two weeks.

Response Options: 1 = Not at all; 2 = A little; 3 = A moderate amount; 4 = Very much; 5 = Extremely

(1) To what extent do you feel that physical pain prevents you from doing what you need to do? (reverse coded)
(2) How much do you need any medical treatment to function in your daily life? (reverse coded)
(3) How much do you enjoy life?
(4) To what extent do you feel your life to be meaningful?
(5) How well are you able to concentrate?
(6) How safe do you feel in your daily life?
(7) How healthy is your physical environment?

The following questions ask about **how completely** you experience or were able to do certain things in the last two weeks

1 = Not at all 2 = A little 3 = Moderately 4 = Mostly 5 = Completely

(1) Do you have enough energy for everyday life?
(2) Are you able to accept your bodily appearance?
(3) Have you enough money to meet your needs?
(4) How available to you is the information that you need in your day-to-day life?
(5) To what extent do you have the opportunity for leisure activities?
(6) How well are you able to get around?

The following questions ask you to say **how good or satisfied** you have felt about various aspects of your life over the last two weeks

Response Options: 1 = Very dissatisfied; 2 = Dissatisfied; 3 = Neither satisfied nor dissatisfied; 4 = Satisfied; 5 = Very satisfied

(1) How satisfied are you with your sleep?
(2) How satisfied are you with your ability to perform your daily living activities?
(3) How satisfied are you with your capacity for work?
(4) How satisfied are you with yourself?
(5) How satisfied are you with your personal relationships?

(6) How satisfied are you with your sex life?
(7) How satisfied are you with the support you get from your friends?
(8) How satisfied are you with the conditions of your living place?
(9) How satisfied are you with your access to health services?
(10) How satisfied are you with your transport?

The following question refers to **how often** you have felt or experienced certain things in the last two weeks

Response Options: 1 = Never; 2 = Seldom; 3 = Quite often; 4 = Very often; 5 = Always

How often do you have negative feelings such as blue mood, despair, anxiety, depression? (reverse coded)

Stress doesn't kill us, it's our reaction: exploring the relationship between coping mechanisms and correctional officer PTSD

Katie Hughes Taylor and Kristin Swartz

ABSTRACT

Developing research demonstrates that correctional officers (CO's) are at a higher risk for Post-Traumatic Stress Disorder (PTSD) than the general population, less is known about the relationship between how CO's cope with stress. Most CO's will be exposed to chronic stress and trauma while working in prisons, with approximately one-third of CO's eventually suffering from PTSD. It is important to explore the relationship between coping and PTSD because if certain coping styles are associated with different levels of PTSD, this could be used to inform training and programming for officers. This study examines officer coping and whether they impact the severity of PTSD symptoms among a group of approximately 245 correctional officers across seven adult state institutions from one Southern state. While controlling for exposure to violence and trauma experienced while on the job and adverse childhood experiences (ACEs), this study explores whether multiple problem-focused and emotion-focused coping mechanisms are associated with the level of PTSD symptoms experienced by CO's. Results indicated multiple problem- and emotion-focused coping mechanisms were significantly related to PTSD symptoms, even when controlling for exposure to violence and trauma, ACEs, and other controls. Implications these findings have for practice, and directions for future research are discussed.

Introduction

Prisons are stressful, violent, and often times traumatic environments in which to work. Correctional officers, as the first responders to any critical incident in the institution, are often the staff most exposed to this violence and trauma. In a nationwide sample, Spinaris, Denhof, and Kellaway (2012) found that corrections professionals experienced 28 exposures to violence, injuries, or deaths across their career at the time of the survey. Denhof and Spinaris (2016) further found that approximately 28% of correctional officers within a statewide sample had extreme exposure levels to violence, injury, and death while on the job. Additionally, correctional officers are expected to serve in various roles in an environment where they have limited resources and are often significantly understaffed. There has been significant media coverage regarding staffing shortages within both state and federal prisons. For example, at a federal prison in Texas, inmates are often locked down in their cells over the weekend because there are not enough staff to effectively supervise them (The Associated Press, 2021). This same article notes that officers in a prison in Illinois are forced to work 60 hours of overtime due to shortages. Officers in Nebraska note that the lack of staffing has led to threats of riots from inmates and that one of their units went from 35 officers down to less than 10 (Safchik, 2021). Finally, an article from *Corrections Today* outlines that there are multiple barriers for recruitment and retention, including the inability to offer competitive pay, increased danger, and the possibility of required overtime (Sumpter, 2008). All the factors – managing a difficult population, exposure to chronic violence and trauma, limited resources, and understaffing – culminate to create a difficult work environment that ultimately impacts correctional officers' physical and mental health. While well overdue, correctional researchers and correctional practitioners have finally begun to focus on these health consequences. However, what is less understood to date are potential protective factors that could help mitigate the effects this stressful, traumatic, and violent environment has on these negative physical and mental health outcomes.

Traditionally correctional staff research has focused on work outcomes, such as job satisfaction and job burnout; however, over the past several years, correctional staff research has begun to shift focus to the negative effects working in corrections has on staff's mental health, and to a lesser degree, their physical health. The bulk of this research has focused on Post-Traumatic Stress Disorder (PTSD) as a result of exposure to violence and trauma on the job. There has been consistent research indicating that approximately one-third of correctional officers suffer from PTSD (Denhof & Spinaris, 2013; Denhof & Spinaris, 2016; Swartz, French, Roberts, & Tolle, 2017) and that the frequency and magnitude of trauma exposure places correctional officers at a higher risk for PTSD. While the body of research on PTSD among correctional staff and the risk factors for PTSD is growing, research regarding possible protective or insulating factors is less developed. For example, research outside of corrections has demonstrated that certain coping repertoires or styles can mitigate the effects of trauma on individuals; or in other words, those who use certain coping mechanisms are less likely to suffer from PTSD (Boden, Bonn-Miller, Vujanovic, & Drescher, 2012; Lee, Park, & Sim., 2018). Therefore, this study aims to fill this gap in the literature by exploring whether a variety of problem-focused and emotion-focused coping mechanisms are associated with lower levels of PTSD symptomology among a group of correctional officers.

Correctional officer traumas and PTSD

Due to the population, they supervise and the difficult working conditions of being under resourced and understaffed, being a correctional officer can be a very stressful job, and the sources and types of stress are varied. Further, correctional officers are exposed to multiple types of trauma that are often chronic in nature while working in prison. Because of these varied stressors, including exposure to trauma, understanding the consequences of exposure to chronic stress and trauma is important.

Research has identified four main stressors that correctional officers face that contribute to their overall exposure to trauma (Bower, 2013). These include: 1) occupational stressors; 2) organizational/administrative stressors; 3) psychosocial stressors; and 4) inmate-related stressors. Occupational stressors encompass the nature of a closed work environment, role ambiguity, hyper-vigilance, and the code of silence that tends to permeate first responders, where asking for help of any kind is seen as a weakness. Organizational or administrative stressors, however, stem from the organization for which the individual works. These include supervisory support and security level on the organizational side, and lack of trust in the administration, no input on decision-making, and mandatory overtime. For example, research has found relationships between increased organizational/administrative stressors and emotional burnout and increased amounts of stress (Griffin, 2006; Lambert et al., 2010a). The third stressors outlined by Bower (2013) are the psychosocial stressors. These can be individual level stressors, such as fear and lack of assertiveness. However, work-family conflict is also mentioned as a psychosocial stressor and has been studied extensively in the correctional system (for example see Higgins, Swartz, & Roberts, 2021; Lambert & Hogan, 2010b; Lambert, Hogan, & Barton, 2004; Lambert, Hogan, Camp, & Ventura, 2006). This research consistently shows that the conflicts that correctional workers face at their jobs negatively bleed over into their personal lives whether it is relationships with family or relationships with friends. Finally, and arguably the most important stressor for correctional officers regarding their exposure to trauma are inmate-related stressors – that is the direct or indirect trauma experienced due to working with the inmate population (Bower, 2013). These include witnessing assaults, attempted or completed suicides and being assaulted by inmates. Further, because over half the prison population suffers from a mental illness, which often manifests with self-harm, correctional officers often play a role in not only supervising but also treating inmates (James & Glaze, 2006). Research has indicated that being exposed to violence and trauma while working in prison is inevitable. For example, Spinaris et al. (2012) found that 100% of their sample (n = 3599) had experienced at least one event involving violence, injury, or death while on the job, with the average number of 28 experiences across their career.

PTSD occurs when an individual directly experiences or is exposed to violent and traumatic events. After individuals encounter violence or trauma, they may start to develop PTSD symptoms, such as avoidance, hyper-vigilance, nightmares, or dissociation from the world around them. Often, PTSD is diagnosed after a singular traumatic event. Examining PTSD among correctional officers is unique because they work in an inherently violent and traumatic profession, lending itself to chronic exposure to trauma.

With trauma being the requirement for PTSD, due to exposure to violence and trauma, it is understandable that correctional officers are at a much higher risk than the general population of suffering from PTSD. Multiple studies have found that approximately one-third of officers meet the criteria for PTSD (Denhof & Spinaris, 2012; Denhof & Spinaris, 2016; Swartz et al., 2017) compared to about only 8% of the general population (APA, 2013; Kilpatrick et al., 2013). Further, the prevalence rates for PTSD symptoms among correctional staff are higher than other similar occupations, such as policing, with prevalence rates between 13% and 19%, (Robinson, Sigman, & Wilson, 1997; West et al.,

2008), and firefighters demonstrating prevalence rates between 26% and 32% (Boffa et al., 2017; Bryant & Harvey, 1996). Therefore, correctional officers are at an increased risk of developing and suffering from PTSD symptoms.

While correctional officers are at a much higher risk for suffering from PTSD than the general population, and even most other first responder groups, still, most do not suffer from PTSD. Therefore, research has also begun to explore potential risk factors for PTSD. For example, the years of service working in corrections or tenure are positively associated with PTSD symptoms (Denhof & Spinaris, 2016; Swartz et al., 2017). That is, the longer an individual works in corrections, the higher the risk they are for suffering PTSD symptoms. Officers who had higher levels of job ambiguity were also at a higher risk of developing PTSD (James & Todak, 2018). Security levels also appear to influence the risk of developing PTSD. Even while controlling for the number of violent and traumatic events experienced, those working in maximum custody institutions were at a significantly higher risk of suffering from PTSD (Swartz et al., 2017). The last, and likely most consistent and important predictor of PTSD symptomology is the number of violent and traumatic events experienced on the job. Specifically, the more exposure to trauma and violence, the more likely the officer is to suffer from PTSD symptoms (James & Todak, 2018; Spinaris et al., 2012; Swartz et al., 2017).

The above listed risk factors for PTSD generally relate to the correctional officer's job within the prison system. There are, however, other risk factors for developing PTSD as an adult. One risk factor that has been identified within the trauma literature is the number of adverse childhood experience someone has. These experiences include witnessing intimate partner violence, neglect, having someone in the home with a mental illness, having someone in the home who is addicted, and having a family member go to prison (Felitti et al., 1998; Widom, Czaja, & Dutton, 2008). Using the Adverse Childhood Experiences scale (ACEs), research has found that individuals who experience more ACEs have a higher likelihood of developing PTSD as an adult (Felitti et al., 1998; Widom et al., 2008). Felitti et al. (1998) also uncovered that individuals who experienced higher levels of adverse childhood experiences were also at a higher risk for smoking, obesity, depression, and suicide attempts. There has been little research on ACEs as risk factors for PTSD among first responder populations. For example, one of the few studies examining Iraq and Afghanistan veterans. Carroll, Currier, McCormick, and Drescher (2017) found that treatment-seeking veterans who were exposed to adverse childhood experiences were more likely to suffer from increased suicide risk. Research surrounding other first responder populations, correctional officers included, regarding exposure to adverse childhood experiences has not been published.

Though this body of research regarding PTSD among correctional officers is growing, we still know rather little about what set those officers who do not suffer from PTSD from those who do. Continued attention on researching the possible protective factors risk factors is warranted. If we have a better understanding of these protective and risk factors, we could better prepare correctional officers for the job based upon these factors. The overall goal of this body of research is ultimately to help officers do their job without suffering from the negative consequences of PTSD. For example, those with PTSD are at a higher risk for also suffering from depression (Breslau, Davis, Peterson, & Schultz, 2000), at a higher risk for suicidality (Chen, Yoon, Harford, & Grant, 2017; Gradus, 2017; Panagioti, Gooding, & Tarrier, 2015) and the symptoms of PTSD often affect one's relationships with family and friends (McFarlane & Bookless, 2001; Ray & Vanstone, 2009) and their job performance (Adler et al., 2011; Regehr & LeBlanc, 2017). One possible avenue to explore is whether the ways in which correctional officers' cope with stress and trauma place them at a higher or lower risk for suffering from PTSD.

Coping

Correctional officers have been identified as having increased amounts of stress and trauma through the work they complete on a daily basis. Stress is often defined as the nonspecific response of the body to any demand (Selye, 1956). Utilizing a learned set of coping skills is one of the ways that individuals handle their perceived and actual stressors. In their 1984 book, *Stress Appraisal, and Coping,* Folkman and Lazarus define coping as 'constantly changing cognitive and behavioral efforts to manage specific external and internal demands that are appraised as taxing or exceeding the resources of the person' (p. 141). Research regarding coping mechanisms surrounding singular stressful or traumatic events is not new, and coping research broadly has brought insight into how individuals work through everyday stressors, increased stress, and traumatic events. Coping has often been broken down into two separate categories. They are known as problem-focused coping mechanisms and emotion-focused coping mechanisms (Folkman and Lazarus, 1984). When coping is problem-focused, individuals feel they have some sense of control over the situation and its outcome. There are several coping mechanisms that fall into this category including making a plan of action and coming up with ways to attack the problem. Emotion-focused coping, however, is generally used when individuals who are under stress feel they have little to no control over the situation and its outcome (Folkman & Lazarus, 1984). Emotion-focused coping mechanisms include responses like avoidance, denial, acceptance, and seeking emotional support. It should be noted that adaptive and maladaptive coping mechanisms have been identified in both the problem- and emotion-focused categories.

While research regarding coping among correctional staff is essentially non-existent, outside of corrections, research has begun to reveal that one's coping style or coping repertoire can impact their risk for suffering from various mental health issues and overall well-being. For example, in a meta-analysis, Moskowitz, Hult, Bessolari, and Acree (2009) found that using positive or adaptive coping mechanisms resulted in better physical and mental health and that maladaptive or negative coping mechanisms were associated with poorer mental and physical health. Studies have also shown that individuals who were depressed were more likely to use maladaptive coping mechanisms, such as self-blame and venting (Faulk, Gloria, & Steinhardt, 2013). Further coping and depression research has found that when adaptive coping mechanisms are used, such as optimism and social support, depressive symptoms decreased (Kolchakian & Sears, 1999). The relationship between coping with anxiety has also been studied, and like depression, individuals who cope by using maladaptive coping mechanisms are more likely to suffer from anxiety. For example, those who utilized denial, behavioral disengagement, and mental disengagement were more likely to suffer from increased anxiety (Liverant, Hofmann, & Litz, 2004; Savitsky, Findling, Ereli, & Hendel, 2020). However, similar to research on coping and depression, using adaptive coping mechanisms resulted in decreased levels of anxiety (Auerbach, Beckerman, & Blanco, 2013). Finally, coping has been examined with individuals who suffer from PTSD symptoms. Similar to both depression and anxiety, when individuals utilize coping mechanisms such as denial and behavioral disengagement, they are more likely to suffer from increased levels of PTSD (Jeavons, De, Horne, & Greenwood, 2000; McNeill & Galovski, 2015). Research has found that first responders that utilize mechanisms such as active coping and using social support correlate with decreased rates of PTSD (Boden et al., 2012; Lee et al., 2018).

Materials and methods

The current study explores several research questions aimed at exploring the relationships between correctional officers' coping skills and the likelihood of suffering from PTSD. The two main research questions for the current study are as follows:

RQ1: Are various problem-focused coping mechanisms associated with PTSD symptomology?

RQ2: Are various emotion-focused coping mechanisms associated with PTSD symptomology?

The data for the current study comes from a much larger National Institute of Justice funded study titled, *Effects of Mindfulness-Based Stress Reduction in Correctional Officers: A Biopsychosocial Approach* (NIJ 2017-R2-CX-0035). However, in this study, the focus is on whether various coping strategies are associated with higher or lower risks of suffering from PTSD while controlling for the correctional officers' exposure to trauma. The data for the current study comes from the baseline survey data collected prior to half of the participants receiving an 8-week Mindfulness-Based Stress Reduction (MBSR) program with each class meeting for 2 hours. The MBSR program was created specifically for the correctional officer population in mind and followed all the major tenents of the MBSR program. Classes did include psychoeducation but were heavily weighted in experiential exercises such as body scans and meditation. The sample includes 245 correctional officers from 7 different adult state institutions, from one Southern state. The average age for the sample was 37.6 years old, approximately 73% of the sample were male. Out of the officers in the study, 50% were married.

Measures

All the variables for the current study came from the survey collected prior to the Mindfulness intervention was given to half of the sample. The scales and distributions for all variables are displayed below in (Table 1). The dependent variable for the current study is the correctional officers' score from the PTSD symptoms Checklist (PCL-5). This is a 20-item questionnaire that focuses exclusively on PTSD. Developed by Weathers and colleagues in 2015, the PCL-5 has three main purposes, which include screening individuals for PTSD, monitoring symptom changes among individuals before and during treatment, and making provisional PTSD diagnoses. The PCL-5 is a self-reported PTSD assessment that takes approximately 5–10 minutes to complete and does not require a clinician. The PCL-5 asks the individual to recall their feelings about stressful events over the past month. The prompt given to the respondents is 'In the past month, how often

Table 1. Descriptive statistics.

Variable	Mean	S.D.	Range	N
Dependent Variable				
PCL-5 Score	30.5	17.9	0–78	243
Independent Variables				
Problem Focused Coping				
Social Support	8.9	3.2	4–16	243
Planning	10.3	2.9	4–16	243
Active Coping	9.8	2.5	4–16	243
Restraint	9.2	2.4	4–16	243
Emotion Focused Coping				
Positive Growth	11.1	2.7	4–16	243
Acceptance	10.7	2.9	4–16	243
Religion	9.0	4.3	3–16	243
Emotional Support	7.7	3.4	3–16	243
Denial	5.7	2.1	3–16	243
Humor	9.7	3.6	4–16	243
Magnitude of Exposure to Trauma	3.2	1.4	1–6.3	243
Control Variables				
ACEs Score	2.6	2.5	0–10	234
Gender	.73	.44	0–1	243
Age	37.6	12.0	21–77	243
Marital Status	.50	.50	0–1	242
Correctional Experience	81.4	77.2	.5–394	242

have you been bothered by . . .,' then the item. The assessment is scored on a Likert scale where 0 = 'Not at all,' 1 = 'A little bit,' 2 = 'Moderately,' 3 = 'Quite a bit,' and 4 = 'Extremely.' The scores for the 20 items PCL-5 were summed to create the total PCL-5 score which serves as the dependent variable in the current study.

The key independent variables for the current study come from the COPE Inventory. The COPE includes 15 subscales that measure various coping mechanisms on a Likert scale of 0 (I usually do not do this at all) to 4 (I usually do this a lot) (Carver, Scheier, & Weintraub, 1989). The COPE Inventory determines how often the respondent utilizes the coping mechanisms described in the item. The items are then grouped into subscales in which there are four items. Although there are 15 subscales within the COPE Inventory, the current analysis focuses on a select number of subscales. The inclusion of the subscales for the current analysis was determined based on two criteria: 1) the coping mechanisms that fall into the two categories designated by Carver as problem-focused or emotion-focused; and 2) had alphas over .6. These subscales, the items within them, and their Cronbach's alpha value are listed in (Table 2) below. The problem-focused subscales used in the current analysis *planning, active coping, social support, and restraint.* Planning focuses on one's ability to make arrangements for the future regarding their stressful situation, while active coping has the individual working through the stressful situation in real time. When social support is utilized, the individual takes the time to seek out others to talk to who have been in their current situation. Finally, using restraint has the individual evaluating the situation until they feel it is appropriate to act. The emotion-focused subscales used are *positive growth, denial, emotional support, acceptance, religion*, and *humor*. Positive growth refers to the individual's willingness and ability to turn negative situations into learning or growing experiences. Denial, on the other hand, is the opposite, where stress-affected individuals deny the situation is having an impact on them. Emotional support is similar to social support, however, the support the individual receives is emotional in nature, such as venting their emotions. Acceptance is the idea

Table 2. COPE inventory scales.

Emotion Focused		Problem Focused	
Name	α	Name	α
Denial	.718	**Active Coping**	.624
I say to myself 'this isn't real' I refuse to believe that it has happened I pretend that it hasn't really happened I act as though it hasn't even happened		I concentrate my efforts on doing something about it. I take additional action to try to get rid of the problem. I take direct action to get around the problem. I do what has to be done, one step at a time.	
Religion	.927	**Planning**	.827
I put my trust in God I seek God's help I try to find comfort in my religion I pray more than usual		I make a plan of action. I try to come up with a strategy about what to do. I think about how I might best handle the problem I think hard about what steps to take.	
Emotional Support	.856	**Social Support**	.795
I discuss my feelings with someone I try to get emotional support from friends or relatives I get sympathy and understanding from someone I talk to someone about how I feel		I try to get advice from someone about what to do. I talk to someone to find out more about the situation. I talk to someone who could do something concrete about the problem. I ask people who have had similar experiences what they did.	
Positive Growth	.764	**Restraint**	.606
I try to grow as a person as a result of the experience I try to see it in a different light, to make it seem more positive I look for something good in what is happening I learn something from the experience		I restrain myself from doing anything too quickly. I hold off doing anything about it until the situation permits. I make sure not to make matters worse by acting too soon. I force myself to wait for the right time to do something.	
Acceptance	.771		
I get used to the idea that it happened. I accept it has happened and that it can't be changed I accept the reality of the fact that it happened I learn to live with it			
Humor	.889		
I laugh about the situation I make jokes about it I kid around about it. I make fun of the situation.			

that the individual understands and accepts what is happening to them. The religious subscale measures the individual's likelihood of turning to religion or prayer for guidance during the situation. Finally, humor is making jokes and lessening the tension through making fun of the situation. In the seminal 1989 article, Carver and colleagues did not identify *humor* as an emotion-focused or problem-focused coping mechanism. However, much of the research has labeled humor as an emotion-focused coping mechanism (Abel, 2002; Rim, 1988). Though some researchers have argued that humor falls into both categories (Kuiper, Rod, & Olinger, 1993; Lefcourt, Davison, Prkachin, & Mills, 1997), *humor* ultimately was placed into the emotion-focused category for this analysis due to many previous studies categorizing it as emotion-focused. The most frequently used coping mechanisms were *positive growth* with a mean of 11.1, followed by *acceptance* with a mean of 10.7, and *planning* with a mean of 10.3. The least used coping mechanism reported by the sample was *denial* with a low mean of 5.7.

Because previous research has consistently demonstrated that the frequency or magnitude of exposure to trauma is strongly predicted with PTSD symptomology, another important independent variable is the *magnitude of exposure to trauma*, which measures the frequency and recency of violent and traumatic events experienced by correctional officers while on the job. This variable comes from the Violence, Injury, and Death Exposure Scale also known as the VIDES (Denhof & Spinaris, 2014). This scale was developed to determine the magnitude of direct and indirect trauma exposure experienced while on the job. The VIDES consists of 12 items, of which seven are direct exposure items, and the remaining five are indirect exposure items. Direct exposure to trauma includes being physically assaulted, encountering deceased individuals, or witnessing attempted or completed suicide. Indirect trauma exposure includes situations such as witnessing an assault and learning about any of the direct trauma incidents against another person (Denhof & Spinaris, 2016). Each item asks how many times the respondent has experienced a specific event. The item responses are recorded on a Likert scale where 0 = 'Never;' 1 = 'Once;' 2 = '2–3 Times;' 3 = '4–6 Times;' 4 = '7–9 Times;' and 5 = '10 + Times.' In addition to measuring the frequency of the exposure to violence or trauma, the VIDES also measures the recency of each experience. The recency component of the measure asks when the most recent exposure of each event occurred. It is measured on a Likert scale, where 0 = 'Never;' 1 = '1–30 Days Ago;' 2 = '2–3 Months Ago;' 3 = '4–6 Months Ago;' 4 = '7–12 Months Ago;' and 5 = 'More Than a Year Ago.' Then, to calculate the exposure to trauma scores the Response-to-Numeric Score Conversion Key created by Denhof and Spinaris (2014) was used. To calculate the *magnitude of exposure to trauma*, the scores from both frequency of exposure and recency are summed. This is done for all 12 items on the VIDES. Once the response from each individual item is determined, they are added together and then divided by 12. This creates the VIDES score which is also the *magnitude of exposure to trauma*. Denhof and Spinaris (2014) note that exposure scores >1 and <2 are slight exposure, ≥ 2 and <3 are fair exposure, ≥ 3 and <4 are moderately high exposure, ≥ 4 and <5 are high exposure, and that scores that are ≥5 are extreme exposure. The mean for the current sample is 3.2, which indicates that the correctional officers in this study have experienced moderately high levels of trauma exposure. The standard deviation for the *magnitude of exposure to trauma* is 1.38 and the minimum is 1.00 and the maximum is 6.28.

Control variables

Control variables for the current study include the basic demographic variables of *age*, measured in years; *gender* (Male = 1; Female = 0); and *marital status* (Married = 1; Not married = 0). Age, gender, and marital status are all important control variables because previous research has demonstrated that these may function as important correlates of PTSD symptomology. For example, previous research using general population samples has found that younger individuals (Breslau, 2009; Perrin et al., 2014) and females (Breslau, 2009; Coronas, García-Parés, Viladrich, Santos, & Menchón, 2008; Kilpatrick et al., 2013; Perrin et al., 2014) are more likely to suffer from PTSD after experiencing trauma. However, among the correctional staff population, research has indicated that males might be at a higher risk than females (Spinaris et al., 2012). Additionally, being married appears to somewhat insulate individuals from PTSD, that is, those who are married are less likely to suffer from PTSD than those who are not married (Berger et al., 2007; Corneil, Beaton, Murphy, Johnson, & Pike, 1999).

Additional job characteristic control variables were also included – correctional experience. *Correctional experience* was measured by the number of months working within the correctional field. The last control variable included in the study comes from the Adverse Childhood Experiences Scale (ACEs). The ACEs is a 10-item questionnaire that measures experiences of abuse, neglect, and other household challenges, such as having a parent incarcerated from childhood. ACEs are measured by summing up the number of adverse experiences, and an individual can experience anywhere from zero to all 10 of the experiences. Previous research has demonstrated that those who have had more adverse childhood experiences are also at a higher risk for PTSD (Frewen, Zhu, & Lanius, 2019; Widom et al., 2008); therefore, it is important to control for these negative childhood experiences.

Analytic strategy

To answer our research questions, we conduct two multivariate linear regression models. Due to the dependent variable, PCL-5 score, being continuous in nature and approximating a normal distribution linear regression, is appropriate. The first model explores whether any of the problem-focused coping mechanisms predicted PTSD symptoms while controlling for exposure experienced on the job, adverse childhood experiences, and relevant demographics and job characteristics. The second model parallels the first model except for Model 2 explores the relationship between the emotion-focused coping mechanisms with PTSD and all controls.

Results

To determine whether various coping mechanisms predict the severity of PTSD symptoms suffered by correctional officers, the various coping mechanisms from the COPE inventory were divided into two categories – problem focused and emotion focused. The first model examined the relationships between the four problem-focused coping mechanisms of *social support, planning, active coping*, and *restraint* with the correctional officers' PCL-5 score while controlling for all relevant controls. The results for this model are displayed below in (Table 3).

The results of this model indicated that the only coping mechanism significantly predicted the PCL-5 score was planning. The model indicated that more frequent use of planning as a coping mechanism was associated with lower levels of PTSD symptoms. The other three coping mechanisms of social support, active coping, and restraint were not found to predict higherPCL-5 scores. However, the model also indicated that the number of ACEs that an officer experienced was significantly and positively predicted a higher PCL-5 score. Furthermore, the VIDEs was also significantly and positively predicted increased levels of PTSD symptoms, according to the PCL-5. This means that, as expected, those correctional officers who had been exposed to more violence, and trauma on the job and had experienced more adverse childhood experiences were also more likely to

Table 3. Trauma and problem-focused coping.

Variable	B	S. E
Magnitude of Exposure to Trauma	3.9**	.853
ACEs Score	1.3**	.429
Social Support	.345	.419
Planning	−2.16**	.528
Active Coping	.327	.614
Restraint	.644	.488
Gender	−4.3	2.4
Age	−.183	.115
Marital Status	.226	.853
Correctional Experience	−.021	.018
	$R^2 = .252$	

**$p \leq 0.01$.

Table 4. Trauma and emotion-focused coping.

Variable	B	S. E
Magnitude of Exposure to Trauma	2.58**	.853
ACEs Score	1.28**	.422
Positive Growth	−1.15**	.475
Acceptance	.381	.454
Religion	.131	.265
Emotional Support	−.604	.076
Denial	2.49**	.480
Humor	.414	.329
Gender	−4.48	2.39
Age	−.129	.113
Marital Status	−.221	2.08
Correctional Experience	−.026	.018
	$R^2 = .310$	

**$p \leq 0.01$.

suffer from higher PTSD symptoms. None of the control variables – *gender, age, correctional experience,* and *marital status* – were significantly related to PTSD symptoms, which is unsurprising given the literature surround correctional officer PTSD.

Model 2- emotion focused model

Model 2, which is outlined in (Table 4), displays theemotion-focused coping mechanisms that were explored along with the outlined control variables. This model also revealed multiple significant associations between the PCL-5 and the independent variables. There is consistency across the models in that both show significant and positive associations between PCL-5 PTSD symptoms and the VIDES score and the total number of ACEs an officer has experienced. There are two significant coping mechanisms in the current model. First, *denial's* significant positive prediction indicates that as officers utilize *denial* as a coping mechanism, they are more likely to suffer from increased PTSD symptoms.

The second significant-coping mechanism within the emotion-focused category is *positive growth*, and the negative association with PTSD symptoms indicates that as officers utilize this inherently prosocial-coping mechanism are less likely to suffer from PTSD symptoms. Consistent with model 1 and previous PTSD literature on correctional staff, the control variables were not significantly related to PTSD symptoms.

Discussion

As indicated by the presented results, there are multiple significant variables when investigating what causes increased likelihood of developing PTSD symptoms. At the same time, there are also variables that present themselves as insulators to the traumatic effects of working in prison. Both of the proposed research questions were answered by the regression models performed. First, it was found that only one of the examined problem-focused coping mechanisms had a significantly predicted PTSD symptomology. *Planning*, was found to have a negative relationship with PTSD symptoms, indicating that as correctional officers took time to plan, they were less likely to suffer from increased PTSD symptoms. The National Institute of Mental Health (2019) notes that having strategies, one of which is the use of planning, to get through traumatic events, is considered a resiliency factor and could contribute to lower levels of PTSD symptoms. Therefore, it has been shown that the use of planning is an important tool in an officer's arsenal to combat PTSD.

The second research question, which explored whether emotion-focused coping mechanisms predicted PTSD symptomology, was also answered in the analysis performed. Although there was only one significant problem-focused coping mechanism, there were two emotion-focused coping mechanisms that were significantly related to PTSD symptoms. Both *positive growth* (-) and *denial* (+) predicted PTSD symptoms.

As the use of *positive growth* increased, the level of PTSD symptoms decreased within the sample. This finding is not unexpected, as the National Institute of Mental Health (2019) found that individuals who try to learn something from their stressful experiences are more likely to be resilient to developing PTSD. Coping programs that focus on the reinterpreting negative stressors into positive growth opportunities could be desirable for correctional officers since they have shown to offer resiliency factors to stress and PTSD.

Denial was found to have a positive relationship with PTSD symptoms, indicating that as officers increased their use of *denial* as a coping mechanism, they were more likely to suffer from increased PTSD symptoms. When examining as to why *denial* leads to an increase in PTSD among military veterans, Kaplan (2008) found that veterans were not seeking PTSD treatment due to the denial of their symptoms. Because undiagnosed PTSD rarely resolves itself, it is logical that as officers fail to seek treatment, they suffer from increased severity of PTSD.

Although it was a cognizant goal of the principal investigator and research team to follow best practice in their design and study implementation, the current study is not without limitations. The current data is cross-sectional in nature. The current analysis, therefore, provides only a snapshot into the difficult and traumatic jobs that correctional officers perform on a daily basis. Additionally, temporal order cannot be determined, and causal inferences cannot be made. Second, all the data used in the current analysis is self-reported data. Though best efforts were made to ensure the importance of complete and honest data, issues of memory and the perception of the questions asked are inherent to survey research. Although arguments are often made about the lack of generalizability, the authors here argue that the analysis and results of this study are generalizable to the larger correctional officer population. The current sample is very close to other correctional officer samples, both state and nationwide. Age and gender makeup are similar across state and nationwide samples (Spinaris et al., 2012; Swartz et al., 2017).

The results regarding coping mechanisms and their impact on PTSD symptoms among correctional officers open up a multitude of implications for policy and practice. It is understood that correctional officers suffer from increased levels of PTSD (Denhof & Spinaris, 2016; Spinaris et al., 2012; Swartz et al., 2017). Exposure to violent and traumatic events (VTEs) has been determined as the top factor in whether officers develop PTSD. The likelihood of officer exposure to violence and trauma decreasing while continuing to work within a prison setting is small, therefore the focus of research and programming should shift to discovering what insulates officers against the negative aftermath of being exposed to violence and trauma. The current analysis did reveal two possible insulating factors, *planning* and *positive growth*. Using these insulating coping mechanisms would help officers decrease their likelihood of developing PTSD after being exposed to VTEs. Therefore, it would be advantageous for correctional departments to invest in programming that focuses on the use of insulating coping mechanisms. One such program would be mindfulness-based stress reduction (MBSR) programming. MBSR focuses on coping with stressors through mindfulness. MBSR has been shown to be effective at reducing PTSD symptoms among populations similar in structure to corrections, including military veterans and police officers (Krick & Felfe, 2020; Stephenson, Simpson, Martinez, & Kearney, 2017).

Future research is surely needed to better understand the issues surrounding correctional officers, their high levels of PTSD, and off the chart's exposure to violence and trauma. Coping can be further explored with the correctional officer literature by expanding the questioning to determine specific coping responses to specific traumatic events. Further, exploring moderators, such as depressive or anxious symptoms and number of ACEs, which have an impact on the relationship between exposure to trauma and PTSD would be a logical advancement of the trauma literature. Finally, although mindfulness-based interventions for correctional officers have begun to be explored on a state-level, more programming and program evaluation is needed.

This study contributes to the current correctional literature, the trauma literature, and the broader-coping literature by providing information about what coping mechanisms have the ability to insulate officers against the likelihood of developing PTSD due to the inherently traumatic job they perform. Further, this work outlined the use of *denial* as a risk factor for the likelihood of developing PTSD. Correctional officers and the work they do are becoming more recognized by researchers and the general public alike. Research has begun to outline and acknowledge the important and difficult jobs that officers perform daily. Officers, who often suffer silently, deserve access to training and treatment to prevent and mitigate the devastating symptoms of PTSD, as well as depression and anxiety. The goal of examining coping and exposure to trauma is to arm correctional officers with tools that will keep them well, both physically and mentally, as they perform their duty to protect the inmates they supervise, one another, and the community as a whole.

Disclosure statement

No potential conflict of interest was reported by the author(s).

Funding

This work was supported by the National Institute of Justice (NIJ) under Grant *Effects of Mindfulness-Based Stress Reduction in Correctional Officers: A Biopsychosocial Approach* (NIJ 2017-R2-CX-0035).

References

Abel, M.H. (2002). Humor, stress, and coping strategies. *Humor*, 15(4), 365–381.

Adler, D.A., Possemato, K., Mavandadi, S., Lerner, D., Chang, H., Klaus, J., ... Oslin, D.W. (2011). Psychiatric status and work performance of veterans of operations enduring freedom and Iraqi freedom. *Psychiatric Services*, 62(1), 39–46.

American Psychiatric Association. (2013). *Diagnostic and statistical manual of mental disorders* (5th (Arlington, VA: APA).)doi: 10.1176/appi.books.9780890425596

Auerbach, C., Beckerman, N.L., & Blanco, I. (2013). Women coping with chronic disease: The psychosocial impact of lupus. *Journal of Social Service Research*, 39(5), 606–615.

Berger, W., Figueira, I., Maurat, A.M., Bucassio, E.P., Vieira, I., Jardim, S.R., ... Mendlowicz, M.V. (2007). Partial and full PTSD in Brazilian ambulance workers: Prevalence and impact on health and on quality of life. *Journal Of Traumatic Stress*, 20(4), 637–642.

Boden, M.T., Bonn-Miller, M.O., Vujanovic, A.A., & Drescher, K.D. (2012). A prospective investigation of changes in avoidant and active coping and posttraumatic stress disorder symptoms among military veteran. *Journal of Psychopathology and Behavioral Assessment*, 34(4), 433–439.

Boffa, J.W., Stanley, I.H., Hom, M.A., Norr, A.M., Joiner, T.E., & Schmidt, N.B. (2017). PTSD symptoms and suicidal thoughts and behaviors among firefighters. *Journal of Psychiatric Research*, 84, 277–283.

Bower, J. (2013). *Correctional officer wellness and safety literature review* 028104 . Washington D.C.: Office of Justice Programs. Accessed 10 November 2020 https://s3.amazonaws.com/static.nicic.gov/Public/244831.pdf.

Breslau, N., Davis, G.C., Peterson, E.L., & Schultz, L.R. (2000). A second look at comorbidity in victims of trauma: The posttraumatic stress disorder–major depression connection. *Biological Psychiatry*, 48(9), 902–909.

Breslau, N. (2009). The epidemiology of trauma, PTSD, and other posttraumatic disorders. *Trauma, Violence & Abuse*, 10(3), 198–210.

Bryant, R.A., & Harvey, A.G. (1996). Posttraumatic stress reactions in volunteer firefighters. *Journal of Traumatic Stress*, 9(1), 51–62.

Carroll, T.D., Currier, J.M., McCormick, W.H., & Drescher, K.D. (2017). Adverse childhood experiences and risk for suicidal behavior in male Iraq and Afghanistan veterans seeking PTSD treatment. *Psychological Trauma: Theory, Research, Practice, and Policy*, 9(5), 583–586.

Carver, C.S., Scheier, M.F., & Weintraub, J.K. (1989). Assessing coping strategies: A theoretically based approach. *Journal of Personality and Social Psychology*, 56(2), 267–283.

Chen, C.M., Yoon, Y.H., Harford, T.C., & Grant, B.F. (2017). Dimensionality of DSM-5 posttraumatic stress disorder and its association with suicide attempts: Results from the National Epidemiologic Survey on Alcohol and Related Conditions-III. *Social Psychiatry and Psychiatric Epidemiology*, 52(6), 715–725.

Corneil, W., Beaton, R., Murphy, S., Johnson, C., & Pike, K. (1999). Exposure to traumatic incidents and prevalence of posttraumatic stress symptomatology in urban firefighters in two countries. *Journal of Occupational Health Psychology*, 4(2), 131–141.

Coronas, R., García-Parés, G., Viladrich, C., Santos, J.M., & Menchón, J.M. (2008). Clinical and socio-demographic variables associated with the onset of posttraumatic stress disorder in road traffic accidents. *Depression and Anxiety*, 25(5), 16–23.

Denhof , M. D., &Spinaris , C. G.(2013). Depression, PTSD, and Comorbidity in United States Corrections Professionals: Prevalence and Impact on Health and Functioning (Desert Waters). Accessed 10 February 2021, https://desertwaters.com/wp-content/uploads/2013/09/Comorbidity_Study_09-03-131.pdf

Denhof, M.D., & Spinaris, C.G. (2016). Prevalence of trauma-related health conditions in correctional officers: A profile of Michigan corrections organization members. Accessed 5 January 2021. Retrieved http://www.mco-seiu.org/files/2016/05/MCO-Paper_FINAL.pdf

Denhof, M.D., & Spinaris, C.G. (2014). The violence, injury, and death exposure scale (VIDES). Accessed 8 January 2021. Retrieved https://desertwaters.com/wp-content/uploads/2014/01/VIDES_Data_Sheet.pdf

Faulk, K.E., Gloria, C.T., & Steinhardt, M.A. (2013). Coping profiles characterize individual flourishing, languishing, and depression. *Anxiety, Stress, and Coping*, 26(4), 378–390.

Felitti, V.J., Anda, R.F., Nordenberg, D., Williamson, D.F., Spitz, A.M., Edwards, V., . . . Marks, J.S. (1998). Relationship of childhood abuse and household dysfunction to many of the leading causes of death in adults. *American Journal of Preventive Medicine*, 14(4), 245–258.

Folkman , S, & Lazarus, R. S.(1984). Stress, Appraisal, and Coping (New York: Springer Publishing Company).

Frewen, P., Zhu, J., & Lanius, R. (2019). *Lifetime traumatic stressors and adverse childhood experiences uniquely predict concurrent PTSD, complex PTSD, and dissociative subtype of PTSD symptoms whereas recent adult non-traumatic stressors do not: Results from an online survey study.*

Gradus, J.L. (2017). PTSD and death from suicide. *PTSD Research Quarterly*, 28(4 1–3).

Griffin, M.L. (2006). Gender and stress: A comparative assessment of sources of stress among correctional officers. *Journal of Contemporary Criminal Justice*, 22(1), 4–25.

Higgins, E.M., Swartz, K., & Roberts, A. (2021). How conflict 'bleeds over' for correctional staff: Exploring work-family conflict through correctional subculture. *Journal of Crime and Justice*, 1–17. doi:10.1080/0735648X.2020.1870526

James, D., & Glaze, L.E. (2006). *Mental health problems of prison and jail inmates*. Washington, DC: Bureau of Justice Statistics.

James, L., & Todak, N. (2018). Prison employment and post-traumatic stress disorder: Risk and protective factors. *American Journal of Industrial Medicine*, 61(9), 725–732.

Jeavons, S., De, L., Horne, D.J., & Greenwood, K.M. (2000). Coping style and psychological trauma after road accidents. *Psychology, Health & Medicine*, 5(2), 213–221.

Kaplan, A. (2008). Untreated vets: A "gathering storm" of PTSD/depression. *Psychiatric Times*, 25(12), n.p.

Kilpatrick, D.G., Resnick, H.S., Milanak, M.E., Miller, M.W., Keyes, K.M., & Friedman, M.J. (2013). National estimates of exposure to traumatic events and PTSD prevalence using DSM-IV and DSM-5 criteria. *Journal of Traumatic Stress*, 26(5), 537–547.

Kolchakian, M.R., & Sears, S.F., Jr. (1999). Religious coping in college students. *Journal of Religion and Health*, 38(2), 115–125.

Krick, A., & Felfe, J. (2020). Who benefits from mindfulness? The moderating role of personality and social norms for the effectiveness on psychological and physiological outcomes among police officers. *Journal of Occupational Health Psychology*, 25(2), 99–112.

Kuiper, N.A., Rod, M.A., & Olinger, J.L. (1993). Coping humor, stress, and cognitive appraisals. *Canadian Journal Of Behavioral Science*, 25(1), 81–96.

Lambert, E.G. Hogan, N.L., & Barton, S.M. (2004). The nature of work-family conflict among correctional staff: An exploratory examination. *Criminal Justice Review*, 29(1), 145–172.

Lambert, E.G. Hogan, N.L., Camp, S.D., & Ventura, L.A. (2006). The impact of work-family conflict on correctional staff: A preliminary study. *Criminology & Criminal Justice*, 6(4), 371–387.

Lambert, E.G. & Hogan, N.L. (2010a). Wanting change: The relationship of perceptions of organizational innovation with correctional staff job stress, job satisfaction, and organizational commitment. *Criminal Justice Police Review*, 21(2), 160–184.

Lambert, E.G. & Hogan, N.L. (2010b). Work-family conflict and job burnout among correctional staff. *Psychological Reports*, 106(1), 19–26.

Lee, J.H., Park, S., & Sim., M. (2018). Relationship between ways of coping and posttraumatic stress symptoms in firefighters compared to the general population in South Korea. *Psychiatry Research*, 270, 649–655.

Lefcourt, H.M., Davison, K., Prkachin, K.M., & Mills, D.E. (1997). Humor as a stress moderator in the prediction of blood pressure obtained during five stressful tasks. *Journal of Research in Personality*, 31(4), 523–542.

Liverant, G.I., Hofmann, S.G., & Litz, B.T. (2004). Coping and anxiety in college students after the September 11th terrorist attacks. *Anxiety, Stress, and Coping*, 17(2), 127–139.

McFarlane, A.C., & Bookless, C. (2001). The effect of PTSD on interpersonal relationships: Issues for emergency service workers. *Sexual and Relationship Therapy*, 16(3), 261–267.

McNeill, S.A., & Galovski, T.E. (2015). Coping styles among individuals with severe mental illness and comorbid PTSD. *Community Mental Health Journal*, 51(6), 663–673.

Moskowitz, J.T., Hult, J.R., Bessolari, C., & Acree, M. (2009). What works in coping with HIV? A meta-analysis with implications for coping with serious illness. *Psychological Bulletin*, 135(1), 121–141.

National Institute of Mental Health. (2019). Post-Traumatic Stress Disorder. Accessed 8 February 2021. Retrieved https://www.nimh.nih.gov/health/topics/post-traumatic-stress-disorder-ptsd/index.shtml

Panagioti, M., Gooding, P.A., & Tarrier, N. (2015). A prospective study of suicidal ideation in post-traumatic stress disorder: The role of perceptions of defeat and entrapment. *Journal of Clinical Psychology*, 71(1), 50–61.

Perrin, M., Vandeleur, C.L., Castelao, E., Rothen, S., Glaus, J., Vollenweider, P., & Preisig, M. (2014). Determinants of the development of post-traumatic stress disorder, in the general population. *Social Psychiatry and Psychiatric Epidemiology*, 49(3), 447–457.

Ray, S.L., & Vanstone, M. (2009). The impact of PTSD on veterans' family relationships: An integrated phenomenological inquiry. *International Journal of Nursing Studies*, 46(6), 838–847.

Regehr, C., & LeBlanc, V.R. (2017). PTSD, acute stress, performance and decision-making in emergency service workers. *The Journal of the American Academy of Psychiatry and The Law*, 45, 184–192.

Rim, Y. (1988). Sense of humor and coping styles. *Personality and Individual Differences*, 9(3), 559–564.

Robinson, H.M., Sigman, M.R., & Wilson, J.P. (1997). Duty-related stressors and PTSD symptoms in suburban police officers. *Psychological Reports*, 81(3), 835–845.

Safchik, J. (2021, September 15). 'It's dangerous, it's scary': Corrections workers speak on staffing shortages. Accessed 18 September 2021. https://www.ketv.com/article/its-dangerous-its-scary-corrections-workers-speak-on-staffing-shortages/37615315

Savitsky, B., Findling, Y., Ereli, A., & Hendel, T. (2020). Anxiety and coping strategies among nursing students during the covid-19 pandemic. *Nurse Education in Practice*, 46, 1–7.

Selye, H. (1956). *The stress of life.* (New York: McGraw Hill Inc.).

Spinaris, C.G., Denhof, M.D., & Kellaway, J.A. (2012). Post-traumatic stress disorder in US corrections professionals: Prevalence and impact on health and functioning. Accessed 5 June 2021. Retrieved http://desertwaters.com/wp-content/uploads/2013/09/PTSD_Prev_in_Corrections_09-03-131.pdf

Stephenson, K.R., Simpson, T.L., Martinez, M.E., & Kearney, D.J. (2017). Changes in mindfulness and posttraumatic stress disorder symptoms among veterans enrolled 126 in mindfulness-based stress reduction. *Journal of Clinical Psychology*, 73(3), 201–217.

Sumpter, M. (2008). The correctional work force faces challenges in the 21st century. *Corrections Today*, August 2008.

Swartz, K., French, A., Roberts, A., & Tolle, H. (2017, April). *Examining the prevalence and correlates of PTSD among Kentucky department of corrections staff.*

The Associated Press. (2021, May 21) Federal prisons forced to use cooks, nurses to guard inmates due to staff shortages. Accessed 7 June 2021. https://www.nbcnews.com/news/us-news/federal-prisons-forced-use-cooks-nurses-guard-inmates-due-staff-n1268138

West, C., Bernard, B., Mueller, C., Kitt, M., Driscoll, R., & Tak, S. (2008). Mental health outcomes in police personnel after Hurricane Katrina. *Journal of Occupational and Environmental Medicine*, 50 (6), 689–695.

Widom, C.S., Czaja, S.J., & Dutton, M.A. (2008). Childhood victimization and lifetime revictimization. *Child Abuse & Neglect*, 32(8), 785–79. doi:10.1016/j.chiabu.2007.12.006

Clarifying the role of officer coping on turnover in corrections

Jessie Harney and Amy E. Lerman

ABSTRACT

Correctional officers are at high risk of exposure to workplace violence, and many report experiencing severe mental health symptoms, including post-traumatic stress disorder, anxiety, and depression. Despite growing concern for these issues, however, we do not yet fully understand the coping mechanisms correctional officers employ to manage work-related stress, or how coping mechanisms affect workplace outcomes. To address these questions, we utilize original survey data about California correctional officers. We draw on the Stress Process Paradigm to model the relationship between exposure to violence and mental health, the impact of occupational stress on the development of coping mechanisms, and whether differential coping mechanism utilization impacts officers' levels of cynicism and desire to leave corrections. Our findings suggest that emotion-focused coping (e.g. having someone to talk to) is associated with lower intention to leave correctional employment, while the opposite is true for avoidant coping (i.e. alcohol abuse). These insights shed light on the problem of officer turnover and retention, and provide potential direction to policymakers and practitioners seeking to create an effective, healthy workforce.

Evidence documenting the deleterious effects of incarceration on well-being is strong and clear. Incarceration has a profound, negative influence on the health of incarcerated individuals (Goff, Rose, Rose, & Purves, 2007; Haney, 2003; Liebling, Durie, van Den Beukel, Tait, & Harvey, 2005). More specifically, the experience of incarceration – including exposure to violence, disruption of social networks, and painful monotony – can lead to enduring effects on mental health (e.g. Haney, 2003; Massoglia, 2008a, 2008b; Novisky & Peralta, 2020; Sykes, 2007; Turney, Wildeman, & Schnittker, 2012).

We know far less about the impacts of the correctional environment on officer physical and mental health (Butler, Tasca, Zhang, & Carpenter, 2019; Brower, 2013). Understanding the occupational health of correctional officers is vital for at least two reasons. First is their substantial presence in the American workforce. Data from the Bureau of Labor Statistics suggests that as of 2020, there were approximately 405,870 correctional officers and jailers employed in the United States. As a point of comparison, in the same year there were roughly 654,900 police officers. A second reason to better understand the well-being of correctional officers is their elevated risk of exposure to violence in the workplace. Correctional officers face some of the highest rates of workplace violence of any occupation in the United States, second only to police officers (Finn, 2000). Emerging evidence suggests that this can take a sizable toll; work-related stress is associated with harm to wellbeing amongst correctional officers (Trounson, Pfeifer, & Skues, 2019), including higher risk of post-traumatic stress disorder (Kunst, Bogaerts, & Winkel, 2009). Yet despite their high risk for work-related mental health problems, studies of correctional officers have so far been limited. In particular, we know little about the psychological coping mechanisms officers employ to deal with workplace stress.

Our purpose in this inquiry is to further the understanding of how officers adapt to deal with work-related stressors, and whether these coping mechanisms influence officers' desire to stay in the field of corrections. This outcome is especially important given the enduring problem of officer turnover. High rates of officer turnover impose substantial costs to correctional departments – resources that could otherwise be allocated to support for programming, re-entry services, and other needs (Finn, 2000). This includes the cost of onboarding new employees, as well the loss of institutional knowledge and experience that can strain the ability of correctional systems to maintain institutional safety.

Coping mechanisms and the stress process paradigm

Individuals utilize a variety of psychological strategies to cope with prolonged stress. Broadly categorized, these include problem-focused, emotion-focused, and avoidant coping (Holahan, Moos, Holahan, Brennan, & Schutte, 2005; Lazarus & Folkman, 1984). Problem-focused coping encompasses a set of strategies aimed at 'managing or altering the problem causing the distress,' (Lazarus & Folkman, 1984, p. 150). Examples of problem-focused coping include behaviors such as thinking through ways to address stress, talking it out with others, and weighing the costs and benefits of different options to reduce the impact of the stressor (Gould, Watson, Price, & Valliant, 2013). In contrast, emotion-focused coping is described as the '[regulation of] emotional responses to the problem' (Lazarus & Folkman, 1984, p. 150). Emotion-focused coping (EC) can be either positive or negative. Positive EC engages self-compassion, including altering thought processes to reframe and reprocess stressful situations, while negative EC is typically characterized by being critical of oneself or ruminating over the difficulties of the situation (Gould et al., 2013; Stanisławski, 2019). This type of negative coping often co-occurs with strategies that fall into the third broad category, avoidant coping. Avoidant coping involves behaviors or thought patterns that facilitate denial or minimization of stressors, such as evading feelings or avoiding certain situations (Holahan et al., 2005). Avoidant coping can also include substance use, which serves to blunt the feelings associated with stressful or traumatic experiences.

Extant literature suggests that the types of coping mechanisms an individual utilizes can profoundly influence their overall health (Folkman, Lazarus, Dunkel-Schetter, DeLongis, & Gruen, 1986; Zaleski, Levey-Thors, & Schiaffino, 1998). In particular, unhealthy coping strategies can exacerbate the detrimental effects of stress. Even relatively passive forms of avoidant coping, such as denial and evasion, can be associated with worse mental health outcomes. One study found that among trauma-exposed refugees, disengagement (i.e. distancing oneself from the stressor) was associated with greater PTSD symptom severity (Hooberman, Rosenfeld, Rasmussen, & Keller, 2010). Amongst police officers, repressed anger has been shown to completely mediate the relationship between the stressors of police work and health outcomes (Can & Hendy, 2014).

Negative emotion-focused coping can similarly shape health-related outcomes. Li and colleagues studied burnout amongst nurses in China to understand the influence of core self-evaluation, which includes traits such as self-efficacy, on burnout. They found that core self-evaluation was positively associated with 'active' or problem-focused coping ($\rho = 0.31$) and negatively associated with avoidant coping ($\rho = -0.25$), including alcohol abuse. Moreover, nurses with lower core self-evaluation tended to score higher for cynicism, defined as 'a negative, callous or excessively detached response to various aspects of the job.' Conversely, those who engaged in problem-focused (or active) coping, utilizing techniques to alter the ways they thought about or reacted to stressors, had lower cynicism scores (Li, Guan, Chang, & Zhang, 2014).

More broadly, and in contrast to negative EC and avoidant coping, the adoption of problem-focused coping strategies can have a protective effect against mental health distress. One especially common problem-focused coping mechanism for dealing with work-related stress involves reaching out for social support (Beh & Loo, 2012). This can include talking over problems with friends or family members, as well as building caring relationships with supervisors. In fact, extant studies find that individuals coping with trauma who have limited access to social support are at increased risk for developing PTSD (Brewin, Andrews, & Valentine, 2000; Ozer, Best, Lipsey, & Weiss, 2003). Likewise, perceived support from institutional actors can affect the experience of workplace stressors (Barnes, Nickerson, Adler, & Litz, 2013; Kelley, Britt, Adler, & Bliese, 2014). In a study of the military, organizational support was found to be negatively related to PTSD (Barnes et al., 2013). Another study found that the more an individual felt supported by their organization, the less stigma they felt in seeking out resources to help manage stress (Kelley et al., 2014).

Correctional officers & the stress process paradigm

While our understanding of coping mechanism utilization specific to correctional officers is limited, some studies suggest that officers frequently make use of negative coping mechanisms that lessen their ability to maintain healthy social ties. For instance, many correctional officers adopt a 'working personality' in response to work-related stress, becoming more isolated from others and cynical about the world (Brower, 2013; Rogers, 2001). This coping strategy might be useful for handling day-to-day situations at work, but can be detrimental to officer well-being in the longer term (Liebling et al., 2005). Avoidant coping is associated with a variety of negative mental health outcomes; when correctional officers experience workplace stressors, including exposure to violence, they are more likely to develop negative psychological outcomes such as severe depression, disordered sleep, and suicidal ideation (James, Todak, & Best, 2017; Morgan, 2009; Ross, 2013; Stack & Tsoudis, 1997). Avoidant coping can also present as alcohol abuse among law enforcement personnel, especially those who experience trauma (Leino,

Eskelinen, Summala, & Virtanen, 2011). One study finds that nearly 30% of officers engaged in binge drinking (defined as consuming six or more drinks on one occasion) either sometimes or often (Lerman, Harney, & Sadin, 2021).[1]

The Stress Process Paradigm (SPP) provides a useful theoretical framework for identifying the potential importance of different coping strategies (Pearlin, 1989; Pearlin, Menaghan, Lieberman, & Mullan, 1981; Thoits, 2010). The SPP theorizes that stressors – including specific events or continual stressful experiences throughout one's life – cumulatively impact health outcomes. Importantly, however, the effects of stress are context-dependent and can be mediated through coping mechanisms and other resources. In other words, the effects of a stressor depend largely on the context and available resources, such as proximity to other stressful events, the magnitude and frequency of the stressor, and also factors like coping strategies and institutional supports (Pearlin et al., 1981).

In previous studies, the SPP framework has been utilized to explain how criminal justice contact, including being stopped by police, charged with a crime, or being incarcerated, can fuel long-lasting disparities in social outcomes. Sugie and Turney (2017) summarize this perspective, stating that: 'a primary stressor such as criminal justice contact can lead to secondary stressors, or reverberating chronic strains, in other domains of life (e.g. employment or relationships)' (p. 720). Three aspects of this framework are especially relevant: 1) the way that stress proliferates, producing secondary stressors, 2) the way that both primary and secondary stressors contribute to health inequalities; and 3) the importance of context in conditioning stress responses and coping.

Correctional officers are confronted with many primary stressors in the workplace, including substantial risk of exposure to violence. This can lead to secondary stressors, such as heightened anxiety and post-traumatic stress disorder (Jaegers et al., 2019; Lerman et al., 2021). In turn, this might reduce the likelihood that officers reach out to others for help managing stress or feel confident they can manage stress effectively (i.e. problem-focused or positive EC), and increase the likelihood that officers turn to less healthy ways of coping (i.e. negative EC or avoidant coping). For example, PTSD has been found to be highly comorbid with both alcohol abuse and avoidance (Debell et al., 2014). The way officers attempt to cope with stressors is also conditioned by correctional norms and culture (e.g. whether talking openly about problems with co-workers is deemed socially acceptable), as well as by the availability of institutional supports, including access to trauma-informed programs or therapy (Lerman et al., 2021).

A handful of studies have attempted to model these types of associations between work-related stress, coping mechanisms, and workplace outcomes for correctional officers. However, most rely on very small samples. For example, Trounson et al. (2019) measure workplace adversity and psychological well-being, as well as workplace outcomes such as absenteeism, presenteeism, and job dissatisfaction among 174 correctional officers. The authors employ a structural equation model to assess whether coping mechanisms moderate the influence of workplace adversity, specifically through (negative) emotional/avoidant or (positive) interpersonal/solution-focused coping. Their findings indicate that workplace adversity increases psychological distress, which contributes to a higher likelihood of negative workplace outcomes. Interpersonal/solution-focused coping, but not emotional/avoidant coping, had a significant indirect impact on psychological and workplace outcomes (Trounson et al., 2019).

Burnout has also been empirically linked to coping mechanisms for correctional officers. An online survey of 208 correctional officers working in Alberta found that burnout was positively associated with maladaptive coping mechanisms, such as venting and behavioral disengagement, and negatively associated with problem-solving coping (Gould et al., 2013). Another study, focused specifically on avoidant coping through alcohol use, employed an online survey of 1,370 correctional officers (Shepherd, Fritz, Hammer, Guros, & Meier, 2019). Using a form of path analysis, the authors demonstrate a positive relationship between the emotional demands of work and burnout as measured by the Oldenburg Burnout Inventory (Demerouti & Bakker, 2008). Emotional demands also appeared to have an indirect effect on the frequency and quantity of alcohol use, operating on the pathway through burnout (Shepherd et al., 2019).

Burnout is especially important because of its potential to increase turnover of staff. Turnover has long been a prevalent issue in government (Shim, Park, & Eom, 2017), and correctional departments are no exception. Yearly turnover rates vary across departments – previous studies estimate a low of 12% (Wells, Minor, Lambert, & Tilley, 2016) or as high as 45% (McShane, Williams, Scbichor, & McClain, 1991) – but rates often fall in the range of about 20–25% (Lambert, 2001; Lambert & Hogan, 2009; Patenaude, 2001; Wright, 1994). As a point of comparison, yearly turnover rates tend to be substantially lower amongst workers in other high-stress occupations, such as teaching – 8% (Kukla-Acevedo, 2009); nursing – 18% (NSI, 2021), and even policing – 11% (Wareham, Smith, & Lambert, 2015).

These high turnover rates can be extremely costly to correctional organizations. Previous research suggests that the cost of turnover per employee ranges from one to two years of salary and benefits (Ramlall, 2004). In a study of correctional officer turnover in Georgia, for example, the monthly rate of turnover ranged from approximately 1.0% to 1.8%, with a cumulative 18% of officers leaving their post in 2003. This was estimated to cost over $27,000,000 in 2007, a sum that would be more than $38,000,000 in 2021 (Udechukwu et al., 2007). Greater turnover in corrections can also mean increased pressures on the officers who remain, requiring the imposition of mandatory overtime in extreme cases. While some officers may welcome additional overtime to supplement their income, increased and involuntary hours at work can add to already high levels of exhaustion, stress, and work-life imbalance.

A model of correctional officer coping

In this paper, we estimate a model of correctional officer stress, coping strategies, and organizational outcomes using the framework of the Stress Process Paradigm. As the SPP suggests, we posit that exposure to violence as a primary stressor will lead to secondary stressors, such as symptoms of post-traumatic stress disorder (PTSD). In addition, both PTSD and violence are likely to catalyze a range of coping mechanisms. This includes problem-focused coping (i.e. social supports), negative emotion-focused coping (i.e. cynicism), and avoidant coping (i.e. alcohol abuse). In this model, we also address the effect of stressors on officers' intention or desire to leave corrections, and whether stress impacts turnover indirectly via the pathway through officer coping.

Within our theoretical framework, we hypothesize that exposure to violence and symptoms of PTSD have a reciprocal relationship. In line with the SPP, greater exposure to violence increases symptoms of PTSD (Fontana & Rosenheck, 1993; Hoge et al., 2004; Thomas et al., 2010; Wieclaw et al., 2006), but PTSD might also increase subsequent exposure to violence. For instance, common residual symptoms of trauma include heightened emotions like anger and aggression (Orth & Wieland, 2006). As a result, increased severity of trauma might plausibly result in officers who are less capable of controlling an aggressive response when presented with a subsequent threat.

We propose two coping strategies that are also reciprocal with PTSD: avoidant coping (i.e. alcohol abuse) and problem-focused coping (i.e. having someone to talk to). PTSD and alcohol abuse are highly comorbid (Fetzner, McMillan, Sareen, & Asmundson, 2011) and individuals with PTSD often report utilizing alcohol to cope with post-trauma symptoms (U.S. Department of Veterans Affairs, 2019), but alcohol abuse may actually worsen the experience of PTSD (Foundations Recovery Network, 2020). Conversely, social support is key to recovering from PTSD. Ironically, however, the experience of PTSD can be isolating, especially if someone does not feel that they have a safe resource to reach out to or someone who will understand their experience (Charuvastra & Cloitre, 2008).[2]

We also suspect that problem-focused coping strategies (i.e. peer support and perceived supervisory support) are related to officers' desire to leave corrections. Previous research suggests a negative relationship between supervisory support and turnover intention (Gillet, Gagné, Sauvagère, & Fouquereau, 2013; Maertz, Griffeth, Campbell, & Allen, 2007) and a positive relationship with organizational commitment (Johnson, 2015). In fact, having socially supportive conversations with supervisors is positively associated with socially supportive conversations with coworkers (Beehr, Farmer, Glazer, Gudanowski, & Nair, 2003). Not surprisingly, supervisory support also indirectly impacts job satisfaction on the pathway through supervisory support (Kula, 2017) and can moderate the effects of violence on negative mental health outcomes (Lerman et al., 2021).

Our final hypotheses are related to negative emotion-focused coping. In particular, we suspect that cynicism interacts with other coping strategies and directly impacts officers' desire to leave corrections. Specifically, we suspect avoidant coping strategies like alcohol abuse are associated with emotions like anger and hostility (Bunde & Suls, 2006; Epstein & McCrady, 2002; McCrady & Epstein, 1995). Conversely, we expect that problem-focused strategies like connecting with co-workers to talk through problems makes officers less likely to incur secondary effects of trauma on the job (Finn, 2000).

Finally, in addition to coping strategies we also control for the ways that financial security might influence an officer's intention to leave the field. Occupational literature has found a consistent association between financial security and emotional strain (Brief & Atieh, 1987) and a significant, negative correlation between financial security and burnout (Munyon, Carnes, Lyons, & Zettler, 2020). Even better established is the empirical link between financial security and workers' desire to leave their profession. Although job transitions have costs outside of the potential change in income (e.g. search and opportunity costs), financial security is still likely to be a key consideration in retention (Allen & Meyer, 1990; McCall, 1970).

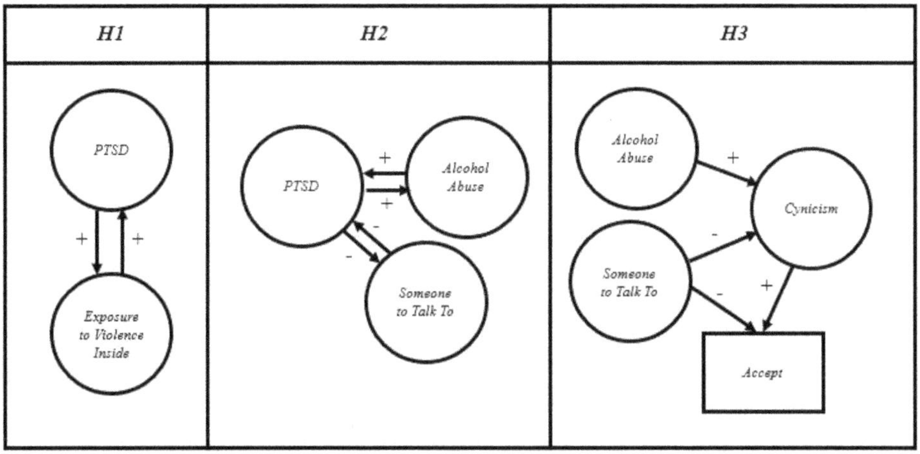

Figure 1. Visual representation of model hypotheses.

To summarize, our model builds on the Stress Process Paradigm to outline a potential framework for understanding how correctional officers cope with occupational stress, and how coping strategies are associated with outcomes like turnover intention. Our primary hypotheses (see Figure 1) include the following:

(1) Greater exposure to violence at work is i) associated with greater severity of PTSD symptoms, and ii) the relationship between exposure to violence at work and PTSD is reciprocal.
(2) PTSD symptoms are associated with i) increased avoidant coping (alcohol abuse) and ii) decreased problem-focused coping (social connectedness). Again, iii) both of these relationships are reciprocal.
(3) Avoidant coping mechanisms are positively associated with i) negative EC (cynicism) and ii) officers' desire to leave the field of corrections.
(4) Problem-focused coping is negatively associated with i) negative EC and ii) desire to leave corrections.
(5) Perceived support from supervisors is positively associated with problem-focused coping.
(6) Experiencing financial stress is associated with an increased desire to leave the field of corrections.

Data

Our analysis utilizes survey data from the California Correctional Officer Survey (CCOS), which we conducted from March to May of 2017 (Lerman, 2017). The survey was fielded to all correctional and parole officers working in the state of California, with a response rate of approximately 42%. The final sample size was 8,334 correctional officer respondents and includes participants from every state prison. Due to missing data, and once we

Table 1. Descriptive statistics of the CCOS 2017 sample.

Variable	Level	Frequency	Percentage	Missing %
Gender	Male	5,088	82.40%	
	Female	1,087	17.60%	25.91%
Race/Ethnicity	Asian or Asian-American	276	4.58%	27.62%
	Black or African-American	581	9.63%	
	Hispanic/Latinx	2,103	34.86%	
	White/Caucasian	2,794	46.32%	
	Native Hawaiian or Pacific Islander	142	2.35%	
	Other	487	8.07%	
Political Party	Republican	2,558	42.42%	27.65%
	Independent	865	14.34%	
	Democrat	1,150	19.07%	
	Other party	105	1.74%	
	No party	1,351	22.40%	
Education Level	GED or High School degree	597	9.72%	26.29%
	Some college (no degree)	2,715	44.20%	
	Associate's degree	1,353	22.03%	
	Bachelor's degree or higher	1,478	24.06%	
Marital Status	Never married	736	12.11%	
	Widowed	56	0.92%	
	Divorced	746	12.27%	27.06%
	Separated	101	1.66	
	Married or domestic partnership	4,440	73.04%	
Veteran Status	Yes	1,606	26.15%	26.31%
	No	4,535	73.85%	
Security Level	I	373	5.57%	19.70%
	II	1,692	25.28%	
	III	1,923	28.74%	
	IV	2,704	40.41%	
Variable		**Mean**	**Std. Dev.**	**Missing %**
Age		47.55	11.46	29.00%
CDCR Tenure		13.16	8.24	52.53%

exclude personnel who are not correctional officers (e.g. parole officers), our analytical sample size is roughly 5,500 officers (67.5% of the sample that has some response recorded).

In order to ensure confidentiality, surveys were mailed to each officer at their home address along with pre-paid return envelopes. Officers were also provided the option to complete the survey online or on a mobile device. As shown in (Table 1), the sample is largely male (82.4%), White (46.3%) and/or Hispanic/Latinx (34.9%), Republican (42.4%) and married (73.0%). Most sample respondents were assigned to high security levels (69.2%), and the average tenure was 13 years.

Our key survey measures are as follows (Appendix A1 includes the specific question text and possible responses for each item):

Exposure to Violence is measured by four binary survey questions, adapted from the Trauma History Questionnaire (THQ) (Green, 1996), which ask whether the officer has experienced various types of violence while working inside prison: 1) having been seriously injured; 2) fearing serious injury or being killed; 3) seeing or handling dead bodies; and 4) seeing someone be seriously injured or killed. The Cronbach's alpha for these items is .67

Post-Traumatic Stress (PTSD) is measured by two survey items, both on a seven-point Likert scale, which are a subset of the PTSD Checklist – Civilian Version (PCL-C). These items address officers' experience of being bothered by repeated, disturbing memories of stressful events and feeling upset when being reminded of such events. Both items are reverse coded such that greater values indicate greater PTSD symptom severity. While there are only two measures included in the PTSD factor, it has a strong Cronbach's alpha of 0.90.

Avoidant coping focuses on alcohol abuse and is measured by three, four-point Likert-scale items adapted from the Alcohol Use Disorders Identification Test (AUDIT).[3] All questions are reverse coded such that greater values indicate greater alcohol abuse symptom severity. The Cronbach's alpha reliability statistic for these items is 0.73.

Negative EC is measured using three, seven-point Likert-scale items measuring the extent to which officers feel they have become harsher and angrier since starting work in corrections, as well as their level of agreement that they would be a better spouse, partner, or parent if they did not work in corrections. These items aim to capture the adaptive 'working personality' adopted by officers in order to cope with correctional work (e.g. Brower, 2013). All items were reverse-coded so that higher scores on this factor indicate greater cynicism, and the resulting Cronbach's alpha is 0.80.

Problem-focused Coping is measured using three survey items. A seven-point Likert scale (reverse coded) addresses the extent to which officers feel there is someone they can talk to about problems in the workplace. A second scale sums the number of resources officers have for talking about problems in the workplace, and a third sums resources for talking about concerns specifically related to health or wellness. The associated Cronbach's alpha is 0.70 for this factor.

Financial Security is measured using three, seven-point Likert scale items with an associated Cronbach's alpha of 0.72. Higher values on each item indicate greater financial security.

Supervisory Support is measured using a seven-point Likert scale capturing the extent to which officers feel their supervisor cares about the feelings of subordinates.

Turnover Intention is measured with a seven-point Likert scale measuring the extent to which officers agree they would take a job outside of corrections if they had an offer with similar salary and benefits.

Methods

We utilized techniques within the structural equation modeling family of methods in Stata 16 (StataCorp, 2019) to assess relationships between variables and whether our proposed application of the Stress Process Paradigm is appropriately fit to the data. Structural equation modeling incorporates a number of different methods, including confirmatory factor analysis, mediation analysis, and path analysis and can address analytical inquiries related to measurement and the relationship between factors within a system (Kline, 2015). Following best practices (Anderson & Gerbing, 1988), we constructed a model via the two-step approach.[4] First, we generated a measurement model with all latent variables allowed to covary (i.e. no inclusion of single-headed arrow pathways specifying the direction of the relationship).[5] Additionally, in line with standard practice, the reference variable method was used, selecting one indicator from each factor to be equal to one (Kline, 2015).

While there is debate about the use of correlated errors, we have included them within our measurement (and subsequent structural) model, as they were *a priori*-specified to be related based on their proximal measurement and theory. Hermida's (2015) seminal paper addressing correlated errors in structural models suggests that much of the justification for including correlated errors in previous studies was purely for improving model fit. Importantly, our inclusion of error correlations is instead based on theory or the presence of a feedback loop (Kline, 2015). Given generally positive fit results and significant pattern coefficients, this model can then be utilized for the structural model, completing the second step in the two-step approach. In this step, we test both direct and indirect effects of model factors.

Results

Descriptive statistics

(Table 2) reports means and standard deviations for each variable in the model. (Correlation matrices are included in Appendix B1.) As the Table shows, the utilization of different coping mechanisms varied, but all were endorsed by substantial segments of officers. While more than a quarter (28.4%) of individuals in the analytical sample indicated that they drank six or more drinks often or sometimes in the last year, the other two alcohol abuse items were less commonly endorsed. Likewise, almost 70% agreed that they had someone to talk to about workplace problems, with a smaller majority indicating they had at least one source to talk to specifically about workplace and health problems. Indicators of cynicism also appeared to be quite common. Of the analytical sample, 39.5% agreed they would be a better spouse, partner, or parent if they did not work in

Table 2. Means and standard deviations of observed variables.

Factor, If Applicable	Observed Variable	Mean	SD	Skew.	Kurt.	Scale	Scaled Mean	Scaled SD
Exposure to Violence Inside (ETV_In)	Inj_In	0.203	0.402	1.479	3.186	0–1	0.203	0.402
	Fear_In	0.563	0.499	−0.108	1.012	0–1	0.563	0.499
	DB_In	0.663	0.473	−0.687	1.473	0–1	0.663	0.473
	Seen_In	0.763	0.425	−1.235	2.526	0–1	0.763	0.425
PTSD	Rep_Mem	1.179	1.211	0.811	2.702	0–4	0.295	0.303
	Upset_R	1.134	1.205	0.863	2.778	0–4	0.284	0.301
Someone to Talk To (Talk_To)	Wrk_Prob	3.626	1.809	−0.622	2.331	0–6	0.604	0.302
	WP_Srcs	1.574	1.542	0.955	3.671	0–8	0.197	0.193
	WB_Srcs	2.156	1.417	1.136	4.365	0–8	0.269	0.177
Alcohol Abuse (Alc_Ab)	6+ Drinks	0.954	1.011	0.687	2.269	0–3	0.318	0.337
	Fail_Norm	0.217	0.543	2.810	11.261	0–3	0.072	0.181
	No_Mem	0.244	0.587	2.665	10.121	0–3	0.081	0.200
Cynicism	Better	3.956	1.907	−0.054	1.894	1–7	0.493	0.318
	Harsh	4.363	1.995	−0.295	1.807	1–7	0.560	0.332
	Anger	3.782	1.893	0.080	1.840	1–7	0.464	0.315
Single Indicator	Sup_Cares	4.504	1.779	−0.295	1.973	1–7	0.584	0.296
Financial Security (Fin_Sec)	JGBF	3.397	1.316	−0.300	1.975	1–5	0.400	0.219
	Not_Last	3.265	1.299	−0.225	1.969	1–5	0.377	0.217
	Unexp	2.839	1.192	0.133	2.214	1–5	0.306	0.199
Single Indicator	Accept	5.202	1.852	−0.813	2.543	1–7	0.700	0.309

Skew = Skewness; Kurt = Kurtosis. Scaled Mean & Standard Deviation indicate the mean and standard deviation (respectively) of the zero-to-one scaled version of each variable. (Note for all exposure to violence variables, these will be the same as the original mean and standard deviation).

corrections; 53.2% agreed they have become harsher or less trusting since they started working in corrections; and 39.1% agreed they have had a harder time controlling their anger since they started correctional work.

Coping mechanism utilization also varied by officer demographics and occupational characteristics. Specifically, males tended to report more alcohol abuse, but also reported greater availability of supportive resources (i.e. having someone to talk to). Relative to whites, minority officers reported less alcohol abuse, as well as greater agreement that they had someone to talk to about workplace problems. Exposure to violence, unsurprisingly, was associated with both higher rates of alcohol abuse and less social support.

Structural equation modeling

On almost all measures of fit, the structural equation model performed well (see Table 3); however, the Likelihood Ratio Test (LRT) was significant, both for the standard and Satorra-Bentler scaled chi-square LRT. While this is a limitation of the model, χ^2 values tend to be somewhat sensitive for larger models (Cheung & Rensvold, 2002; Meade, Johnson, & Braddy, 2008). On all other measures of fit, the model performs quite well. The Root Mean Squared Error of Approximation (RMSEA or $\hat{\varepsilon}$) or 'badness-of-fit statistic' 95% confidence interval suggests that this model is well within an acceptable range.[6]

(Table 3) also includes the Comparative Fit (CFI) and Tucker-Lewis (TLI) Indices, both the standard and Satorra-Bentler adjusted measures, as well as the Standardized Root Mean Squared Residual (SRMR). The CFI and TLI both range from zero to one, with values closer to one indicating better fit, while the SRMR is another 'badness-of-fit' index, with values closer to zero indicating better fit. As suggested by the structural equation modeling literature, the CFI/TLI and SRMR should be interpreted in conjunction; specifically, the CFI should be greater than or equal to 0.95 and the SRMR should be less than or equal to 0.08 (Hu & Bentler, 1999). This model meets these benchmarks (see Table 3). Additionally, significance of all pattern coefficients in the first step measurement model

Table 3. Measurement model fit statistics.

Fit Statistic		Value	CI or p-value
Likelihood Ratio			
Model vs. Saturated	χ^2_{146}	1,256.40	< 0.0001
Baseline vs. Saturated	χ^2_{190}	34,086.40	< 0.0001
Satorra-Bentler			
Model vs. Saturated	χ^2_{143}	1,215.99	
Baseline vs. Saturated	χ^2_{190}	32,481.73	
Population Error			
Root Mean Squared Error of Approximation (RMSEA)		0.037	(0.035, 0.039)
Probability RMSEA < 0.05		1.00	
Satorra-Bentler			
RMSEA (Satorra-Bentler)		0.036	
Baseline Comparison			
Comparative Fit Index (CFI)		0.967	
Tucker-Lewis Index (TLI)		0.958	
Satorra-Bentler			
Satorra-Bentler Comparative Fit Index (SB-CFI)		0.967	
Satorra-Bentler Tucker-Lewis Index (SB-TLI)		0.957	
Size of Residuals			
Standardized Root Mean Squared Residual (SRMSR)		0.027	

provides evidence of the convergent validity of model indicators (Anderson & Gerbing, 1988). With these acceptable fit results and significant pattern coefficients, we proceed with creating a structural model.

Structural model results

We constructed a non-recursive structural model with correlated errors (Cole, Ciesla, & Steiger, 2007), reference coding to ensure an identified model with Satorra-Bentler standard errors. (Figure 2) diagrams the non-recursive structural model with correlated errors, including pattern coefficients and the overall model estimates (i.e. direct effects for the structural and measurement components of the model). Covariance residuals are provided in Appendix C. Model estimation of direct effects is also reported in (Table 4). Notably, all direct effects are significant and we find evidence in support of each of our hypotheses. First, we see that greater to *Exposure to Violence* has a significant, positive impact on PTSD symptom severity and we see evidence of a feedback loop as predicted by Hypothesis 1. The positive pattern coefficient for *PTSD* to *Exposure to Violence* is significant, suggesting that greater exposure to violence while working inside prison is associated with greater symptom severity.

Similarly, and in line with Hypothesis 2, the model also finds support for feedback loops between PTSD and two coping mechanisms: *Avoidant* and *Problem-focused Coping*. The directionality of these reciprocal effects is in line with predictions: the pattern coefficient on the *PTSD* to *Problem-focused Coping* pathway was significant and negative, indicating that greater PTSD symptom severity was associated with lower social connectedness. The pattern coefficient on the pathway back to *PTSD* was also significant and negative, in line

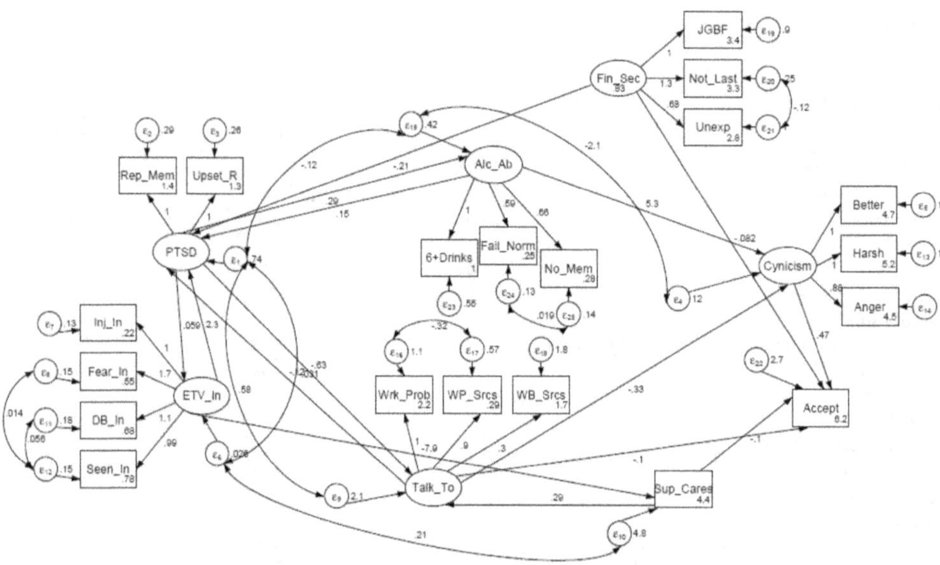

Figure 2. Coping mechanisms structural model diagram. *Note: N = 5,627; Likelihood Ratio Test (Satorra-Bentler) χ^2_{143} = 1,215.99.

Table 4. Overall model results (direct effects).

Factor or Variable	Measure or Indicator	Std. Coeff.	UnStd. Coeff.	UnStd. SB+ Standard Error	UnStd. Z	UnStd. p-value	UnStd. 95% Confidence Interval (LB and UB)	
Structural								
Accept	Sup_Cares	−0.097	−0.101	0.014	−7.41	< 0.001*	−0.127	−0.074
	Talk_To	−0.082	−0.102	0.021	−4.90	< 0.001*	−0.143	−0.061
	Cynicism	0.381	0.470	0.019	24.85	< 0.001*	0.433	0.507
	Fin_Sec	−0.040	−0.082	0.028	−2.93	0.003*	−0.137	−0.027
Sup_Cares	ETV_In	−0.827	−7.889	1.251	−6.31	< 0.001*	−10.341	−5.437
PTSD	ETV_In	0.400	2.326	0.155	15.04	< 0.001*	2.023	2.629
	Talk_To	−0.169	−0.123	0.032	−3.79	< 0.001*	−0.186	−0.059
	Alc_Ab	0.092	0.146	0.032	4.49	< 0.001*	0.082	0.209
	Fin_Sec	−0.172	−0.205	0.013	−16.03	< 0.001*	−0.230	−0.180
ETV_In	PTSD	0.342	0.059	0.006	9.36	< 0.001*	0.046	0.071
Talk_To	Sup_Cares	0.342	0.287	0.017	17.02	< 0.001*	0.254	0.320
	PTSD	−0.455	−0.626	0.066	−9.50	< 0.001*	−0.755	−0.497
Alc_Ab	PTSD	0.456	0.289	0.027	10.88	< 0.001*	0.237	0.341
Cynicism	Talk_To	0.039	−0.329	0.047	−7.02	< 0.001*	−0.421	−0.237
	Alc_Ab	0.212	5.264	0.504	10.44	< 0.001*	4.275	6.252
Measurement								
JGBF	Fin_Sec	0.691	*1.000*	–	–	–	–	–
Not_Last	Fin_Sec	0.922	1.316	0.064	20.59	< 0.001*	1.191	1.442
Unexp	Fin_Sec	0.519	0.681	0.040	16.97	< 0.001*	0.602	0.759
Rep_Mem	PTSD	0.896	*1.000*	–	–	–	–	–
Upset_R	PTSD	0.905	1.005	0.013	77.07	< 0.001*	0.979	1.030
Better	Cynicism	0.788	*1.000*	–	–	–	–	–
Harsh	Cynicism	0.779	1.035	0.018	59.03	< 0.001*	1.000	1.069
Anger	Cynicism	0.701	0.883	0.017	51.92	< 0.001*	0.850	0.916
Inj_In	ETV_In	0.464	*1.000*	–	–	–	–	–
Fear_In	ETV_In	0.630	1.688	0.077	21.89	< 0.001*	1.537	1.840
DB_In	ETV_In	0.433	1.098	0.056	19.52	< 0.001*	0.988	1.209
Seen_In	ETV_In	0.434	0.989	0.057	17.38	< 0.001*	0.878	1.101
Wrk_Prob	Talk_To	0.823	*1.000*	–	–	–	–	–
WP_Srcs	Talk_To	0.873	0.904	0.029	31.15	< 0.001*	0.847	0.960
WB_Srcs	Talk_To	0.320	0.304	0.30	10.19	< 0.001*	0.246	0.363
6+ Drinks	Alc_Ab	0.679	*1.000*	–	–	–	–	–
Fail_Norm	Alc_Ab	0.747	0.590	0.032	18.31	< 0.001*	0.527	0.654
No_Mem	Alc_Ab	0.766	0.656	0.035	18.59	< 0.001*	0.586	0.725
Covariances								
cov(Not_Last, Unexp)		0.105	−0.116	0.039	−3.00	0.003*	−0.192	−0.040
cov(Fear_In, Seen_In)		0.018	0.014	0.003	4.82	< 0.001*	0.008	0.019
cov(Sup_Cares, ETV_In)		0.064	0.212	0.038	5.61	< 0.001*	0.138	0.287
cov(Fear_In, DB_In)		0.016	0.0555	0.003	19.01	< 0.001*	0.050	0.061
cov(e.Wrk_Prob, WP_Srcs)		0.287	−0.317	0.156	−2.03	0.043*	−0.623	−0.010
cov(Fail_Norm, No_Mem)		0.059	0.019	0.009	2.10	0.036*	0.001	0.037
cov(PTSD, ETV_In)		0.027	−0.031	0.004	−8.51	< 0.001*	−0.038	−0.024
cov(PTSD, Talk_To)		0.035	0.575	0.064	8.95	< 0.001*	0.449	0.701
cov(PTSD, Alc_Ab)		0.025	−0.122	0.015	−8.18	< 0.001*	−0.151	−0.093
cov(Alc_Ab, Cynicism)		0.013	−2.050	0.206	−9.98	< 0.001*	−2.453	−1.647

*Note: Constants, reference indicators, and variance output not reported here for efficiency.

with our hypothesis that PTSD can be isolating. Higher prevalence of PTSD symptoms was also associated with more *Avoidant Coping*, and vice versa, in line with previous literature (Prigerson, Maciejewski, & Rosenheck, 2002).

Focusing specifically on the impact of coping mechanisms, we find that both *Avoidant Coping* and *Problem-focused Coping* had significant pattern coefficients on the pathway to *Negative EC*, as predicted by Hypothesis 3. In turn, *Negative EC* significantly and positively impacted *Turnover Intention* (i.e. greater cynicism is associated with a stronger desire to leave corrections). Specifically, *Problem-focused Coping* was significantly, negatively associated with *Negative EC*, and *Avoidant Coping* was positively associated with *Negative EC*. Additionally, as expected given extant literature (e.g. Tetrick, Slack, Da Silva, & Sinclair, 2000), *Problem-focused Coping* had a significant, direct impact on *Turnover Intention*, showing the impact of social support on intention to quit. Findings also supported Hypothesis 4. Supervisory support had a significant, negative impact on turnover intention, such that greater supervisory support was negatively associated with an officer's likelihood of accepting a job offer outside corrections. Lastly, financial stress was significantly and positively associated with turnover intention, supporting Hypothesis 5.

Additionally, all indirect effects in the model were significant. This is unsurprising, given our theoretical framework. The impact of a traumatic experience – in this case, *Exposure to Violence* – appears to have a direct impact on *PTSD* and, through this pathway, can precipitate alcohol use (i.e. promoting *Avoidant Coping*). *Avoidant Coping* also had a negative impact on *Problem-focused Coping*, suggesting that coping styles are not utilized independently of one another, but can be closely linked. Lastly, these effects also include the significant indirect influence of *Avoidant Coping* and *Problem-focused Coping* on intention to quit.[7] In other words, these coping styles had an impact on officers' desire to leave corrections on the pathway through *Negative EC*.

Focusing on the standardized coefficients, we see that the largest relative contribution to the average for each factor corresponds well with model hypotheses. Unsurprisingly, *Exposure to Violence* had the largest standardized coefficient for its direct effect on *PTSD*. Importantly, while *PTSD* had the strongest relative contribution to *Problem-focused Coping* (−0.46), supervisory support was not far behind at 0.34. For direct effects on intention to quit, *Negative EC* had the largest coefficient in terms of absolute value, suggesting the significant contribution of cynicism to officers' intention to leave corrections.

Conclusion

In this paper, we use structural equation modeling and original survey data to examine the use of coping mechanisms among a large sample of California correctional officers. Our results help clarify the correctional stress process – including the impact of exposure to violence on the development of post-trauma symptoms, the influence of violence and trauma on the utilization of specific coping mechanisms, and ultimately the impact of stress on the likelihood that officers intend to stay within the field of corrections. In line with the Stress Process Paradigm, we find that exposure to a traumatic incident is positively associated with post-traumatic stress symptoms, but also that exposure to violence and PTSD symptoms directly and substantially impact coping styles. Specifically, greater PTSD symptom severity means a lower likelihood of engaging in *Problem-focused Coping* (i.e. talking with others about work-related problems) and a higher likelihood of turning to *Avoidant Coping* strategies (i.e. alcohol abuse).

The adoption of these coping mechanisms then impacts officers' desire to leave corrections, primarily through their impact on *Negative Emotional-Coping* (e.g. cynicism). Specifically, the effect of alcohol abuse appears to operate fully through its impact on perpetuating cynicism, while having someone to talk to both lowers cynicism and directly reduces the desire to leave corrections. As proposed by the Stress Process Paradigm, this highlights the importance of context and resources in shaping the consequences of stressors. Within the correctional environment, traumatic events are associated with post-traumatic stress symptoms, which tend to coincide with adoption of *Avoidant Coping*. However, when an officer can engage in *Problem-focused Coping*, this seems to reduce the experience of stress.

There are of course limitations to our inquiry. First and foremost, structural equation modeling relies heavily on the analysts' ability to properly specify the model. Thus, using theory to guide model building is essential. While our model is informed by available empirical evidence and rooted in extant theory, the topic of mental health in the correctional workplace is only recently a burgeoning field of study. In the future, as more data are collected that can speak to specific impacts of violence, mental health, and coping on correctional officers' intentions to stay in the field, we can begin to refine our model specification.

Additionally, our analytical sample size was determined by available data. Our results might vary to the extent that responses to some questions are not missing at random. We did not employ any imputation methods to address missing data, so we are working with approximately two-thirds of the overall sample. We may therefore be underestimating the impact of correctional officers' experience of mental health symptoms and/or exposure to violence, or have introduced bias into our estimates of structural relationships. Additionally, we did not have objective measures of exposure to violence to utilize for this study. Future studies could benefit from administrative data on violence and other factors to help validate or refine the model.

On-going research efforts should continue to study the correctional environment and prison workforce to build upon, revise, and further clarify the cognitive processes presented here. Future empirical work would ideally utilize exogenous variation in context and resources to help advance this line of inquiry. For example, a randomized controlled trial of mental health programs for correctional officers would be useful for understanding how changes to the quality or availability of mental health supports can influence coping and turnover. Separately, exogenous variation might also be leveraged from pre-existing data where outside shocks have been experienced, such as in prisons with sporadic upticks in exposure to violence.

Finally, future work could expand the model presented here to include other outcomes that might result from the stress process we have described. In particular, this could focus on officers' professional orientations and behavior when interacting with incarcerated individuals (Lerman & Harney, 2019). To the extent correctional institutions can facilitate the adoption of coping mechanisms that minimize (rather than exacerbate) the psychological burdens of working in corrections, they might profoundly impact the way a correctional workforce cares for those confined to prison.

Nevertheless, our results provide a useful framework, one that is likely close to the truth based on fit, and one that can inform the way policymakers, correctional leadership, and other stakeholders make decisions about how best to support their correctional staff. In particular, our findings highlight specific pain points in the correctional stress process that prison administrators might target for intervention. Starting from the end of our stress process, health and wellness initiatives could focus on *Negative EC* and its impact on the desire to leave corrections. Cynicism likely impacts officers across a variety of domains – not only in their interactions with coworkers and incarcerated individuals, but also family members and friends. Thus, providing family-based interventions may be a promising way to counteract *Negative EC* and promote *Problem-focused Coping*. Moreover, these interventions might be efficacious for addressing symptoms of trauma more broadly (Cukor, Spitalnick, Difede, Rizzo, & Rothbaum, 2009). Given the significant indirect effect of PTSD on officers' desire to leave corrections, this could prove impactful for reducing turnover.[8]

Taking a step further into the model, the opportunity for officers to build their social support systems may be particularly powerful in the prison context. The more the correctional institution can encourage *Problem-focused Coping*, such as by increasing access to therapists or others who can support officers in dealing with post-trauma symptoms, the more willing officers may be to stay in corrections. Another promising intervention could be a peer support program (Hundt, Robinson, Arney, Stanley, & Cully, 2015; Pfeiffer, Heisler, Piette, Rogers, & Valenstein, 2011),[9] which would provide an alternative for officers seeking support, but who are concerned about having a therapy appointment that might appear in their medical records.[10]

In addition, our model shows a direct impact of supervisory support on the likelihood officers utilize *Problem-focused Coping*. Supervisors can lead by example, showing vulnerability by discussing their own struggles, expressing support for the use of mental health resources, and providing personal support to the employees who report to them. As part of departmental policy, supervisors could also engage in specific training targeting their own mental health, as well as targeted mental health crisis intervention training (Mental Health First Aid, 2020). For the greatest effect, this training should be designed to address the needs and concerns of corrections workers specifically. Having a supervisor who can show meaningful leadership, not simply manage day-to-day workplace activities, is likely to build a broader supportive and collaborative environment, which appears key to employee retention.

Finally, we find that financial security is an important factor in whether officers desire to stay in corrections, but it does not fully explain intentions to leave the field for other employment. The 2018 median base pay for correctional officers in California was approximately $75,000, a figure that is high relative to both correctional officers in other states and to workers in jobs with similar occupational entry requirements (Transparent California, 2021). Yet while pay raises are often the primary (and sometimes even the sole) focus of labor negotiations, our results suggest that this alone will not be sufficient to help combat the turnover problem in corrections. Instead, additional support services are needed to retain and protect employees.

Understanding how officers cope with the stresses of their job, and how this impacts their desire to stay in the field, is important. At the same time, the primary onus cannot be on individual officers to manage the intense stress associated with prolonged exposure to workplace violence. Future research would benefit from exploring whether and how improving the correctional work environment might help reduce institutional violence and its correlates. Ultimately, understanding how to reduce violence in prison is crucial to improving outcomes for officers, for incarcerated individuals, and for the correctional system as a whole.

Notes

1. Although not a directly comparable measure, approximately 17% of US adults report binge drinking about four times in a month (CDC, 2019).

2. In order to substantively warrant inclusion of reciprocal effects in a cross-sectional design, the following must be true: first, the model is in a steady state and second, reciprocal effects must essentially be simultaneous and therefore better modeled in a single timepoint versus longitudinal data (Wong & Law, 1999). Unfortunately, there are no methods that will allow us to justify the steady state assumption from a statistical standpoint (Kaplan, Harik, & Hotchkiss, 2001). Overall, however, we have no reason to suspect that the nature of these relationships would change over time, which justifies conceptualizing this process as being in a steady state for modeling purposes.
3. The original response scale for these questions in the AUDIT questionnaire was a five-point scale, with possible responses of 'Never', 'Less than monthly', 'Monthly', 'Weekly', 'Daily or almost daily' (Babor & Grant, 1989).
4. We also conducted a confirmatory factor analysis (CFA) using all of our indicators. The CFA model retained nine factors, eight of which appeared to be meaningful (the ninth having quite low factor loadings). Given these results, we proceed with our model as hypothesized.
5. Note that single-indicator variables, *Supervisory Support* and *Turnover Intention*, were also allowed to covary.
6. Note that the RMSEA tends to inflict stricter penalties upon smaller models (Nevitt & Hancock, 2001).
7. Indirect results for problem-focused coping and avoidant coping on desire to leave corrections: *Problem-focused coping* (Estimate = −0.315, SE = 0.026, p-value < 0.001); *Avoidant coping* (Estimate = 2.664; SE = 0.288, p-value < 0.001).
8. Indirect effect of PTSD on desire to leave corrections: Estimate = 1.313, SE = 0.079, p-value < 0.001.
9. The meta-analysis focused primarily on symptoms of depression. While we did not explicitly include depression in our model, depression and PTSD are highly comorbid (O'Donnell, Creamer, & Pattison, 2004).
10. Mental health treatment is the most reliable intervention for PTSD and stress-related mental health disorders (Lenz, Bruijn, Serman, & Bailey, 2014; Seidler & Wagner, 2006). Thus, providing access to these services – and ensuring officers feel safe enough to make use of them – is vital to mitigating the escalation of trauma symptom severity and its impact on officer coping. This will require improving correctional culture and trust, which is of course no easy task.

Disclosure statement

No potential conflict of interest was reported by the author(s).

References

Allen, N.J., & Meyer, J.P. (1990). The measurement and antecedents of affective, continuance and normative commitment to the organization. *Journal of Occupational Psychology*, 63(1), 1–18.

Anderson, J.C., & Gerbing, D.W. (1988). Structural equation modeling in practice: A review and recommended two-step approach. *Psychological Bulletin*, 103(3), 411.

Babor, T.F., & Grant, M. (1989). From clinical research to secondary prevention: International collaboration in the development of the Alcohol Disorders Identification Test (AUDIT). *Alcohol Health and Research World*, 13(4), 371–374.

Barnes, J.B., Nickerson, A., Adler, A.B., & Litz, B.T. (2013). Perceived military organizational support and peacekeeper distress: A longitudinal investigation. *Psychological Services*, 10(2), 177.

Beehr, T.A., Farmer, S.J., Glazer, S., Gudanowski, D.M., & Nair, V.N. (2003). The enigma of social support and occupational stress: Source congruence and gender role effects. *Journal of Occupational Health Psychology*, 8(3), 220.

Beh, L.S., & Loo, L.H. (2012). Job stress and coping mechanisms among nursing staff in public health services. *International Journal of Academic Research in Business and Social Sciences*, 2(7), 131.

Brewin, C.R., Andrews, B., & Valentine, J.D. (2000). Meta-analysis of risk factors for posttraumatic stress disorder in trauma-exposed adults. *Journal of Consulting and Clinical Psychology*, 68(5), 748–766.

Brief, A.P., & Atieh, J.M. (1987). Studying job stress: Are we making mountains out of molehills? *Journal of Organizational Behavior*, 8(2), 115–126.

Brower, J. (2013). *Correctional officer wellness and safety literature review*. Washington, DC: U.S. Department of Justice Office of Justice Programs Diagnostic Center.

Bunde, J., & Suls, J. (2006). A quantitative analysis of the relationship between the Cook-Medley Hostility Scale and traditional coronary artery disease risk factors. *Health Psychology*, 25(4), 493–500.

Butler, H.D., Tasca, M., Zhang, Y., & Carpenter, C. (2019). A systematic and meta-analytic review of the literature on correctional officers: Identifying new avenues for research. *Journal of Criminal Justice*, 60, 84–92.

Can, S.H., & Hendy, H.M. (2014). Police stressors, negative outcomes associated with them and coping mechanisms that may reduce these associations. *The Police Journal*, 87(3), 167–177.

Centers for Disease Control. (2019). *Binge drinking*. Alcohol and Public Health. Retrieved August 25, 2021, from https://www.cdc.gov/alcohol/fact-sheets/binge-drinking.htm

Charuvastra, A., & Cloitre, M. (2008). Social bonds and posttraumatic stress disorder. *Annual Review of Psychology*, 59(1), 301–328.

Cheung, G.W., & Rensvold, R.B. (2002). Evaluating goodness-of-fit indexes for testing measurement invariance. *Structural Equation Modeling*, 9(2), 233–255.

Cole, D.A., Ciesla, J.A., & Steiger, J.H. (2007). The insidious effects of filing to include design-driven correlated residuals in latent-variable covariance structure analysis. *Psychological Methods*, 12(4), 381–398.

Cukor, J., Spitalnick, J., Difede, J., Rizzo, A., & Rothbaum, B.O. (2009). Emerging treatments for PTSD. *Clinical Psychology Review*, 29(8), 715–726.

Debell, F., Fear, N.T., Head, M., Batt-Rawden, S., Greenberg, N., Wessely, S., & Goodwin, L. (2014). A systematic review of the comorbidity between PTSD and alcohol misuse. *Social Psychiatry and Psychiatric Epidemiology*, 49(9), 1401–1425.

Demerouti, E., & Bakker, A.B. (2008). The oldenburg burnout inventory: A good alternative to measure burnout and engagement. In J.R.B. Halbesleben (Ed.), *Handbook of stress and burnout in health care*. Hauppauge, NY: Nova Science 78 .

Epstein, E.E., & McCrady, B.S. (2002). Couple therapy in the treatment of alcohol problems. In A.S. Gurman & N.S. Jacobson (Eds.), *Clinical handbook of couple therapy* (Vol. 3, pp. 597–628). New York: Guilford Press.

Fetzner, M.G., McMillan, K.A., Sareen, J., & Asmundson, G.J. (2011). What is the association between traumatic life events and alcohol abuse/dependence in people with and without PTSD? Findings from a nationally representative sample. *Depression and Anxiety*, 28(8), 632–638.

Finn, P. (2000). *Addressing correctional officer stress: Programs and strategies*. Washington, DC: US Department of Justice, Office of Justice Programs, National Institute of Justice.

Folkman, S., Lazarus, R.S., Dunkel-Schetter, C., DeLongis, A., & Gruen, R.J. (1986). Dynamics of a stressful encounter: Cognitive appraisal, coping, and encounter outcomes. *Journal of Personality and Social Psychology*, 50(5), 992.

Fontana, A., & Rosenheck, R. (1993). A causal model of the etiology of war-related PTSD. *Journal of Traumatic Stress*, 6(4), 475–500.

Foundations Recovery Network. (2020). *How alcohol affects PTSD*. Retrieved 16 August 2020. https://dualdiagnosis.org/how-alcohol-affects-ptsd

Gillet, N., Gagné, M., Sauvagère, S., & Fouquereau, E. (2013). The role of supervisor autonomy support, organizational support, and autonomous and controlled motivation in predicting employees' satisfaction and turnover intentions. *European Journal of Work and Organizational Psychology*, 22(4), 450–460.

Goff, A., Rose, E., Rose, S., & Purves, D. (2007). Does PTSD occur in sentenced prison populations? A systematic literature review. *Criminal Behavior & Mental Health*, 17(3), 152–162.

Gould, D.D., Watson, S.L., Price, S.R., & Valliant, P.M. (2013). The relationship between burnout and coping in adult and young offender center correctional officers: An exploratory investigation. *Psychological Services*, 10(1), 37.

Green, B.L. (1996). Trauma history questionnaire. In *Measurement of stress, self-report trauma, and adaptation* (pp. 366–369). Sidran Press.

Haney, C. (2003). The psychological impact of incarceration: Implications for post-prison adjustment. *Prisoners once Removed: The Impact of Incarceration and Reentry on Children, Families, and Communities*, 33, 66.

Hermida, R. (2015). The problem of allowing correlated errors in structural equation modeling: Concerns and considerations. *Computational Methods in Social Sciences*, 3(1), 5–17.

Hoge, C.W., Castro, C.A., Messer, S.C., McGurk, D., Cotting, D.I., & Koffman, R.L. (2004). Combat duty in Iraq and Afghanistan, mental health problems, and barriers to care. *New England Journal of Medicine*, 351(1), 13–22.

Holahan, C.J., Moos, R.H., Holahan, C.K., Brennan, P.L., & Schutte, K.K. (2005). Stress generation, avoidance coping, and depressive symptoms: A 10-year model. *Journal of Consulting and Clinical Psychology*, 73(4), 658.

Hooberman, J., Rosenfeld, B., Rasmussen, A., & Keller, A. (2010). Resilience in trauma-exposed refugees: The moderating effect of coping style on resilience variables. *American Journal of Orthopsychiatry*, 80(4), 557.

Hu, L., & Bentler, P.M. (1999). Cutoff criteria for fit indexes in covariance structure analysis: Conventional criteria versus new alternatives. *Structural Equation Modeling*, 6(1), 1–55.

Hundt, N.E., Robinson, A., Arney, J., Stanley, M.A., & Cully, J.A. (2015). Veterans' perspectives on benefits and drawbacks of peer support for posttraumatic stress disorder. *Military Medicine*, 180 (8), 851–856.

Jaegers, L.A., Matthieu, M.M., Vaughn, M.G., Werth, P., Katz, I.M., & Ahmad, S.O. (2019). Posttraumatic stress disorder and job burnout among jail officers. *Journal of Occupational and Environmental Medicine*, 61(6), 505–510.

James, L., Todak, N., & Best, S. (2017). The negative impact of prison work on sleep health. *American Journal of Industrial Medicine*, 60(5), 449–456.

Johnson, R.R. (2015). Police organizational commitment: The influence of supervisor feedback and support. *Crime and Delinquency*, 61(9), 1155–1180.

Kaplan, D., Harik, P., & Hotchkiss, L. (2001). Cross-sectional estimation of dynamic structural equation models in disequilibrium. In *Structural equation modeling: Present and future* (pp. 315–339). Skokie, IL: Scientific Software International, Inc.

Kelley, C.L., Britt, T.W., Adler, A.B., & Bliese, P.D. (2014). Perceived organizational support, posttraumatic stress disorder symptoms, and stigma in soldiers returning from combat. *Psychological Services*, 11(2), 229.

Kline, R.B. (2015). *Principles and practice of structural equation modeling*. New York, NY: Guilford Publications.

Kukla-Acevedo, S. (2009). Leavers, movers, and stayers: The role of workplace conditions in teacher mobility decisions. *The Journal of Educational Research*, 102(6), 443–452.

Kula, S. (2017). Occupational stress, supervisor support, job satisfaction, and work-related burnout: Perceptions of Turkish National Police (TNP) members. *Police Practice and Research*, 18(2), 146–159.

Kunst, M.J., Bogaerts, S., & Winkel, F.W. (2009). Peer and inmate aggression, type D-personality and post-traumatic stress among Dutch prison workers. *Stress and Health: Journal of the International Society for the Investigation of Stress*, 25(5), 387–395.

Lambert, E.G. (2001). To stay or quit: A review of the literature on correctional staff turnover. *American Journal of Criminal Justice*, 26(1), 61–76.

Lambert, E., & Hogan, N. (2009). The importance of job satisfaction and organizational commitment in shaping turnover intent: A test of a causal model. *Criminal Justice Review*, 34(1), 96–118.

Lazarus, R.S., & Folkman, S. (1984). *Stress, appraisal, and coping*. New York, NY: Springer.

Leino, T., Eskelinen, K., Summala, H., & Virtanen, M. (2011). Work-related violence, debriefing and increased alcohol consumption among police officers. *International Journal of Police Science & Management*, 13(2), 149–157.

Lenz, S., Bruijn, B., Serman, N., & Bailey, L. (2014). Effectiveness of cognitive processing therapy for treating posttraumatic stress disorder. *Journal of Mental Health Counseling*, 36(4), 360–376.

Lerman, A.E. (2017). *California correctional officer survey [Data file]*.

Lerman, A.E., Harney, J., & Sadin, M. (2021). Prisons and mental health: Violence, organizational support, and the effects of correctional work. *Criminal Justice and Behavior*, 009385482110377. doi:10.1177/00938548211037718

Lerman, A.E., & Harney, J. (2019). Feedback effects and the criminal justice bureaucracy: Officer attitudes and the future of correctional reform. *The ANNALS of the American Academy of Political and Social Science*, 685(1), 227–249.

Li, X., Guan, L., Chang, H., & Zhang, B. (2014). Core self-evaluation and burnout among nurses: the mediating role of coping styles. *PloS One*, 9(12), e115799.

Liebling, A., Durie, L., van Den Beukel, A., Tait, S., & Harvey, J. (2005). Revisiting prison suicide: The role of fairness and distress. In *The effects of imprisonment* (pp. 209–231). London: Willan Publishing.

Maertz, C.P., Jr, Griffeth, R.W., Campbell, N.S., & Allen, D.G. (2007). The effects of perceived organizational support and perceived supervisor support on employee turnover. *Journal of Organizational Behavior: The International Journal of Industrial, Occupational and Organizational Psychology and Behavior*, 28(8), 1059–1075.

Massoglia, M. (2008a). Incarceration as exposure: The prison, infectious disease, and other stress-related illnesses. *Journal of Health and Social Behavior*, 49(1), 56–71.

Massoglia, M. (2008b). Incarceration, health, and racial disparities in health. *Law & Society Review*, 42 (2), 275–306.

McCall, J.J. (1970). Economics of information and job search. *The Quarterly Journal of Economics*, 84 (1), 113–126.

McCrady, B.S., & Epstein, E.E. (1995). Directions for research on alcoholic relationships: Marital- and individual-based models of heterogeneity. *Psychology of Addictive Behaviors*, 9(3), 157–166.

McShane, M.D., Williams, F.P., III, Scbichor, D., & McClain, K. (1991). Early exits: Examining employee turnover. *Corrections Today*, 53, 220–225.

Meade, A.W., Johnson, E.C., & Braddy, P.W. (2008). Power and sensitivity of alternative fit indices in tests of measurement invariance. *Journal of Applied Psychology*, 93(3), 568–592.

Mental Health First Aid. (2020). *Mental health first aid public safety*. Retrieved 16 August 2020. https://www.mentalhealthfirstaid.org/population-focused-modules/public-safety

Morgan, W. (2009). Correctional officer stress: A review of the literature 1977-2007. *American Jails*, 23 (2), 33–34, 36–43.

Munyon, T.P., Carnes, A.M., Lyons, L.M., & Zettler, I. (2020). All about the money? Exploring antecedents and consequences for a brief measure of perceived financial security. *Journal of Occupational Health Psychology*, 25(3), 159.

Nevitt, J., & Hancock, G.R. (2001). Performance of bootstrapping approaching to model test statistics and parameter standard error estimation in structural equation modeling. *Structural Equation Modeling*, 8(3), 353–377.

Novisky, M.A., & Peralta, R.L. (2020). Gladiator school: Returning citizens' experiences with secondary violence exposure in prison. *Victims & Offenders*, 1–25. doi:10.1080/15564886.2020.1721387

NSI Nursing Solutions, Inc. (2021). *2021 NSI National Health Care Retention & RN staffing report*. Retrieved August 25, 2021, from https://www.nsinursingsolutions.com/Documents/Library/NSI_National_Health_Care_Retention_Report.pdf

O'Donnell, M.L., Creamer, M., & Pattison, P. (2004). Posttraumatic stress disorder and depression following trauma: Understanding comorbidity. *American Journal of Psychiatry*, 161(8), 1390–1396.

Orth, U., & Wieland, E. (2006). Anger, hostility, and posttraumatic stress disorder in trauma-exposed adults: A meta-analysis. *Journal of Consulting and Clinical Psychology*, 74(4), 698.

Ozer, E.J., Best, S.R., Lipsey, T.L., & Weiss, D.S. (2003). Predictors of posttraumatic stress disorder and symptoms in adults: A meta-analysis. *Psychological Bulletin*, 129(1), 52–73.

Patenaude, A.L. (2001). Analysis of issues affecting correctional officer retention within the Arkansas department of correction. *Corrections Management Quarterly*, 5, 49–67.

Pearlin, L.I., Menaghan, E.G. Lieberman, M.A., & Mullan, J.T. (1981). The stress process. *Journal of Health and Social Behavior*, 22(4), 337–356.

Pearlin, L.I. (1989). The sociological study of stress. *Journal of Health and Social Behavior*, 30(3), 241–256.

Pfeiffer, P.N., Heisler, M., Piette, J.D., Rogers, M.A., & Valenstein, M. (2011). Efficacy of peer support interventions for depression: A meta-analysis. *General Hospital Psychiatry*, 33(1), 29–36.

Prigerson, H.G., Maciejewski, P.K., & Rosenheck, R.A. (2002). Population attributable fractions of psychiatric disorders and behavioral outcomes associated with combat exposure among US men. *American Journal of Public Health*, 92(1), 59–63.

Ramlall, S. (2004). A review of employee motivation theories and their implications for employee retention within organizations. *Journal of American Academy of Business*, 5, 52–63.

Rogers, J.B. (2001). *FOCUS survey and final report: A summary of the findings: Families officers and corrections understanding stress.*

Ross, J.I. (2013). Deconstructing correctional officer deviance: Toward typologies of actions and controls. *Criminal Justice Review*, 38(1), 110–126.

Seidler, G.H., & Wagner, F.E. (2006). Comparing the efficacy of EMDR and trauma-focused cognitive-behavioral therapy in the treatment of PTSD: A meta-analytic study. *Psychological Medicine*, 36 (11), 1515–1522.

Shepherd, B.R., Fritz, C., Hammer, L.B., Guros, F., & Meier, D. (2019). Emotional demands and alcohol use in corrections: A moderated mediation model. *Journal of Occupational Health Psychology*, 24 (4), 438.

Shim, D.C., Park, H.H., & Eom, T.H. (2017). Street-level bureaucrats' turnover intention: Does public service motivation matter?. *International Review of Administrative Sciences*, 83(3), 563–582.

Stack, S., & Tsoudis, O. (1997). Suicide risk among correctional officers: A logistic regression analysis. *Archives of Suicide Research*, 3(3), 183–186.

Stanisławski, K. (2019). The coping circumplex model: An integrative model of the structure of coping with stress. *Frontiers in Psychology*, 10. doi:10.3389/fpsyg.2019.00694

StataCorp. (2019). *Stata statistical software: Release 16*. College Station, TX: Author.

Sugie, N.F., & Turney, K. (2017). Beyond incarceration: Criminal justice contact and mental health. *American Sociological Review*, 82(4), 719–743.

Sykes, G.M. (2007). *The society of captives: A study of a maximum security prison*. Princeton, NJ: Princeton University Press.

Tetrick, L.E., Slack, K.J., Da Silva, N., & Sinclair, R.R. (2000). A comparison of the stress–strain process for business owners and nonowners: Differences in job demands, emotional exhaustion, satisfaction, and social support. *Journal of Occupational Health Psychology*, 5(4), 464.

Thoits, P.A. (2010). Stress and health: Major findings and policy implications. *Journal of Health and Social Behavior*, 51(S), S41–S53.

Thomas, J.L., Wilk, J.E., Riviere, L.A., McGurk, D., Castro, C.A., & Hoge, C.W. (2010). Prevalence of mental health problems and functional impairment among active component and National Guard soldiers 3 and 12 months following combat in Iraq. *Archives of General Psychiatry*, 67(6), 614–623.

Transparent California. (2021). *California's largest public pay and pension database. [Data file.]* Retrieved 16 August 2020 https://transparentcalifornia.com

Trounson, J.S., Pfeifer, J.E., & Skues, J.L. (2019). Perceived workplace adversity and correctional officer psychological well-being: An international examination of the impact of officer response styles. *The Journal of Forensic Psychiatry & Psychology*, 30(1), 17–37.

Turney, K., Wildeman, C., & Schnittker, J. (2012). As fathers and felons: Explaining the effects of current and recent incarceration on major depression. *Journal of Health and Social Behavior*, 53(4), 465–481.

Udechukwu, I., Harrington, W., Manyak, T., Segal, S., & Graham, S. (2007). The Georgia department of corrections: An exploratory reflection on correctional officer turnover and its correlates. *Public Personnel Management*, 36(3), 247–268.

United States Department of Veterans Affairs. (2019). *PTSD and problems with alcohol use*. Retrieved 16 August 2020. https://www.ptsd.va.gov/understand/related/problem_alcohol_use.asp

Wareham, J., Smith, B.W., & Lambert, E.G. (2015). Rates and patterns of law enforcement turnover: A research note. *Criminal Justice Policy Review*, 26(4), 345–370.

Wells, J.B., Minor, K.K., Lambert, E.G. & Tilley, J.L. (2016). A model of turnover intent and turnover behavior among staff in juvenile corrections. *Criminal Justice and Behavior*, 43(11), 1558–1579.

Wieclaw, J., Agerbo, E., Mortensen, P.B., Burr, H., Tüchsen, F., & Bonde, J.P. (2006). Work related violence and threats and the risk of depression and stress disorders. *Journal of Epidemiology and Community Health*, 60(9), 771–775.

Wong, C.S., & Law, K.S. (1999). Testing reciprocal relations by nonrecursive structural equation models using cross-sectional data. *Organizational Research Methods*, 2(1), 69–87.

Wright, K. (1994). *Effective prison leadership*. Binghamton, NY: William Neil.

Zaleski, E.H., Levey-Thors, C., & Schiaffino, K.M. (1998). Coping mechanisms, stress, social support, and health problems in college students. *Applied Developmental Science*, 2(3), 127–137.

Appendix A1. Survey item question text.

Factor/ Indicator (Model Abbreviation)	Question Prompt	Indicator Abbreviation: Question Text	Response Options
Accept	To what extent do you agree or disagree with the following statements?	**Accept**$^{+}$: If I received an offer for a job outside of corrections with a similar salary and benefits, I would immediately accept it.	7-Point Agreement Likert
Alcohol Abuse (Alc_Ab)	Please describe how often any of the following has occurred over the last year	**6+ Drinks**$^{+}$: I had six or more drinks on one occasion. **Fail_Norm**$^{+}$: I failed to do what was normally expected from me because of drinking. **No_Mem**$^{+}$: I was unable to remember what happened the night before because I had been drinking	Often, Sometimes, Rarely Never
Cynicism (Cynicism)	To what extent do you agree or disagree with the following statements?	**Better**$^{+}$: I would be a better parent, spouse, or partner if I did not work in corrections. **Harsh**$^{+}$: I have become harsher or less trusting towards friends or family members since I took this job **Anger**$^{+}$: I have a harder time controlling my anger since I started working in corrections.	7-Point Agreement Likert
Exposure to Violence Inside (ETV_In)	At any time in your life, have you been in a situation in which ...	**Inj_In**: At any time in your life, have you been in a situation in which you were seriously injured? **Fear_Inj**: When you were in a situation in which you feared you might be killed or seriously injured? Please mark all that apply. **DB_In**: When you were in a situation in which you were seriously injured? Please mark all that apply. **Seen_In**: When you were in a situation in which you were seriously injured? Please mark all that apply.	*Binary indicator for endorsed*: After I started working for CDCR, while working inside the prison
Financial Security (Fin_Sec)	How well does each of the following statements describe you or your situation?	**JGBF**: I am just getting by financially. **Not_Last**: I am concerned that the money I have or will save won't last. **Unexp**$^{+}$: I am confident that I could handle an unexpected expense.	5-Point Likert from Describes me completely to Does not describe me at all
Supervisor Cares	(Sup_Cares)	To what extent do you agree or disagree with the following statements:	**Sup_Cares**: My direct supervisors shows very little interest in feelings of subordinates.
7-Point Likert	Agreement		

(*Continued*)

(Continued).

Factor/ Indicator (Model Abbreviation)	Question Prompt	Indicator Abbreviation: Question Text	Response Options
PTSD	Please read each one carefully, and indicate how much you have been bothered by that problem in the last month.	**Rep_Mem**$^{+}$: Repeated, disturbing memories, thoughts, or images of a stressful experience from the past. **Upset**$^{+}$: Feeling very upset when something reminded you of a stressful experience from the past.	A great deal, A lot, A moderate amount, A little, Not at all
Someone to Talk To (Talk_To)	To what extent do you agree or disagree with the following statement:	**Wrk_Prob**$^{+}$: When I have a problem at work, there is someone I can talk to who will really help me solve it.	7-Point Agreement Likert
	Sum of endorsed	**WP_Srcs**: When you have a problem at work, who do you feel you can talk to who will really help you solve it? Please mark all that apply. **WB_Srcs**: If you were to have concerns specifically about your personal health and well-being, who might you consider talking to in order to get help? Please mark all that apply.	A co-worker, A supervisor, A prison administrator, A family member or friend, A member of the clergy, A union rep or someone from CCPOA, A counselor or therapist, A doctor or medical professional, Other

+ Indicates a reverse-coded item. Agreement scales from 'Strongly Agree' to 'Strongly Disagree.'

Appendix B1. Pearson correlations of observed variables

Variable	2	3	4	5	6	7	8	9	10	11	12	13	14	15	16	17	18	19	20
1. Inj_In	0.28*	0.20*	0.19*	0.27*	0.26*	−0.12*	−0.05	−0.00	0.03	0.08*	0.05*	0.15*	0.15*	0.15*	−0.07*	−0.02	−0.07*	−0.03	0.12*
2. Fear_In	1	0.29*	0.34*	0.32*	0.29*	−0.14*	−0.06*	0.01	0.09*	0.10*	0.09*	0.24*	0.26*	0.24*	−0.07*	−0.04	−0.13*	−0.05	0.18*
3. DB_In		1	0.47*	0.19*	0.17*	−0.09*	−0.05*	−0.01	0.09*	0.07*	0.08*	0.17*	0.20*	0.17*	−0.00	−0.00	−0.06*	−0.02	0.12*
4. Seen_In			1	0.21*	0.18*	−0.09*	−0.06*	−0.01	0.09*	0.07*	0.07*	0.17*	0.20*	0.18*	−0.02	0.00	−0.05	−0.02	0.12*
5. Rep_Mem				1	0.81*	−0.22*	−0.14*	−0.04	0.20*	0.25*	0.22*	0.43*	0.46*	0.45*	−0.15*	−0.14*	−0.21*	−0.09*	0.24*
6. Upset_R					1	−0.24*	−0.15*	−0.04	0.19*	0.27*	0.22*	0.44*	0.47*	0.47*	−0.16*	−0.16*	−0.22*	−0.10*	0.26*
7. Wrk_Prob						1	0.61*	0.16*	−0.01	−0.08*	−0.06	−0.24*	−0.24*	−0.22*	0.33*	0.08*	0.14*	0.09*	−0.23*
8. WP_Srcs							1	0.37*	−0.03	−0.06	−0.03	−0.17*	−0.18*	−0.15*	0.26*	0.06*	0.10*	0.07*	−0.18*
9. WB_Srcs								1	−0.05	−0.03	−0.02	−0.05	−0.06*	−0.03	0.11*	0.02	0.03	0.03	−0.09*
10. 6+ Drinks									1	0.50*	0.53*	0.17*	0.16*	0.22*	−0.03	−0.09*	−0.11*	−0.07*	0.12*
11. Fail_Norm										1	0.63*	0.20*	0.18*	0.22*	−0.07*	−0.09*	−0.11*	−0.06*	0.12*
12. No_Mem											1	0.17*	0.16*	0.19*	−0.05	−0.07*	−0.08*	−0.05	0.10*
13. Better												1	0.63*	0.54*	−0.15*	−0.18*	−0.24*	−0.10*	0.41*
14. Harsh													1	0.55*	−0.14*	−0.14*	−0.21*	−0.08*	0.30*
15. Anger														1	−0.12*	−0.13*	−0.21*	−0.11*	0.27*
16. Sup_Cares															1	0.09*	0.13*	0.05*	−0.20*
17. JGBF																1	0.64*	0.37*	−0.13*
18. Not_Last																	1	0.40*	−0.18*
19. Unexp																		1	−0.04
20. Accept																			1

* Indicates significance at the $\alpha = 0.05$ level. All significant correlations were significant for both Spearman and Pearson correlations with a Bonferroni correction. Correlations are only including the 5,627 officers for which all model observed variables were non-missing.

Appendix C1. Covariance residuals.

Variable	1	2	3	4	5	6	7	8	9	10	11	12	13	14	15	16	17	18	19	20
JGBF	.0																			
Not_Last	.0	.0																		
Unexp	.0	.0	.0																	
Accept	.0	−.1	.1	.0																
Rep_Mem	.0	.0	.0	.0	.0															
Upset_R	.0	.0	.0	.0	.0	.0														
Better	.0	−.1	.0	.3	−.1	−.1	.0													
Harsh	.0	.0	.1	−.1	.0	.0	.1	.0												
Anger	.0	.0	.0	−.1	.1	.1	−.1	.0	.0											
Inj_In	.0	.0	.0	.0	.0	.0	.0	.0	.0	.0										
Fear_In	.0	−.1	.0	.0	.0	.0	.0	.0	.0	.0	.0									
Sup_Cares	.1	.2	.0	.0	.0	.0	−.1	−.1	.0	.0	.0	.0								
DB_In	.0	.0	.0	.0	.0	.0	.0	.0	.0	.0	.0	.0	.0							
Seen_In	.0	.0	.0	.0	.0	.0	.0	.0	.0	.0	.0	.0	.0	.0						
Wrk_Prob	.0	.1	.1	−.1	−.1	−.1	−.2	−.2	−.2	.0	.0	.2	.0	.0	.0					
WP_Srcs	.0	.0	.0	.1	.1	.1	.1	.1	.1	.0	.0	−.1	.0	.0	.0	.0				
WB_Srcs	.0	.0	.0	.0	.1	.0	.1	.0	.1	.0	.0	.0	.0	.0	−.3	.2	.0			
6+ Drinks	.0	−.1	.0	.1	.0	.0	.0	.0	.1	.0	.0	.0	.0	.0	.0	.0	−.1	.0		
Fail_Norm	.0	.0	.0	.0	.0	.0	.0	.0	.1	.0	.0	.0	.0	.0	.0	.0	.0	.0	.0	
No_Mem	.0	.0	.0	.0	.0	.0	.0	.0	.0	.0	.0	.0	.0	.0	.0	.0	.0	.0	.0	.0

Leading zeros were removed only for space. For reference: 1 = JGBF; 2 = Not_Last; 3 = Unexp; 4 = Accept; 5 = Rep_Mem; 6 = Upset_R; 7 = Better; 8 = Harsh; 9 = Anger; 10 = Inj_In; 11 = Fear_In; 12 = Sup_Cares; 13 = DB_In; 14 = Seen_In; 15 = Wrk_Prob; 16 = WP_Srcs; 17 = WB_Srcs; 18 = 6+ Drinks; 19 = Fail_Norm; 20 = No_Mem.

Barriers to help-seeking among correction officers: examining the influence of institutional culture and structure

Candence Wills, Kayla Bates, Natasha A. Frost and Carlos. E. Monteiro

ABSTRACT

Correction officers experience a challenging work environment that increases the risk of encountering violence, physical danger, and traumatic events such as inmate violence and potential assaults by inmates. The demanding work climate can lead to stress and mental health concerns. However, officers are reluctant to seek help for their own mental health concerns and avoid employer provided services, including peer-to-peer support units. This study seeks to explore the underlying institutional barriers to help-seeking for mental health concerns among correction officers. Content analysis is applied to qualitative data from 42 semi-structured interviews with family members and friends of correction officers who died by suicide and 395 interviews with officers working for a state department of corrections answering open-ended questions. Two overarching themes emerged and within these themes were a series of subthemes revealing institutional barriers to help-seeking for mental health concerns. Institutional culture centers around stigma related to mental health and hypermasculinity perpetuated in the work environment. Institutional structure contains institutional organization, confidentiality, and punitive responses as subthemes. Correctional settings could benefit from reducing stigma of mental health related encouraged by hypermasculinity, restructuring organizational hierarchies, enforcing confidentiality, and creating supportive environments for officers to seek help for mental health concerns.

Introduction

Correction officers work in a challenging occupational context with an elevated risk of exposures to traumatic and dangerous events. Officers witness violence between inmates, respond to inmate self-harm and suicide, and have to remain hypervigilant due to the potential for assaults on themselves. Most officers experience extensive violence exposures and some exhibit symptoms of psychological distress including anxiety, depression, and suicidal ideation that are often left untreated (Frost and Monteiro, 2020). Stress from working in correctional facilities derives not only from potential violence exposures but also from overcrowding, shift work, long or irregular hours, exhaustion, strained relationships with colleagues and supervisors, and limited organizational support (Finney, Stergiopoulos, Hensel, Bonato, & Dewa, 2013). Despite the many challenges associated with this type of work, those within corrections and other protective services are reluctant to engage in help-seeking behaviors. The lack of perceived support or access to services within institutional environments discourages officers from addressing compounding stress and psychological distress that accompanies working in protective services.

Gourash (1978, p. 413) explains that when individuals are confronted with issues that necessitate more coping resources than they can access on their own, they engage in help-seeking behaviors. Help-seeking is understood to be 'any communication about a problem or troublesome event which is directed toward obtaining support, advice, or assistance in times of distress' (Gourash, 1978, p. 414), which Lee (1997) expands with the addition of an interpersonal interaction between one party requesting help from another party and a proactive help-seeker wanting to resolve an issue. In the context of intimate partner violence (IPV), Liang, Goodman, Tummala-Narra, and Weintraub (2005) discuss help-seeking as a process with specific stages, including 'defining a problem, deciding whether to seek help, and choosing a support provider,' that can occur in any order. Social location including gender, culture, lower socioeconomic status, and minority race can impact the likelihood of help-seeking (Kennedy et al., 2012; Liang et al., 2005). Although the studies focus on sexual assault and IPV, the process of help-seeking is generalizable to occupational help-seeking and help-seeking for victimization.

Help-seeking behavior may involve simply wanting someone to listen and provide comfort, but those with more complex and serious issues may need to seek professional mental health support from an expert. Mental health professionals and resources remain largely underutilized by those experiencing psychological distress and other mental health concerns within the general population and especially among protective services (Barney, Griffiths, Jorm, & Christensen, 2006; Haugen, McCrillis, Smid, & Nijdam, 2017; Jetelina, Molsberry, Gonzalez, Beauchamp, & Hall, 2020; Jones, Agud, & McSweeney, 2020). This study seeks to explore the underlying institutional barriers, including cultural and structural factors, to help-seeking for mental health concerns among correction officers.

Literature review

Institutional culture

Protective services include those who protect a population and provide services to help a community, such as law enforcement, military personnel, and correction officers (Ricciardelli, Czarnuch, Carleton, Gacek, & Shewmake, 2020). Due to the cumulative impact of their work, those who work in protective services have an increased likelihood of psychological distress from continuous exposure to high-stress environments and can ultimately experience both family issues and various mental and physical health issues (Finn, 1998; Finney et al., 2013; Jetelina et al., 2020; Papazoglou & Tuttle, 2018).

Negative perceptions of mental health, including stigma associated with having mental health concerns and seeking help for mental health, often prevents those in need from reaching out for help. Stigma involves labeling, separating, endorsing stereotypes, supporting prejudice and discrimination within an environment of uneven social, economic, or political influence (Clement et al., 2015; Link & Phelan, 2001). In the context of mental health, stigma impacts the willingness to seek help by provoking feelings of embarrassment. Individuals may also believe that peers or employers will react negatively to seeking help for mental health, which prohibits the individual from reaching out to managers at work, peers and friends, or health professionals for their psychological distress (Barney et al., 2006; Chew-Graham, Rogers, & Yassin, 2003).

Studies have found there are reasons for the reluctance to among protective service employees. Fox et al. (2012) reported that 40% of the officers in their sample acknowledged symptoms of psychological distress, though did not utilize the department's mental health services due to the stigma associated with seeking help. A second study reported similar findings among police officers, with two-thirds of officers acknowledging that they did not seek help for stress or their mental health concerns due to the stigma associated with counseling (Carlan & Nored, 2008). Officers also recognized stress was natural and unavoidable, yet still feared the stigma surrounding mental health services (Carlan & Nored, 2008).

Part of the explanation for the enhanced stigma surrounding seeking mental health services in protective service occupations is a fear of being perceived as weak or unfit for the job due to needing help. Help-seeking goes against the hypermasculine institutional work culture of protective services, which emphasizes being tough and independent (Carlan & Nored, 2008; Morgan, Van Haveren, & Pearson, 2002). Officers report feeling weak and maintaining their own stereotypes regarding mental health; these perceptions lead to officers being less likely to receive treatment for their stress and trauma (Heffren & Hausdorf, 2016; Morgan et al., 2002).

The correctional environment impacts the development of hypermasculinity due to this continual emphasis on toughness, dangerousness, and aggression in prisons (Morgan et al., 2002). Among inmates, hypermasculinity is used as a tool for survival and protection, reinforcing s toughness and aggression in the prison environment while also increasing inmates and officer stress (Karp, 2010). Characteristics that are considered more feminine or 'soft' such as being more caring, and sensitive are believed to be potentially harmful for the officer in the corrections facilities (Crawley, 2004). They are expected to be 'resilient, courageous, authoritative, and fearless,' prohibiting them from acknowledging non-masculine feelings, like stress (Crawley, 2004, p. 132).

Suppressing qualities labeled as more *feminine* oppresses women in hypermasculine work environments, leading to male officers resisting women entering or being promoted within the profession (Brown, Baldwin, Dierenfeldt, & McCain, 2020; Waddington, 1999). In policing, the 'ideal officer' possesses more aggressive, hypermasculine traits, and as a result women officers are expected to dissolve their femininity in order to establish competency and capability among their peers (Brown et al., 2020). The institutional culture of corrections, similarly leads to a working environment that emphasizes suppression of emotion and being independent and tough, and these values are instilled in officers from their earliest days of their careers. During the academy, training highlights the need for self-reliance, aggression, toughness, independence, and the suppression of any appearance of weakness (Papazoglou & Tuttle, 2018; Soomro & Yanos, 2019). Those who identify with or are immersed in more masculine environments are then less likely to seek help when facing difficult situations or experiencing stress and other emotional or psychological distress (Crawley & Crawley, 2013).

Occupationally, individuals within protective services fear that by reaching out for professional help they will also be deemed unable to perform their job and unfit to serve (Jetelina et al., 2020). Officers reported not seeking help because they do not want to harm their chances of getting a promotion or have any clinical diagnosis impact the way they are perceived at work (White, Shrader, & Chamberlain, 2016). One study examined police officers and found by interacting with a high rate of individuals with mental illness, officers developed a negative stereotype towards individuals with mental illness and had more negative attitudes toward seeking help (Soomro & Yanos, 2019). Police officers reported viewing those with mental illness as dangerous and unpredictable; these stereotypes led to officers to avoid seeking help themselves so as to not be similarly perceived (Soomro & Yanos, 2019).With the prevalence of mental health issues among the incarcerated population, correction officers likely perceive the same mental health stigma as police officers based on their interactions (Wilper et al., 2009).

Corrections is one of several high stress fields in which an occupational reluctance to seek help has been documented. In other high stress fields, such as medicine, general practitioners have reported growing rates of psychological distress including, depression, anxiety, and suicidal ideation (Braquehais et al., 2014; Spiers et al., 2017). The stigma associated with being a physician and having mental illness has created barriers to help-seeking in that occupation as well (Spiers et al., 2017). Once negative beliefs associated with mental health help-seeking are internalized, the stigma embeds in the institutional culture. Conversely, institutions which promote more positive perceptions of seeking help for mental concerns and psychological distress lead to improved help-seeking outcomes. In a study involving active duty military personnel, those who perceive a climate of support for finding help for mental health concerns within the military have more positive and accepting beliefs towards mental health help-seeking (Britt, Wilson, Sawhney, & Black, 2020).

Institutional barriers to help-seeking

Institutional culture within departments of corrections plays a role in shaping the perceptions of mental health and help-seeking and can be institutionalized by actors within the workplace organization. Over time, institutions develop internal cultures that reflect the values of the organization and are spread throughout the organization through imposed institutional norms, goals, and beliefs on the actors. These values remain consistent as seasoned institutional actors, who have adopted the cultural norms and behaviors, pass on the culture to later generations (Meyers, 2004; Zucker, 1991, p. 83). Within organizations that have strongly embedded institutional cultures, individual actors internalize the interests and norms of the organization and behave in a manner that upholds the cultural norms and values regardless of the individual's personal beliefs (Meyers, 2004). Within the context of help-seeking for mental health concerns, organizations may have a culture that promotes mental health and encourages help-seeking behaviors rather than stigmatizing outreach.

Among correction officers, help from providers is better received when the officers perceive the provider as understanding the unique workplace context of working in prisons. As a result, those working in high stress institutions are often more willing to seek help from colleagues than from health care professionals and peer-to-peer support services have flourished (Brower, 2013). Though most departments of correction offer mental health services to combat negative coping mechanisms and offer support and training, research suggests that officers do not utilize the services (Frost, 2020).

Research has identified several barriers to help-seeking in protective services. One significant barrier to seeking help is a lack of confidentiality in the workplace, particularly among superiors and those providing employee mental health services (Fox et al., 2012; Jetelina et al., 2020). Superiors who maintain confidentiality or are perceived to be fair may encourage subordinates to reach out to them or other actors within the organization when issues or challenges arise. Employees are more likely to seek help within their organizations from those who are accessible, trustworthy, and perceived to be knowledgeable (Van Der Rijt et al., 2013). Those in higher ranking positions or positions handling confidential information (e.g. HR, counseling) need to be supportive and promote cultural values which destigmatizes mental health help-seeking and reinforces confidentiality for those reaching out for help and disclosing sensitive personal information.

Current study

Current literature on correction officers recognizes that officers experience traumatic and stressful events in their work environment leading to mental health concerns and suicidal ideation; however, officers are often reluctant to seek help for their own mental health. The current research seeks to identify some of the underlying issues that impact help-seeking behaviors among correction officers.

Using qualitative data from interviews with officers working for a state department of corrections, the study explores how workplace institutionalized culture and institutional structures play a role in promoting or inhibiting help-seeking behaviors. This approach prioritizes the voice of correction officers to provide a participant-led understanding of how institutional environments impact officer access and willingness to seek help. Themes which emerged from the interviews with officers and their loved ones provided rich context for understanding how institutional environments can create barriers to help-seeking or promote reaching out for help for mental health concerns.

Methodology

Qualitative interview sample

This article draws on data from a study of correction officer suicide and wellbeing funded by the National Institute of Justice in 2016 that involved two phases.[1] In the first phase, we sought to develop a nuanced understanding of crisis-level distress and suicide among officers within this state. We conducted 42 semi-structured interviews with family members and friends of correction officers who had worked for the department and had died by suicide between 2010 and 2015. Interviews were conducted in person with the individual(s) in a private location. The location was typically their home but occasionally at their workplace or at a location identified for the purpose of conducting a private in-person interview. Interviews ranged from one to three hours, and most were audio-recorded and transcribed. A few participants asked not to be recorded – these were primarily the current or former employees of the department of correction. In those instances, one or more research assistants took extensive notes during the interview and those notes were transcribed.

In the second phase, the research team interviewed a total of 440 officers who were still working for this department. The phase two interviews were designed to understand the impact of the officer suicides on officers who still work for the department. This phase involved structured interviews that included a series of questions about workplace experiences, proximity to suicide, self-report assessments of emotional and mental health and wellbeing, and opportunities to suggest how the department can improve responses to officer wellbeing. Additional sections of the interview focused on concern about officer health, wellbeing, suicide, and help-seeking for self and others. Although much of the data collected during these interviews was quantitative, 395 of the 440 participants answered open-ended questions designed to elicit their own perspectives of officer health and wellbeing and the qualitative analyses here relies upon those narrative responses.

Table 1 includes the descriptive statistics on the characteristics of the interview respondents across both phases. Among the phase one friends and families of correction officers who died by suicide, 64% were family members or relatives and 36% were friends. Fifty-two percent of the interviewees were male and just over a third (36%) were also current or former employees of this department. By contrast, an overwhelming majority of the phase two officer interview participants are male (83.8%) and White (86.3%) with 5.3% Black, and 5.6% identifying as Latinx. Although respondents are mixed in rank, the vast majority are officers (76.5%) with only 9.1% of respondents ranked as sergeant, 6.8% lieutenant, 4.3% captain, and 3.3% in administration. The phase two respondents are representative of the population of sworn officers within this department, who are overwhelmingly White (88.5%), male (84.4%), line-level officers (76.4%) (Frost et al., 2020).

Analytic strategy

Since the study is largely exploratory, both phases of the study employ qualitative content analysis in order to gain a more detailed and in-depth understanding of how institutions impact officer help-seeking for mental health concerns through the genuine voices of officers themselves and of family and friends of officers who died by suicide (Forman & Damschroder, 2007). In the first phase of interviews with family members and friends of correction who died by suicide, research assistants transcribed the recorded interviews and interview notes and uploaded to QSR NVivo 12 qualitative software. Two research assistants then applied qualitative content analysis techniques to independently code each interview transcription or notes file for emergent themes using QSR NVivo12 software. Each transcript was inductively coded using a systematic, iterative process. General themes that emerged through inductive coding included coping mechanisms, institutional culture, department structure, employee stress, family and homelife problems, and help-seeking among officers.

In the second phase, all officers interviewed were asked a series of open-ended questions about officer health and wellbeing and what the department could or should be doing to address correction officer wellbeing in the department such as, 'In your

Table 1. Characteristics of respondents.

Family & Friends Characteristics	Study Group (N = 42) n (%)
Relationship to Officer	
Family Member	27 (64)
Friend	15 (36)
Gender	
Male	22 (52)
Female	20 (48)
Current or Former DOC Employee	15 (36)
Officer Characteristics	**Study Group (N = 395) n (%)**
Age at Interview, mean (SD)	41 (9.14)
Age at Hire, mean (SD)	27.2 (7.7)
Gender	
Male	331 (83.8)
Female	64 (16.2)
Race/Ethnicity	
White	341 (86.3)
African American/Black	21 (5.3)
Hispanic/ Latinx	22 (5.6)
Asian American	8 (2.0)
Other/ Not Specified	3 (0.8)
Rank	
Officer	302 (76.5)
Sergeant	36 (9.1)
Lieutenant	27 (6.8)
Captain	17 (4.3)
Administrator	13 (3.3)
Veteran Status	122 (40)
Tenure, mean (SD)	13.3 (9.5)
Security Level of Facility	
Not a Facility*	21 (5.3)
Pre-Release and Minimum	19 (4.8)
Minimum and Medium	113 (28.6)
Medium	151 (38.2)
Maximum	91 (23.0)
Gender of Incarcerated Population at Facility	
Male	361 (91.4)
Female	34 (8.6)
Educational Level	
High School or Equivalent	118 (29.9)
Some College	107 (27.1)
Associate degree	54 (13.7)
Bachelor's degree	93 (23.5)
Master's degree	16 (4.1)
Missing	7 (1.8)

*Officers are assigned to transportation, assigned to region rather than facility, or work at administration

opinion, what is the most challenging aspect of working in corrections?' and 'In your opinion, what can (or should be) done to address correctional officer wellbeing within the Ma DOC?' The narrative data from the open-ended responses were also coded by at least two coders using qualitative content analysis techniques to identify emergent themes using QSR NVivo12 software. Overwhelmingly, the issues of cultural and structural barriers to help-seeking emerged as common themes. Many officers identified the associated stigma as ongoing issues in need of addressing and the officers' responses parallel the findings related to help-seeking from the interviews with friends and family members of officers who died by suicide.[2]

Results

Two overarching themes emerged from the content analysis that related to help-seeking: institutional culture and institutional structure were identified by the respondents as problematic. Both were identified as barriers to help-seeking for correction officers and within these overarching themes were a series of subthemes that similarly emerged during the coding analysis process. Table 2 contains themes and subthemes related to the current study. Problems in the institutional culture largely centered around the subthemes of stigma related to mental health and hypermasculinity perpetuated in the work environment. Within the theme of institutional structure, institutional organization, confidentiality, and punitive responses emerged as subthemes.

Institutional culture

Stigma

As in policing, the stigma associated with mental health and with reaching out for help for mental health concerns often prevents correction officers from seeking help. In an interview with a family member of a correction officer who died by suicide, the participant explained that perceptions of mental health concerns inhibit help-seeking:

> that's what it was for him; it was all the perception and the stigma that's associated with it, and here these guys are . . . – they don't want to be perceived [as needing help]– that was my feeling kind of like it's almost like it, that part of it got in the way of getting help . . . (Interview 10-03)

Mental health stigma proliferates throughout correction facilities and reinforces an environment that attaches negative ideas to seeking help for treatable symptoms and illness. Even when officers are struggling with familial and substance issues, many find it difficult to get help. As one officer explained:

Table 2. Thematic analysis of qualitative interview data.

Themes	Sub-themes
(1) **Institutional and workplace culture preventing help-seeking among correction officers**	(a) Stigma associated with mental health and help-seeking for mental health concerns (b) Hypermasculine culture within male dominated corrections
(1) **Institutional structures that inhibit officers from accessing or seeking help for mental health concerns**	(a) Institutional organization of hierarchical structure of employee support staff reporting to personnel (b) Violating confidentiality by supervisors and department administrators (c) Punitive response to help-seeking for revealing mental health concerns

> It's hard because we're in a job where you want to be closed off and not talk to anybody, but those people might benefit from being less closed-off. If people are struggling with substance abuse, divorce, etc. and were more open to counseling, substance abuse rehab, talking to someone about a career change, etc., they might be better off. You should realize that and leave, but some people don't. (Interview 1245)

The occupation fosters an environment that emotionally isolates individuals and prevents them from discussing common personal and mental health concerns. Officers grappling with their own personal issues may not consider reaching out to peers or a formal employee service. As one officer noted, 'in order to get help you have to want the help, but [correction officers] teach you to be desensitized' (Interview 1246). Officers may be able to acknowledge their own potential mental health concerns as they are socialized to ignore internal alarms raising red flags to seek help. They are prevented from not just receiving and accessing help but recognizing that they need it or may want it as a positive approach to managing mental health. The walls of stigma that silence officers from voicing their pain and challenges further prohibits them from engaging in formal support or recognizing that their career is potentially the foundation of their personal and mental health concerns.

Hypermasculinity

Correctional work environments promote a hypermasculine complex that perpetuates stigma associated with seeking help for mental health, and the reinforcement of masculine norms and ideals begins during the hiring phase. One interview explained, '... it's pretty clear when we go through the academy what you're getting yourself into – first responders job attracts alpha-males – a certain type of person. If guys don't take advantage of it, it's all for naught' (Interview 1248). According to this officer, corrections attracts hypermasculine people and therefore hypermasculine norms are embedded within the institution beginning with the self-selection process for entering correction officers. The masculine culture is further propagated throughout the work environment where officers are expected to suppress feelings of mental distress. Many believe that they cannot perform their job duties adequately if they acknowledge their emotions and mental state. Officers expressed feeling pressured into '[k]eeping up the façade of being tough and not weak' (Interview 1049) preventing them from recognizing their own red flags for mental health conditions.

Correction officers associate weakness and femininity with seeking help due to masculine complexes throughout the DOC. In an interview with a friend of a deceased officer, the friend highlighted the negative associations with reaching out for help among officers emphasizing 'He didn't want any help. He didn't want to be labeled as *soft* or ... *a pussy*. He didn't want to be labeled ... [Officers are] scared to go and seek help' (Interview 06–01). There is a common theme among officer responses that masculinity plays an important role with preventing help-seeking for mental health concerns so to appear to be both physically and mentally strong; whereas, seeking help might lead to becoming a target for other officers to scrutinize. Fear of being perceived as having weakness builds the barrier to seeking help. For those already facing distress, the added pressure to ignore personal psychological concerns and to conform to hypermasculine roles becomes a necessity in the workplace to avoid potential harassment. Officers who consider reaching out feel discouraged because of the institutionalized masculine culture stigmatizing mental health and seeking help within the DOC. One interviewee expressed that especially in female prisons, stigma prevents help-seeking behaviors:

> The idea of working in a female facility also may have played an important role. The idea of asking for help in a female facility is looked down upon. [He] may have not spoken up because of the pressures from coworkers and the stereotypes of correctional officer culture. (Interview 1107)

Stereotypes and stigma driven by institutionalized hypermasculinity perpetuate the perception that officers will be ridiculed for addressing their own mental health concerns. They are expected to appear 'strong' and to mentally 'suck it up' in their field of work (Frost & Monteiro, 2020). Another officer asserted that 'Everyone deals with it in their own way- [it's] not discussed, [it's] private, [and it's a] sign of weakness to discuss emotional well-being' (Interview 1079). The officer recognized the private nature of mental health and alluded to socialization of stigma associated with mental health and acknowledging concerns openly as 'a sign of weakness.' This perception of mental health as evidence of *weakness* encourages keeping the issue private and prevents officers from getting necessary mental health care.

Unfortunately, institutional cultures in work environments that perpetuate hypermasculinity may have adverse mental health effects and may contribute to suicidal behaviors, ideation, and death by suicide. Several officers expressed wanting psychologically distressed colleagues to break through hypermasculine belief systems and seek help for mental health concerns. One officer emphasized that in the aftermath of a cluster of suicides they are 'More aware that shit's going on' (Interview 1142) regarding correction officers struggling silently with their mental health. The same officer acknowledged that hypermasculine culture among officers discourages help-seeking behaviors for all officers irrespective of gender 'Hopefully they see if they start feeling like that [suicidal] they need to talk to somebody. Problem with COs is that they're all macho – [the] girls and guys' (Interview 1142). Many officers expressed a willingness to support their colleagues in seeking help and finding avenues for correction officers to receive psychological help. In one interview an officer suggested 'Getting people to talk openly, honestly, and not worry about macho-ism or anything else and get that information to the right person – [you] would otherwise need to read behavioral signs' (Interview 1061) allows supervising officers to recognize when they are suffering in silence and find support for the officers.

Institutional structure

Institutional organization

The structure and organization of institutions can negatively impact willingness to seek formal help. Institutional hierarchies, policies, and punitive procedures may determine if an officer feels comfortable approaching employer-provided institutional services. Organizational hierarchies can deter corrections personnel from approaching employee services. Officers expressed, in particular, a concern with having the Employee Assistance Services Unit (EASU) reporting to the personnel. The EASU provides peer-to-peer counseling to Department of Corrections employees and their extended families for stressful and challenging life events; this can include substance abuse, work or personal stress, feelings of anxiety and depression, and traumatic events or injuries. Officers were reluctant to disclose mental health concerns, fearing the organizational structure of the department's reporting hierarchy, which has the EASU reporting to personnel. Specifically, they expressed concern that those in the personnel department might have access to a private matter that they expected to remain confidential. They further indicated they would withhold information regarding their mental health state to avoid potential negative consequences, such as being demoted or having their responsibilities as an officer taken away by higher ranking officers or administrators.

In some instances, the rigid structure of the institution created an impersonal nature between supervisors and administrators in the DOC and the officers, resulting in officers expressing feeling unsupported. One officer, for example, lamented 'feeling like you're just a number and want to replace yourself, and the DOC doesn't care' (Interview 1043). A common theme among officers was the feeling of not being valued by the department administration or supervisors. In the workplace, officers perceive the department as considering their lives as less worthy than that of incarcerated persons. An officer highlights this notion when stating:

> If an inmate suicide happens on my watch, they're [department administrators] looking for reasons why it's my fault [or other COs faults]. If a CO kills themselves nobody looks to the administrations' role in the matter - or their accountability. (Interview 1255)

Officers frequently mentioned that they are not appreciated and are held to a double standard that the administration is not held to. They further believe that the department's concerns for inmate mental health are taken more seriously than that of the correction officers.

Confidentiality

One of the more notable issues emerging out of these rich conversations was that of institutional barriers to help-seeking by personnel and the structural hierarchy within the department. The department offers limited avenues for officers to seek help for personal matters. In this department, a peer-to-peer counseling unit was formed to help officers struggling with a number of challenges ranging from personal problems, including alcohol and drug dependency concerns, familial issues, job stress, marital support, and mental health referrals. Peer staff in the unit are trained officers who assist and refer fellow officers to alternative resources and specialized services, if needed. Employees can either self-select into the program or be referred by colleagues, friends, and family members. Unfortunately, the peer-to-peer support unit in this department has struggled to shift a longstanding negative perception primarily tied to concerns about confidentiality, boundaries, and dual role challenges. The change in perception of the peer-to-peer support unit has been slow, which has unfortunately left officers who need help seeking services with limited options.

Within the Department of Corrections, issues regarding confidentiality, structural hierarchical concerns, and punitive responses towards those who expressed having mental health concerns have dissuaded officers from engaging with formal employer-provided help-seeking services. Interviews with officers revealed that employees were reluctant to use the EASU for mental health concerns fearing a lack of confidentiality and too much communication between the EASU and supervising staff. In a group interview, the family member of a correction officer who died by suicide noted that they felt that information that was confidential was getting to everyone else in the department. [His supervisors] were telling him that he would have to write an incident report about his comments about his feelings about hurting himself. Although there is the capacity for confidential reports to go only to the superintendent, in this situation, the trust built between the employee and the employee service providers was broken. Officers also emphasized the need for 'safe places' specifically for correction officers to have as an option for seeking help. Explaining the need for specialized services reserved for officers, the officer states:

> some meetings [services provided by the department, such as AA] have inmates; there's no confidentiality. If you're struggling, you need that confidentiality. People on the stress unit who have had struggles [are necessary providers] instead of people who haven't walked in their [correction officers] shoes. A mixture of experience and education [are needed]; you need somebody who's been there. (Interview 9003)

Employees seeking help from employer provided services need to feel that the service provider can understand their unique position working in prisons. Officers need to believe that the staff is handling their information with the highest regard toward confidentially in order to feel comfortable enough to reach out for help. In explaining his understanding of department-wide issues, one officer described his perspective:

> The department, the department's biggest problem is, is when people are having problems at home, and they try to reach out and use the stress unit [EASU]. Back in the day there was no such thing as confidentiality. Everybody knew your business, and then you have these captains that take it upon themselves to belittle people, to spread rumors, and make peoples' lives miserable. And there was one particular captain ... who literally told – and I didn't witness this, there's other people that have talked to me about this that were really close to him – That he says, 'maybe you should kill yourself' – and ultimately, he did. (Interview 1301)

Breaching the trust of employees has an effect beyond the immediate employee struggling; other correction officers learn of the violation in confidentiality and lose trust and potentially respect for EASU and the department.

In another interview, an officer described how frequently the department violated confidentiality, 'the confidential ... nothing is really confidential in the department, so you can like Alex, everyone knew the personal business, everyone knew that [he] was having a struggle with the paperwork from administration, everyone knew' (Interview 05–01). Officers have further expressed frustration when there is a lack of confidence and support from the department, '[It] opens up your eyes to how there's nobody in the department who's there for you. They have the EASU but almost because they have to – it's not confidential. Try to deal with issues on your own to save your reputation' (Interview 1019). Institutions that neglect offering support for mental health create an environment that discourages employees from help-seeking behaviors. Officers express the lack of professionalism among administrators in the department that builds trust in employee services, protects confidentiality of sensitive information, and ultimately promotes help-seeking among officers in stressful or unhealthy situations.

Punitive responses

Correction officers have indicated that there have been negative repercussions for those who engage in help-seeking behaviors to address their mental health concerns. When discussing the events leading up to a correction officer's suicide, a family member of the deceased officer explains that the officer was removed from his duties and placed in the 'tower' (Interview 01–03 and 01–04). The tower is known in corrections to be a punishment and further signals to the other officers that the officer is being punished for experiencing personal or professional difficulties. According to numerous officers who were interviewed, if DOC supervisors do not trust officers, they send them to work in the tower in isolation.

Instead of referring the officer to a mental health professional, the department administrators are perceived to be punishing officers who are struggling. The respondents expounded on the issue recognizing that the corrections personnel did not properly train the staff or staff the unit with mental health professionals who could make appropriate decisions about employees struggling with mental health. Supervisor' tools were to protect the employee by removing the officer from stressful work environments and placing them in a secure space free from potential emotional trigger or dangerous objects. This suggests that even supervisors in this department feel that they have limited options for helping officers who are struggling.

Some officers also believe that the administration in corrections purposefully discipline some who are struggling while overlooking others in similar circumstances. An officer expounded stating, 'There's a lot of games that are played – investigations with no merit. If they don't like you as a person – and we all make mistakes – they find things to discipline them on ... ' (Interview 1289). From the perspective of the officer, favoritism determines if an officer who is experiencing psychological distress will receive punishment. The same officer continues his statement with a request to improve the culture and management in the department and suggestions to dissuade favoritism and punitive responses to help-seeking. He suggests, 'it's a dirty business to be in with dirty stuff going on. Managers should be fined when investigations are dismissed for being *dirty*. [As an officer you are] Always watching your back and [you] have to keep records' (Interview 1289). Additional institutional stress from mistrust in supervisors and administrators allows some officers to feel as if they are placed in a defensive position and must prepare for potential punishments if they seek help for personal or mental health concerns.

Associated consequences for help-seeking may lead to officers hiding psychological distress and avoiding reaching out to formal resources, particularly those provided by employers. To highlight this, an officer described how those who do seek formal or professional help tend to hide their behavior and issues from their employer, 'And same thing with my uncle. I mean, he got help outside. I don't believe his work is aware of his drinking problem for that reason – because he doesn't want any trickle effect coming from it' (Interview 06–01). Officers are aware that there may be career consequences if the department learns that they seek help or have concerns for their behavioral or mental health. Fear of professional consequences from their supervisors or the personnel office prohibit many officers from utilizing the peer-to-peer support unit or other services offered by the department. This finding differs from prior literature on help-seeking within protective services. Police help-seeking research does emphasize the same punitive response as correction officers when seeking help for mental health concerns within the workplace (Jetelina et al., 2020). However, police may not perceive the reaction to mental health concerns by the department supervisors and administrators as punitive, and instead may recognize the regular need for time away from patrol and investigations.

Discussion

Correctional scholars have made great strides in building the body of work examining the occupational demands of correctional work; however, to our knowledge, none of the existing studies have been developed specifically to explore perceptions of mental health stigma and challenges correction officers experience within institutions that discourage help-seeking for mental health concerns. The present study's overarching aim was to provide context surrounding the barriers to help-seeking that exist within correctional environments and offer practical, officer-informed assessments of the factors that influence decisions to seek out mental health services. Through the interviews, themes surface to reveal institutional barriers to help-seeking. The major themes which develop are institutional culture with emergent subthemes of stigma and hypermasculinity and institutional structure including institutional organization, confidentiality, and punitive responses. The collective voices of officers in our sample identify specific barriers that delay or discourage treatment for mental health related problems. Given the high likelihood of social desirability bias in responding to questions about willingness to seek help, the findings in this study demonstrate a general reluctance to help-seeking for mental health concerns and indicated that correction officers are overwhelmingly skeptical of stress and mental health management services offered by the department.

Discussions with participating officers indicated that stigma associated with seeking treatment for mental health related was entrenched in the organizational culture. Predominantly homogenous white, male officer population contributes to the collective culture which supports hypermasculinity and deters help-seeking for mental health. Respondents repeatedly pointed to an unofficial department wide mantra that those in need of care are unsuitable for the job. Officers who openly seek out mental health treatment are labeled as weak, soft, unfit, and even perceived to be a potential safety risk to their colleagues. This finding is consistent with both former work on correction officers (Crawley, 2004) and prior help-seeking literature noting that such hypermasculine institutionalized cultures and labeling leads to constrained opportunities, resources, and well-being for the stigmatized group (Hatzenbuehler & Link, 2014; Ricciardelli et al., 2020). The unfortunate outcome of these stigmatizing practices is that officers are dissuaded from even considering counseling or other forms of help-seeking.

While stigma played an important role in dissuading officers from seeking help, within institutions, the structure and processes can influence willingness of individuals to seek help or to recognize signs of mental health distress. The conversations with officers revealed a work environment that is far from traditional, where violence and trauma is common, but where officers are expected to be unmoved and unaffected by their daily experiences. It is very clear that features of correctional work, including the demanding hours, shift work, and isolation, negatively affect officers' physical and mental health. However, despite the harms associated with the job such as the risks of being physically assaulted, correction officers participating in this study were generally averse to pursuing help in dealing with challenges stemming from their demanding work. Several officers indicated that the structural hierarchy of the department dissuaded them from using employer provided services. As such, departments are discouraged from having staff in the employee peer-to-peer services report directly to the personnel department. Due to the sensitive nature of disclosing mental health concerns, departments should organize the employee services staff under an alternative office that is unrelated to employee relations. Building a professional atmosphere that establishes trust in employee services and protects confidentiality can promote employee help-seeking from formal resources.

Responses from officers describe the organization as apathetic. The organizational hierarchy allows for impersonal interactions between the administration and the officers and seemingly disinterest in their mental health. The organizational staff and administration are repeatedly referred to as indifferent or rigid in reference to officer wellbeing. Even where the departmental efforts to enhance officer wellbeing were acknowledged, participants described the organizational response as unimaginative and perfunctory. An officer summed up this sentiment 'they do help. If you have addiction problems, they'll ship you out and try to get you the help, but I don't think they reach out enough. I think they cover themselves enough to keep the media and keep everyone at bay, I don't think they really say "we could've done more." I think they should do a lot more, for these people [correction officers]. There are people that are struggling' (Interview 05_02). Fostering a more supportive institutional environment by relaxing rigid and impersonal institutional structures may help prevent or alleviate job stress, burnout, and perceptions of worthlessness, while restoring trust in the department. Employees seeking help from employer-provided services need to feel that the service provider can understand their unique position working in prisons. Further, programs available to correction officers should be separate from the programs designated for the inmate population. Conjoining inmate and officer support programs discourages officers from reaching out for help as their personal information should be kept confidential from the inmates that they are guarding.

Nonetheless, there are important silver-linings in what officers reported. Although generally reluctant to avail themselves of the employee peer-to-peer services with only 19% of officers identifying the service as a source of help they would seek, the officers were notably more willing to reach out to this unit on behalf of another officer (42%). Changing the institutional organization of the department and placing the employee services unit under an office or division that does not have the capacity to impact employee positions and job security could facilitate officer help-seeking behavior. Reorganizing to ensure distance between the personnel office and the employee assistance unit would signal that sensitive personal information will remain confidential and out of employee personnel files. Cultural change in hierarchal organizations with power concentrated at the higher ends of the organizational chart requires a shift in both mindset and level. Officers might be convinced to rely on and trust formal resources and use the employee services if they were guaranteed that their help-seeking behavior would not result in a punitive response from department supervisors.

Although certain policies or programs may be in place, the reality of what those in higher positions enforce may deviate from what is documented in policies. Given their power and influence, it is paramount that those in decision-making positions in the organization, support policies that create avenues for help-seeking through their interactions with peer and lower-level actors and foster an environment that promotes help-seeking, particularly for sensitive mental health concerns.

Notes

1. For more extensive detail regarding the methodology of the overall project, please see [Frost et al. 2020].
2. Quotes derived from phase one interviews can be identified by interview numbers with two digits, a dash, and two digits (e.g. Interview 01–01). Quotes derived from phase two interviews can be identified by four-digit interview numbers (e.g. Interview 1234)

Disclosure statement

No potential conflict of interest was reported by the author(s).

Funding

The research reported in this article was supported by the National Institute of Justice under Grant #2016-MU-MU-0010. The content is solely the responsibility of the authors and does not represent the official views of the National Institute of Justice or the U.S. Department of Justice.

References

Barney, L.J., Griffiths, K.M., Jorm, A.F., & Christensen, H. (2006). Stigma about depression and its impact on help-seeking intentions. *Australian and New Zealand Journal of Psychiatry*, *40*(1), 51–54.

Braquehais, M.D., Valero, S., Matalí, J.L., Bel, M.J., Montejo, J.E., Nasillo, V., ... Casas, M. (2014). Promoting voluntary help-seeking among doctors with mental disorders. *International Journal of Occupational Medicine & Environmental Health*, *27*(3), 435–443.

Britt, T.W., Wilson, C.A., Sawhney, G., & Black, K.J. (2020). Perceived unit climate of support for mental health as a predictor of stigma, beliefs about treatment, and help-seeking behaviors among military personnel. *Psychological Services, 17*(2), 141.

Brower, J. (2013). *Correctional officer wellness and safety literature review*. USDOJ.

Brown, T.C., Baldwin, J.M., Dierenfeldt, R., & McCain, S. (2020). Playing the game: A qualitative exploration of the female experience in a hypermasculine policing environment. *Police Quarterly, 23*(2), 143–173.

Carlan, P.E., & Nored, L.S. (2008). An examination of officer stress: Should police departments implement mandatory counseling? *Journal of Police and Criminal Psychology, 23*(1), 8–15.

Chew-Graham, C.A., Rogers, A., & Yassin, N. (2003). 'I wouldn't want it on my CV or their records': Medical students' experiences of help-seeking for mental health problems. *Medical Education, 37* (10), 873–880.

Clement, S., Schauman, O., Graham, T., Maggioni, F., Evans-Lacko, S., Bezborodovs, N., … Thornicroft, G. (2015). What is the impact of mental health-related stigma on help-seeking? A systematic review of quantitative and qualitative studies. *Journal of Psychological Medicine, 45*(1), 11–27.

Crawley, E., & Crawley, P. (2013). Understanding prison officers: Culture, cohesion and conflicts. In J. Bennett, B. Crewe, and A. Wahidin (Eds.), *Understanding Prison Staff* (2nd edition, pp. 134-152). New York: Routledge .

Crawley, E. (2004). *Doing prison work: The public and private lives of prison officers*. Cullompton, UK: Willan Publishing.

Finn, P. (1998). Correctional officer stress-a cause for concern and additional help. *Journal of Federal Probation, 62*, 65.

Finney, C., Stergiopoulos, E., Hensel, J., Bonato, S., & Dewa, C.S. (2013). Organizational stressors associated with job stress and burnout in correctional officers: A systematic review. *BMC Public Health, 13*(1), 82.

Forman, J., & Damschroder, L. (2007). Qualitative content analysis. In L. Jacoby, and L.A. Siminoff (Eds.), *Empirical methods for bioethics: A primer* (Vol. II). Bingley: Emerald Group Publishing Limited 39–62. doi:10.1016/S1479-3709(07)11011-6

Fox, J., Desai, M.M., Britten, K., Lucas, G., Luneau, R., & Rosenthal, M.S. (2012). Mental-health conditions, barriers to care, and productivity loss among officers in an urban police department. *Connecticut Medicine, 76*(9), 525.

Frost, N. A, Monteiro , C. E., & Stowell , J. I.(2020). *Final Summary Overview: The Impact of Correction Officer Suicide on the Institutional Environment and on the Wellbeing of Correctional Employees.* Washington, D.C.: U.S. Department of Justice, National Institute of Justice.

Frost, N.A. (2020, April). Understanding the impacts of corrections officer suicide. *Corrections Today.*

Frost, N.A., & Monteiro, C.E. (2020). The interaction of personal and occupational factors in the suicide deaths of correction officers. *Justice Quarterly, 37*(7), 1277–1302.

Gourash, N. (1978). Help-Seeking: A review of the literature. *American Journal of Community Psychology, 6*(5), 413–423.

Hatzenbuehler, M.L., & Link, B.G. (2014). Introduction to the special issue on structural stigma and health. *Social Science & Medicine, 103*, 1–6.

Haugen, P.T., McCrillis, A.M., Smid, G.E., & Nijdam, M.J. (2017). Mental health stigma and barriers to mental health care for first responders: A systematic review and meta-analysis *Journal of Psychiatric Research 94*, 218–229. doi: 10.1016/j.jpsychires.2017.08.001

Heffren, C.D., & Hausdorf, P.A. (2016). Post-traumatic effects in policing: Perceptions, stigmas and help seeking behaviours. *Police Practice and Research, 17*(5), 420–433.

Jetelina, K.K., Molsberry, R.J., Gonzalez, J.R., Beauchamp, A.M., & Hall, T. (2020). Prevalence of mental illness and mental health care use among police officers. *JAMA, 3*(10), e2019658–e2019658.

Jones, S., Agud, K., & McSweeney, J. (2020). Barriers and facilitators to seeking mental health care among first responders:"Removing the darkness" *Journal of the American Psychiatric Nurses Association . 26*(1), 43–54.

Karp, D.R. (2010). Unlocking men, unmasking masculinities: Doing men's work in prison. *The Journal of Men's Studies, 18*(1), 63–83.

Kennedy, A.C., Adams, A., Bybee, D., Campbell, R., Kubiak, S.P., & Sullivan, C. (2012). A model of sexually and physically victimized women's process of attaining effective formal help over time: The role of social location, context, and intervention. *American Journal of Community Psychology, 50*(1–2), 217–228.

Lee, F. (1997). When the going gets tough, do the tough ask for help? Help seeking and power motivation in organizations. *Organizational Behavior & Human Decision Processes, 72*(3), 336–363.

Liang, B., Goodman, L., Tummala-Narra, P., & Weintraub, S. (2005). A theoretical framework for understanding help-seeking processes among survivors of intimate partner violence. *American Journal of Community Psychology, 36*(1–2), 71–84.

Link, B.G., & Phelan, J.C. (2001). Conceptualizing stigma. *Annual Review of Sociology, 27*(1), 363–385.

Meyers, C. (2004). Institutional culture and individual behavior: Creating an ethical environment. *Science Engineering Ethics, 10*(2), 269–276.

Morgan, R.D., Van Haveren, R.A., & Pearson, C.A. (2002). Correctional officer burnout: Further analyses. *Criminal Justice & Behavior, 29*(2), 144–160.

Papazoglou, K., & Tuttle, B.M. (2018). Fighting police trauma: Practical approaches to addressing psychological needs of officers. *SAGE Open, 8*(3), 3.

Ricciardelli, R., Czarnuch, S., Carleton, R.N., Gacek, J., & Shewmake, J. (2020). Canadian public safety personnel and occupational stressors: How PSP interpret stressors on duty. *International Journal of Environmental Research and Public Health, 17*(13), 4736.

Soomro, S., & Yanos, P.T. (2019). Predictors of mental health stigma among police officers: The role of trauma and PTSD. *Journal of Police and Criminal Psychology, 34*(2), 175–183.

Spiers, J., Buszewicz, M., Chew-Graham, C.A., Gerada, C., Kessler, D., Leggett, N., … Riley, R. (2017). Barriers, facilitators, and survival strategies for GPs seeking treatment for distress: A qualitative study. *British Journal of General Practice, 67*(663), e700–e708.

Van Der Rijt, J., Van Den Bossche, P., Van De Wiel, M.W., De Maeyer, S., Gijselaers, W.H., & Segers, M.S. (2013). Asking for help: A relational perspective on help seeking in the workplace. *Vocations & Learning, 6*(2), 259–279.

Waddington, P.A. (1999). Police (canteen) sub-culture. An appreciation. *The British Journal of Criminology, 39*(2), 287–309.

White, A.K., Shrader, G., & Chamberlain, J. (2016). Perceptions of law enforcement officers in seeking mental health treatment in a right-to-work state. *Journal of Police and Criminal Psychology, 31*(2), 141–154.

Wilper, A.P., Woolhandler, S., Boyd, J.W., Lasser, K.E., McCormick, D., Bor, D.H., & Himmelstein, D.U. (2009). The health and health care of US prisoners: Results of a nationwide survey. *American Journal of Public Health, 99*(4), 666–672.

Zucker, L.G. (1991). The role of institutionalization in cultural persistence. In W.W. Powell, and P. J. DiMaggio (Eds.), *The new institutionalism in organizational analysis* (pp. 83–107). Chicago: The University of Chicago Press.

OPEN ACCESS

Job demands, organizational justice, and emotional exhaustion in prison officers

Andrew James Clements and Gail Kinman

ABSTRACT

Prison officers experience a number of occupational and organizational stressors, and are at considerable risk of burnout. There has been limited research examining the processes by which the demands officers experience impact on their burnout risk. Drawing on the job demands-resources model, we tested distributive justice perceptions as a mediator for the relationship between workload and violence with emotional exhaustion. We further tested whether supervisor-focused interactional justice perceptions would be associated with reduced emotional exhaustion via stress culture (i.e. a perceived ability to discuss stress-related problems with managers). UK prison officers (N = 1792) completed an online survey. Findings indicated that, while workload was associated with emotional exhaustion directly and via distributive justice, experiences of violence was only directly linked with emotional exhaustion. Interactional justice was significantly associated with emotional exhaustion via the ability to discuss stress-related problems, but the association was weak. Findings suggest positive manager-subordinate relationships are not sufficient to meaningfully enhance psychological wellbeing. Instead we highlight the need to manage officers' workload.

Introduction

In the UK and globally prisons are under pressure due to increasing prisoner numbers and reduced funding (Clements & Kinman, 2020). While in recent years there has been an improvement in living conditions in UK prisons, there remain concerns about the amount of time prisoners spend locked up (rather than in purposive activity), rising levels of self-harm, and violence both between prisoners and on staff (HM Chief Inspector of Prisons for England and Wales, 2020). The lack of purposeful activity for prisoners has been linked to low staffing levels (Her Majesty's Inspectorate of Prisons, 2019). Overcrowding and low staffing levels are a major source of stress for prison officers (Martin, Lichtenstein, Jenkot, & Forde, 2012). These findings indicate that the wellbeing of prisoners and prison officers is interconnected, so there is a business case as well as a moral case for addressing the working conditions of staff.

Work-related stress has significant costs to individuals, organisations, and societies. Individuals are at risk of poor physical and mental health (Li, Zhang, Loerbroks, Angerer, & Siegrist, 2015; Siegrist & Li, 2016), while organisations may face impaired employee performance (Gilboa, Shirom, Fried, & Cooper, 2008), and increased absenteeism (Darr & Johns, 2008) and turnover (Podsakoff, Lepine, & Lepine, 2007). Prison officers are at particular risk of work-related stress (Johnson et al., 2005; Kunst, 2011) and burnout – a state of exhaustion resulting from long-term exposure to stress (Maslach, Schaufeli, & Leiter, 2001). This is due to the job-related stressors that officers can experience, such as heavy workloads (Finney, Stergiopoulos, Hensel, Bonato, & Dewa, 2013), unsociable working hours, (S. Hu et al., 2015) and pressure to work overtime at short notice (Lee, Henning, & Cherniack, 2019). Officers are also at risk of physical assault (Misis, Kim, Cheeseman, Hogan, & Lambert, 2013) verbal abuse and intimidation (Kinman, Clements, & Hart, 2014), and exposure to prisoner self-harm (Wright, Borrill, Teers, & Cassidy, 2006). The exposure to traumatic experiences poses risks to officers, with evidence that they are at similar risk for post-traumatic stress disorder as war veterans (James & Todak, 2018).

Job demands-resources model

The job demands-resources (JDR) model (Demerouti, Bakker, Nachreiner, & Schaufeli, 2001) predicts that stress arises from an imbalance between the demands of the job and the resources that employees have available to deal with them. The model categorises job characteristics as demands, requiring a response from individuals, and resources, which individuals may use to cope with demands. The JDR model predicts that demands and resources explain aspects of psychological wellbeing such as burnout, as job demands deplete the personal resources of individuals over time (Nahrgang, Morgeson, & Hofmann, 2011). Recent research suggests that job demands lead to burnout via reduced adaptive coping and increased maladaptive coping (Bakker & de Vries, 2021). This may be partly a consequence of psychological strain impairing decision making, resulting in the selection of poor strategies, e.g. problem avoidance.

Some scholars have proposed that the JDR model be extended by considering the role of appraisals (Crawford, LePine, & Rich, 2010; Q. Hu, Schaufeli, & Taris, 2013). For example, Hu and colleagues (Q. Hu et al., 2013) have suggested that demands and resources influence primary and secondary appraisals: appraisals of a threat and one's ability to cope, respectively (Lazarus & Folkman, 1984). They found partial support for the role of equity perceptions (i.e. perceived balance between efforts and rewards) in mediating the relationship between both demands and resources and burnout (Q. Hu et al., 2013). Two key demands experienced by prison officers are workload (Finney et al., 2013) and aggression from prisoners (Ferdik, 2016). We suggest that it is important to consider how these demands may shape prison officers' appraisals of their work. For example, higher perceived levels of workload and aggression are likely to be important indicators that officers' health and home lives are threatened (Kinman, Clements, & Hart, 2017b).

Heavy and intense workloads are associated with emotional exhaustion (Aronsson et al., 2017; Boekhorst, Singh, & Burke, 2017). As noted above, prison officers experience heavy demands associated with workload (Kinman, Clements, & Hart, 2017a). This is particularly harmful when workload exceeds officers' capacity to complete it and when conflicting expectations are placed upon them (Schiff & Leip, 2019). Meta-analysis has identified that higher workload is associated with reduced job satisfaction, and poorer physical and psychological health (Bowling, Alarcon, Bragg, & Hartman, 2015). Research conducted with UK prison officers has previously found dissatisfaction with support from managers, both generally and in relation to the stress they experience (Kinman et al., 2014). It is also important to note that managers in prisons are also susceptible to stress (Schiff & Leip, 2019), with meta-analysis suggesting that stress experienced by managers influences their behaviour and relationships with subordinates, thereby influencing subordinate stress (Harms, Credé, Tynan, Leon, & Jeung, 2017). Thus workload pressure may also directly and indirectly influence the quality of relationships between officers and their managers.

In addition to high workloads, prison officers are exposed to various forms of aggression including verbal abuse and physical assault (Kinman et al., 2014). Unsurprisingly, those working with more dangerous prisoners report higher levels of work-related stress (Misis et al., 2013). In a South Korean study, Choi and colleagues found that verbal abuse significantly predicted burnout (Choi, Kruis, & Kim, 2020). This reflects a pattern found in research outside the prison context (Aguglia et al., 2020; Deery, Walsh, & Guest, 2011). There is some evidence to suggest that the relationship between aggression and burnout is mediated by psychological climate, i.e. the way the organisation is experienced and interpreted (Bedi, Courcy, Paquet, & Harvey, 2013).

It is important to also consider the role of resources in the work lives of prison officers, as these may help identify ways to enhance officer wellbeing. For example, one study found the individual level variables hope, optimism, as well as perceptions of social support were associated with reduced burnout in prison officers, mediated by resilience (Klinoff, Van Hasselt, Black, Masias, & Couwels, 2018). Of particular relevance to the present study, justice perceptions have been treated as a job resource in longitudinal research outside the prison context, with both supervisor-related justice perceptions (Kinnunen, Feldt, Siltaloppi, & Sonnentag, 2011) and procedural justice (Boyd et al., 2011) contributing to psychological wellbeing.

Organisational justice

Organisational justice represents a strand of research investigating fairness within organisations. The organisational justice literature primarily draws upon social exchange theory (Colquitt, 2012), which posits that individuals seek to reciprocate for services offered by others (Blau, 1964). In this approach it is assumed that employees are likely to reciprocate when they perceive their organisations and supervisors as fair (Colquitt, 2012; He, Fehr, Yam, Long, & Hao, 2017). Distinction is often made between distributive justice and procedural justice (Colquitt, Conlon, Wesson, Porter, & Ng, 2001; Greenberg, 1990). Distributive justice refers to the fairness of rewards (e.g. is one paid fairly compared to colleagues) while procedural justice considers the fairness of systems (e.g. are promotion processes transparent?). Interactional justice is a third type of organisational justice, emerging from procedural justice (Colquitt, 2012), referring to treatment of employees (e.g. respect) and whether honest explanations are provided to them, e.g. about management decisions (Ambrose & Schminke, 2003; Holtz & Harold, 2009). Interactional justice can be further divided into interpersonal justice, focusing on respect and dignity, and informational justice, e.g. the provision of honest explanations (Colquitt, 2001).

Previous research has identified a relationship between organisational justice perceptions and wellbeing, although evidence regarding the precise nature of this relationship is mixed. For example, studies have variously found that procedural and interpersonal justice perceptions were associated with stress via work-family conflict (Judge & Colquitt, 2004), that only distributive and interpersonal justice were negatively associated with emotional exhaustion (Cole, Bernerth, Walter, & Holt, 2010), and that distributive, procedural, and interactional justice were all associated with job stress (Pérez-Rodríguez, Topa, & Beléndez, 2019). Therefore it is important to build the evidence base to help determine the mechanisms that account for these mixed findings.

A small number of studies have explored the role of justice perceptions in prison officer wellbeing, but these are also produced mixed findings. In a study conducted with 322 corrections staff, Lambert and colleagues reported that interpersonal, procedural, and distributive justice were negatively associated with reported job stress (Lambert et al., 2019). By contrast, Boateng and Hsieh (2019) reported that interactional justice was negatively related to stress, whilst procedural and distributive justice were not. One possible explanation is that in Boateng and Hsieh's study a small majority of items for the procedural and distributive justice measures focused on perceptions of performance appraisal systems and procedures relating to misconduct investigations. By contrast, Lambert et al. (2019) measured justice perceptions more broadly. The variables in these two studies therefore may not have been equivalent. Taxman and Gordon (2009) found that procedural justice, but not distributive justice, was associated with reduced fear and perceived risk of attack by prison inmates or retaliation by officers for disclosing misconduct. They suggested that this was linked to perceptions of equity in the organisation and trust in supervisors, although their measure of perceived justice only included one item that explicitly referred to supervisors. Therefore it seems possible that the findings may reflect broader conditions in the environment. Reflecting the importance of context, Lambert and colleagues used a prison (i.e. organisation)-oriented measure of interpersonal justice. By contrast we argue it is important to consider perceptions of interactional justice in terms of line manager-subordinate relationships rather than organisation-employee relationships. Leader behaviours are considered to be an important theoretical antecedent of justice perceptions, because leaders are important connections within organisations, and because they may be the source of injustice experienced (Karam et al., 2019). Perceived transformational leadership style has been found to correlate with interactional and procedural justice perceptions (Alamir, Ayoubi, Massoud, & Hallak, 2019). Our paper builds upon this existing research by using a supervisor-focused measure of interactional justice perceptions and by using a measure of distributive justice that is more broadly focused on fairness in the allocation of workload, responsibilities, and rewards.

Support from colleagues, and particularly manager support, has been associated with reduced experience of emotional exhaustion in prison officers (Lambert, Altheimer, & Hogan, 2010). However, individuals do not always seek support when they need it. The reporting of mental health challenges is stigmatised in 'macho' types of work, where strength, resilience, and self-sufficiency are prioritised (Iversen et al., 2011), such as uniformed services (White, Aalsma, Holloway, Adams, & Salyers, 2015). There is evidence that officers may be reluctant to discuss stress-related challenges with managers (Kinman et al., 2014). We suggest that when managers are seen as showing consideration for subordinates, reflected in interactional justice perceptions, officers may be more willing to discuss any problems they may be experiencing. In turn, we expect that the ability to discuss stress with managers should be associated with reduced experience of emotional exhaustion.

Project aims and hypotheses

This study aimed to contribute to the literature on job demands and burnout in prison officers by considering the role of appraisals, reflected in distributive and interactional justice perceptions. We see distributive justice as reflecting an appraisal of the work environment, influenced by the experience of workload and experiences of violence from prisoners. By contrast, we see interactional justice as reflecting a job resource in the form of management support, but the availability of which may be affected by the demands present in the work environment. The appraisal of fairness in the organisation, and in relation to one's line manager, may in turn influence a subordinate's willingness to discuss stress-related problems and thereby seek support.

Hypotheses:

- 1a. Perceived workload and experience of violence shall predict distributive justice
- 1b. Perceived workload shall predict interactional justice
- 2. Distributive justice and interactional justice shall predict ability to discuss stress-related problems
- 3. Ability to discuss stress-related problems shall predict emotional exhaustion

Method

Design

We adopted a cross-sectional correlational design in an online survey of prison officers. The variables measured were job demands, experiences of violence and intimidation, justice perceptions (distributive and interactional), the ability to discuss stress-related problems with managers, and burnout.

Participants

Prison officers (N = 1792) were recruited via the POA (formerly the Prison Officer's Association), the trade union for prison, correctional, and secure psychiatric workers. The POA provided a link to the online survey on the website for members. While the POA has over 30,000 members (POA, 2021), it is not possible to know how many saw the link. Therefore, as with much online research, it is not possible to calculate a response rate (Van Selm & Jankowski, 2006). The sample was predominantly male (87.3%), white (97.4%), not disabled (84.3%), heterosexual (90.1%), and married, in a civil partnership, or living with a partner (83.3%). The majority worked in the public sector (99.7%). The age of the sample ranged from 19 to 66 years, with a mean age of 48.18 years (SD = 9.48).

Materials

Subjective workload was measured using the demands subscale of the Health and Safety Executive Management Standards Indicator Tool (Cousins et al., 2004). The subscale consists of eight items on a five-point Likert scale measuring aspects of workload such as working hours, time pressure, and incompatible demands from competing stakeholders. An example item is 'I have unachievable deadlines' (1 = Always to 5 = Never). The scoring was reversed for the purpose of data analysis, such that a higher score represents greater dissatisfaction with workload.

Experiences of aggression were measured using a scale developed by Kinman et al. (2017b). The measure consisted of six items, measuring experiences of verbal abuse and threats, physical assault, and sexual harassment and assault. Items used a five-point Likert scale (1 = Never to 5 = Regularly (e.g. once a day or more)). Higher scores represented more frequent experiences of these events.

Justice perceptions were measured using the distributive justice and interactional justice subscales of Niehoff and Moorman (1993) Organizational Justice measure. Distributive justice consisted of five items measuring perceptions of workload, responsibilities, and rewards as fair. Interactional justice consisted of nine items measuring perceptions of supervisor's behaviour as considerate and perceptions that management decisions were appropriately explained. Both scales were measured using a five-point Likert scale (1 = Strongly disagree to 5 = Strongly agree), with higher scores representing greater levels of perceived justice.

Stress disclosure was measured using a single item. Participants were asked 'to what extent can you discuss stress-related problems with your line manager?' This item was measured on a four-point Likert scale (1 = Never to 4 = Always), with higher scores representing a greater perceived ability to discuss stress-related problems.

Emotional exhaustion was measured using a subscale from the abbreviated version of the Maslach Burnout Inventory (Maslach, Jackson, & Leiter, 1996) which has been used to study wellbeing across a range of occupational groups (Dewa, Jacobs, Thanh, & Loong, 2014). The subscale consists of three items using a seven-point Likert scale (0 = Never to 6 = Every day) measuring frequency of experiences of emotional exhaustion. Higher scores represent higher levels of emotional exhaustion.

Cronbach alpha for scales are reported in Table 1.

Procedure

Ethical approval was granted by the second author's university ethics committee. A link to the online survey was then advertised to POA members by the trade union. Individuals were advised prior to participation that they were invited to complete a survey about their experiences of work with a focus on their wellbeing. They were reassured that participation was voluntary, and that there would be no consequences for them as a result of their decision to participate (or not). They were advised that all data were anonymous, and that their data would be stored on a password-protected computer, with access only available to the research team. We analysed the data using Structural Equation Modeling (SEM) via

Smart PLS to test our hypotheses through the use of competing models. Following guidance (L. Hu & Bentler, 1998) we adopted SRMR as our primary fit index, and supplemented with use of NFI. Table 2 shows the performance of our models with the fit indices.

Results

We began by inspecting the data for multicollinearity using SPSS. Correlation analysis showed a strong relationship between job demands and distributive justice, but not enough to suggest a multicollinearity problem. Table 1 shows the descriptive data for each scale used and the relationships between variables. Workload and aggression both had negative correlations with distributive justice, and to a lesser extent interactional justice. Stress disclosure was positively correlated with both distributive justice and interactional justice, although the latter relationship was stronger. Emotional exhaustion was negatively correlated with distributive justice, interactional justice, and stress disclosure. Having inspected the data, we next conducted hypothesis testing using SEM.

Table 1.

	M	SD	1	2	3	4	5	6	7
(1) Age	48.18	9.48	-						
(1) Workload	3.19	.69	−.12*	(.86)					
(1) Aggression	2.53	.70	−.22*	.52*	(.83)				
(1) Distributive justice	2.30	.75	−.01	−.66*	−.42*	(.84)			
(1) Interactional justice	2.70	.98	−.10*	−.36*	−.27*	.46*	(.97)		
(1) Stress disclosure	1.79	.91	−.01	−.22*	−.22*	.27*	.53*	-	
(1) Emotional exhaustion	3.98	1.69	.01	.58*	.52*	−.55*	−.31*	−.20*	(.86)

Notes: N = 1644–1786
* = p < .001, alpha coefficients are reported along the diagonal

We first tested a model (Figure 1) in which job demands and violence predicted perceptions of distributive justice, distributive justice and interactional justice both predicted ability to discuss stress with line managers, which in turn predicted emotional exhaustion. All pathways were significant, except that between violence and distributive justice (p = .35) and between distributive justice and discussion (p = .40). This model showed a poor fit to the data. We next tested a modification of the model in which violence and interactional justice were predicted by job demands, and violence in turn predicted distributive justice. As with model 1, all pathways were significant, except that between violence and distributive justice (p = .36) and between distributive justice and stress discussion (p = .36). Similarly, this model showed a poor fit to the data.

We next tested a variant of model 1 in which violence directly predicted burnout, rather than being mediated by distributive justice, and the link between job demands and interactional justice was retained (model 3). In this model all pathways were significant, with the exception of that between distributive justice and stress discussion (p = .39). This model showed an improvement in fit.

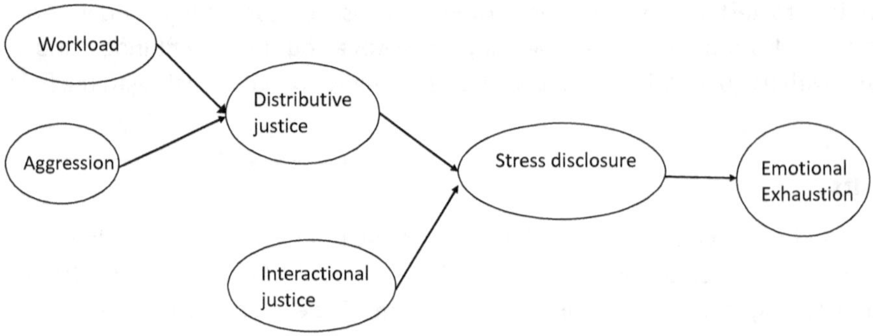

Figure 1. Model 1.

We next tested a version of model 3 in which distributive justice (model 3) and interactional justice had a direct path to emotional exhaustion in addition to the pathway via stress discussions (model 4). This model showed an improved fit, with SRMR falling within the recommended cut-off of .08 (L. Hu & Bentler, 1999). All pathways were significant, save for that between distributive justice and stress discussion ($p = .39$) and between interactional justice and stress discussion ($p = .59$).

In model 5 we tested a more parsimonious model in which stress discussion was removed, and both distributive and interactional justice had direct pathways to emotional exhaustion. In this model all pathways were significant, save that between interactional justice and emotional exhaustion ($p = .07$). However, while there was little change to the SRMR, there was a decrement to the NFI, and therefore we retained model 4.

In model 6 we tested a variant of model 4 in which job demands was permitted a direct pathway to emotional exhaustion, to examine the effects that this had on the pathways via distributive and interactional justice perceptions. The weak positive pathway between job demands and emotional exhaustion was significant ($\beta = .25$, $p < .001$), and the strength of the pathway between distributive justice and emotional exhaustion was reduced from moderate to weak compared to model 4 ($\beta = -.38$, $p < .001$; $\beta = -.21$, $p < .001$, model 4 and 6 respectively). We retained model 6 given that a direct effect was identified, and without detriment to the NFI and SRMR scores. Model 6 is depicted in Figure 2. Model 6 predicted 54.5% of the variance in emotional exhaustion.

Table 2.

Model	X^2	NFI	SRMR
1	10,763.96	.78	.13
2	10,766.85	.78	.13
3	10,114.85	.79	.09
4	9809.11	.80	.07
5	11,785.29	.76	.07
6	9772.93	.80	.07

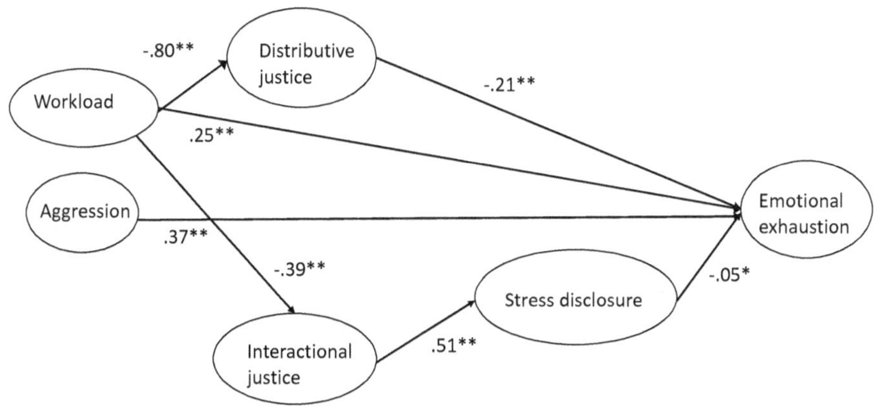

Figure 2. Model 6. Note: * = p < .05, ** = p < .001

Discussion

This study aimed to examine the role of organisational justice perceptions, namely distributive and interactional justice, in prison officer wellbeing. We examined distributive justice as a mediator for the relatonship between job demands and emotional exhaustion, and stress disclosure as a mediator between justice perceptions and emotional exhaustion. Our findings suggest that distributive and interactional justice play different roles in the wellbeing process. We found that workload was associated with emotional exhaustion both directly and indirectly via distributive justice. However, hypothesis 1a was only partially supported; while workload negatively predicted distributive justice, personal experiences of aggression and violence did not. While previous research has shown aggression can influence burnout through psychological climate, i.e. interpretations of the work environment (Bedi et al., 2013), it may be important to consider the source of aggression. It is possible prison officers accept aggression as part of the job, and therefore do not perceive it as representing organisational unfairness. However, violence did directly predict emotional exhaustion, and so it remains an important job demand in the prison context. Workload was also found to negatively predict perceptions of interactional justice, supporting hypothesis 1b. As noted previously, the stress experienced by leaders may impact their subordinates as a result of leader behaviours and the quality of leader-subordinate relationships (Harms et al., 2017). This may explain why higher perceived workload was associated with lower perceived interactional justice, but there are other possibilities. For example, subordinates may be concerned that they are adding to the burden of their line managers' existing heavy workload. However, we did not directly measure line manager stress. Future research could fruitfully explore the inter-relationship between manager and officer stress.

Hypothesis 2 was only partially supported; while interactional justice had a strong positive association with the ability to discuss stress-related problems with one's line manager, distributive justice did not. This may be because, unlike the measure of interactional justice, distributive justice was not supervisor-focused. We may expect distributive justice to have a stronger association with behaviours directed at the organisation as a whole rather than relationships between individuals, e.g.

counterproductive work behaviours (Liu, Luksyte, Zhou, Shi, & Wang, 2015) or withdrawal behaviours such as turnover (Poon, 2012; Soltis, Agneessens, Sasovova, & Labianca, 2013).

While interactional justice was associated with the perceived ability to discuss stress-related problems with line managers, it should be noted that the relationship between perceived ability to discuss stress and emotional exhaustion was weak. The use of null hypothesis significance testing has been debated at length in the social sciences (Szucs & Ioannidis, 2017). Some scholars recommend using the more stringent $p < .005$ as the threshold for accepting significant findings (Benjamin et al., 2018), where the pathway between stress disclosure and emotional exhaustion found in the current study would have been considered nonsignificant. Consequently, we consider the results to provide poor support for hypothesis 3.

While we may expect the ability to discuss stress-related problems would help protect officers against emotional exhaustion, the relationship may be more complicated. Firstly, line managers do not necessarily possess the competencies required to deal with stress experienced by their employees. Responsibility for employee wellbeing is typically devolved to line managers, but they are often not supported for this (Renwick, 2003). They also may be unable or reluctant to manage employee wellbeing due to insufficient time amidst competing demands (Guest & Woodrow, 2012). While line managers may be approachable and offer support, accessability is only one of the stress management competencies needed by managers (Lewis, Yarker, Donaldson-Feilder, Flaxman, & Munir, 2010; Toderi, Gaggia, Balducci, & Sarchielli, 2015), and some managers may lack other competencies needed to help subordinates. There is evidence, however, that these competencies can be trained (Adachi, Sekiya, Imamura, Watanabe, & Kawakami, 2020). It would be useful to test the impact of such training in prison officers' managers.

Secondly, feeling able to discuss stress-related problems with line managers does not necessarily lead to actually doing so. For example, workers may in principle believe it is useful to disclose depression to line managers, they may wish to do so in practice only when 'necessary' (Sallis & Birkin, 2014). There is evidence of mental health stigma in a number of 'masculine' work environment (Iversen et al., 2011; White et al., 2015), which may contribute to this challenge. We suggest that future research could examine help-seeking behaviour in prison officers, in order to determine when officers seek help, and what manager behaviours contribute to positive outcomes. This could, for example, examine the role of subordinates' agentic behaviour. A recent study found that employees' ingratiating behaviour with leaders could produce higher quality relationships, and thereby enhance justice perceptions (Koopman, Matta, Scott, & Conlon, 2015).

As well as considering leader and subordinate agency, it is important to also consider the restrictions upon agency. While leaders may have more power than subordinates, we should consider the potential impacts on prison managers, who may lack the ability to address resource-related challenges, e.g. understaffing and a heavy workload, or to reduce the incidence of aggressive and violent behaviours. There are different forms of support, such as instrumental – i.e. the provision of resources, emotional, and informational support (Jolly, Kong, & Kim, 2021), so it would be useful to identify what officers' managers provide.

Our findings suggest that to address psychological wellbeing in the prison sector, the focus should be on reducing job demands. Both workload and experienced aggression contributed to the variance in emotional exhaustion. One factor driving unsafe conditions is understaffing (Penal Reform International, 2019), and therefore there is a need to increase the workforce through recruitment and retention efforts. This is likely to require significant investment by governments. At the organisational level, attention could turn to interventions that might reduce workload demands. One approach could involve prioritising the allocation of existing staff to tasks that are more labour intensive (Steiner & Wooldredge, 2015). We would also recommend reviewing how tasks are performed to identify ways to reduce demands. We recommend a participatory approach, involving officers in the identification of solutions to workload concerns and how any interventions are evaluated. The importance of employee 'voice' in shaping effective stress-reduction interventions has been highlighted and a report of two such participatory approaches suggest that prison manager support is crucial for the success of such methods (Dugan et al., 2016). Interventions targeting causes of stress, such as workload, can be combined with initiatives that enhance individuals' ability to cope. Research suggests that such multi-level approaches are more effective than targeting organisational factors (e.g. workload) or individuals in isolation (LaMontagne, Keegel, Louie, Ostry, & Landsbergis, 2007). Individual-level interventions could include resilience training (Robertson, Cooper, Sarkar, & Curran, 2015), particularly if aimed at those at greater risk of stress (Vanhove, Herian, Perez, Harms, & Lester, 2016). However, such individualistic approaches should not be used in place of action addressing the causes of stress.

Our paper also contributes to the wider literature of the JDR model. The JDR model predicts that resources moderate the relationship between demands and psychological strain, in this case emotional exhaustion, such that resources buffer the impact of demands (Bakker & Demerouti, 2017). However, this prediction has not been consistently supported, with some studies finding a moderation effect (Bakker, Demerouti, & Euwema, 2005) and others not (Q. Hu, Schaufeli, & Taris, 2011). Further, some studies have reported that demands and resources may both be directly associated with burnout (Q. Hu et al., 2013; Huang, Wang, & You, 2016). This finding has further been supported by a meta-analysis of longitudinal studies (Lesener, Gusy, & Wolter, 2019). However, while we found a direct association between job demands, related to both workload and experiences of violence and intimidation, and emotional exhaustion, there was no direct link between interactional justice and emotional exhaustion. Our findings are more consistent with studies finding separate paths from job demands to strain and from job resources to work engagement (Schaufeli, 2015). In this light, it may be more appropriate to consider interactional justice as a theoretical antecedent to work engagement. Exploration of this process may inform opportunities to enhance positive outcomes within prison workforces.

Limitations and future directions

Although our study contributes to the literature on prison officer wellbeing, there are a number of limitations. Firstly, like much of the literature on prison officers, our data were correlational in nature, and therefore cannot establish causal relationships. Longitudinal designs can provide tests of causality (de Lange, Taris, Kompier, Houtman, & Bongers,

2003). Longitudinal research could test the influence of workload, experienced aggression, and other demands on justice perceptions over time, along with the resources that may buffer against strain. Diary studies can be a useful method for examining the dynamics of change over time (Eatough et al., 2016). Such approaches could also identify specific experiences of injustice at work. However, officers may be concerned about the possibility of being identified through their data (Dollard & Winefield, 1998), which can present a barrier to collecting longitudinal data.

Secondly, our research is based upon self-report data. It has been argued that occupational-specific surveys may encourage over-reporting of problems in an effort to improve working conditions (Goodwin et al., 2013). However, given the stigma related to disclosing stress in work environments such as prisons, there may also be a competing tendency to under-report one's own mental health challenges. However, it would be beneficial to consider additional research designs to broaden our understanding of the field. Intervention studies would help advance the literature. At present there are few studies reporting interventions in the prison sector, and these generally focus on individual-level interventions (Evers, Ogloff, Trounson, & Pfeifer, 2019), i.e. secondary interventions. In other words, there is a need for more research on interventions that directly target the source of stress in prison work, i.e. primary interventions. Research suggests that the combination of both primary and secondary interventions is more effective than either alone (LaMontagne et al., 2007), so there is a need to identify primary interventions that are appropriate for the sector. Following Nielsen and colleagues (Nielsen & Miraglia, 2017) we suggest the use of critical realist research, which would offer the opportunity to investigate not only what interventions may enhance wellbeing, but under what circumstances they are likely to work.

Thirdly, our sample was predominantly white and male and worked for the public sector. While this reflects the current reality of the UK prison service (Ministry of Justice, 2021), it limits our ability to examine psychological wellbeing for groups that are less represented. Qualitative methods, with less emphasis on participant numbers and generalisability, could offer the means to examine the challenges faced by women, people of colour, and lesbian, gay, bisexual and transgender (LGBT) officers. Officers in such under-represented groups may have unique predictors of perceived organisational justice, such as experiences of discrimination (Buttner, Lowe, & Billings-Harris, 2010; Le, Palmer Johnson, & Fujimoto, 2021).

Conclusions

Our study contributes to the literature by examining the role job demands and organisational justice perceptions might together play in shaping prison officer experiences of emotional exhaustion. Our findings suggest that job demands, in the form of workload and experienced violence, contribute significantly to emotional exhaustion, with workload having some of its effects via officer evaluations of the fairness of work. By contrast, the relations officers have with their line managers, reflected in interactional justice perceptions, seems to have a negligible relationship with emotional exhaustion. This suggests that working conditions should be prioritised to enhance prison officer wellbeing. Our findings also raise new questions in relation to the role played by manager support in officer wellbeing. In particular, we suggest that a closer examination of the relationship dynamics between officers and line managers would be beneficial, with a particular focus on help-seeking behaviours and the content and outcomes of discussion of stress-related problems.

Disclosure statement

No potential conflict of interest was reported by the author(s).

ORCID

Andrew James Clements http://orcid.org/0000-0003-0265-0376
Gail Kinman http://orcid.org/0000-0002-0130-1708

References

Adachi, H., Sekiya, Y., Imamura, K., Watanabe, K., & Kawakami, N. (2020). The effects of training managers on management competencies to improve their management practices and work engagement of their subordinates: A single group pre- and post-test study. *Journal of Occupational Health*, *62*(1), 1–10.

Aguglia, A., Murri, M.B., Conigliaro, C., Cipriani, N., Vaggi, M., Di Salvo, G., ... Amore, M. (2020). Workplace violence and burnout among mental health workers. *Psychiatric Services*, *71*(3), 284–288.

Alamir, I., Ayoubi, R.M., Massoud, H., & Hallak, L.A. (2019). Transformational leadership, organizational justice and organizational outcomes: A study from the higher education sector in Syria. *Leadership and Organization Development Journal*, *40*(7), 749–763.

Ambrose, M.L., & Schminke, M. (2003). Organization structure as a moderator of the relationship between procedural justice, interactional justice, perceived organizational support, and supervisory trust. *Journal of Applied Psychology*, *88*(2), 295–305.

Aronsson, G., Theorell, T., Grape, T., Hammarström, A., Hogstedt, C., Marteinsdottir, I., ... Hall, C. (2017). A systematic review including meta-analysis of work environment and burnout symptoms. *BMC Public Health*, *17*(1), 1–14.

Bakker, A.B., & de Vries, J.D. (2021). Job Demands–Resources theory and self-regulation: New explanations and remedies for job burnout. *Anxiety, Stress and Coping*, *34*(1), 1–21.

Bakker, A.B., Demerouti, E., & Euwema, M.C. (2005). Job resources buffer the impact of job demands on burnout. *Journal of Occupational Health Psychology*, *10*(2), 170–180.

Bakker, A.B., & Demerouti, E. (2017). Job demands–resources theory: Taking stock and looking forward. *Journal of Occupational Health Psychology*, *22*(3), 273–285.

Bedi, A., Courcy, F., Paquet, M., & Harvey, S. (2013). Interpersonal aggression and burnout: The mediating role of psychological climate. *Stress and Health*, *29*(5), 350–359.

Benjamin, D.J., Berger, J.O., Johannesson, M., Nosek, B.A., Wagenmakers, E.-J., Berk, R., ... Johnson, V. E. (2018). Redefine statistical significance. *Nature Human Behaviour*, *2*(1), 6–10.

Blau, P.M. (1964). *Exchange and power in social life*. New York: Wiley.

Boateng, F.D., & Hsieh, M.L. (2019). Misconduct within the "four walls": Does organizational justice matter in explaining prison officers' misconduct and job stress? *International Journal of Offender Therapy and Comparative Criminology, 63*(2), 289–308.

Boekhorst, J.A., Singh, P., & Burke, R. (2017). Work intensity, emotional exhaustion and life satisfaction: The moderating role of psychological detachment. *Personnel Review, 46*(5), 891–907.

Bowling, N.A., Alarcon, G.M., Bragg, C.B., & Hartman, M.J. (2015). A meta-analytic examination of the potential correlates and consequences of workload. *Work and Stress, 29*(2), 95–113.

Boyd, C.M., Bakker, A.B., Pignata, S., Winefield, A.H., Gillespie, N., & Stough, C. (2011). A longitudinal test of the job demands-resources model among Australian university academics. *Applied Psychology, 60*(1), 112–140.

Buttner, E.H., Lowe, K.B., & Billings-Harris, L. (2010). Diversity climate impact on employee of color outcomes: Does justice matter? *Career Development International, 15*(3), 239–258.

Choi, J., Kruis, N.E., & Kim, Y. (2020). The impact of occupational characteristics and victimization on job burnout among South Korean correctional officers. *Criminal Justice and Behavior, 47*(7), 905–923.

Clements, A.J., & Kinman, G. (2020). A forgotten profession: The need to invest in the wellbeing of prison officers. In P. Birch, and L.A. Sicard (Eds.), *Prisons and community corrections: Critical issues and emerging controversies* (pp. 86–99). Oxon: Routledge.

Cole, M.S., Bernerth, J.B., Walter, F., & Holt, D.T. (2010). Organizational justice and individuals' withdrawal: Unlocking the influence of emotional exhaustion. *Journal of Management Studies, 47*(3), 367–390.

Colquitt, J.A., Conlon, D.E., Wesson, M.J., Porter, C.O.L.H., & Ng, K.Y. (2001). Justice at the millennium: A meta-analytic review of 25 years of organizational justice research. *Journal of Applied Psychology, 86*(3), 425–445. 10.1037//0021-9010.86.3.425.

Colquitt, J.A. (2001). On the dimensionality of organizational justice: A construct validation of a measure. *Journal of Applied Psychology, 86*(3), 386–400.

Colquitt, J.A. (2012). Organizational justice. In S.W.J. Kozlowski (Ed.), *The Oxford Handbook of Organizational Psychology* (pp. 526–547). New York: Oxford University Press.

Cousins, R., Mackay, C.J., Clarke, S.D., Kelly, C., Kelly, P.J., & Mccaig, R.H. (2004). 'Management Standards' and work-related stress in the UK: Practical development. *Work & Stress, 18*(2), 113–136.

Crawford, E.R., LePine, J.A., & Rich, B.L. (2010). Linking job demands and resources to employee engagement and burnout: A theoretical extension and meta-analytic test. *Journal of Applied Psychology, 95*(5), 834–848.

Darr, W., & Johns, G. (2008). Work strain, health, and absenteeism: A meta-analysis. *Journal of Occupational Health Psychology, 13*(4), 293–318.

de Lange, A.H., Taris, T.W., Kompier, M.A.J., Houtman, I.L.D., & Bongers, P.M. (2003). "The very best of the millennium": Longitudinal research and the demand-control-(support) model. *Journal of Occupational Health Psychology, 8*(4), 282–305.

Deery, S., Walsh, J., & Guest, D. (2011). Workplace aggression: The effects of harassment on job burnout and turnover intentions. *Work, Employment and Society, 25*(4), 742–759.

Demerouti, E., Bakker, A.B., Nachreiner, F., & Schaufeli, W.B. (2001). The job demands-resources model of burnout. *Journal of Applied Psychology, 86*(3), 499–512.

Dewa, C.S., Jacobs, P., Thanh, N.X., & Loong, D. (2014). An estimate of the cost of burnout on early retirement and reduction in clinical hours of practicing physicians in Canada. *BMC Health Services Research, 14*(1), 1–9.

Dollard, M.F., & Winefield, A.H. (1998). A test of the demand–control/support model of work stress in correctional officers. *Journal of Occupational Health Psychology, 3*(3), 243–264.

Dugan, A.G., Farr, D.A., Namazi, S., Henning, R.A., Wallace, K.N., El Ghaziri, M., … Cherniack, M.G. (2016). Process evaluation of two participatory approaches: Implementing total worker health® interventions in a correctional workforce. *American Journal of Industrial Medicine, 59*(10), 897–918.

Eatough, E.M., Meier, L.L., Igic, I., Elfering, A., Spector, P.E., & Semmer, N.K. (2016). You want me to do what? Two daily diary studies of illegitimate tasks and employee well-being. *Journal of Organizational Behavior, 37*(1), 108–127.

Evers, T.J., Ogloff, J.R.P., Trounson, J.S., & Pfeifer, J.E. (2019). Well-being interventions for correctional officers in a prison setting: A review and meta-analysis. *Criminal Justice and Behavior*, 1–19. doi:10.1177/0093854819869975

Ferdik, F.V. (2016). An investigation into the risk perceptions held by maximum security correctional officers. *Psychology, Crime and Law, 22*(9), 832–857.

Finney, C., Stergiopoulos, E., Hensel, J., Bonato, S., & Dewa, C.S. (2013). Organizational stressors associated with job stress and burnout in correctional officers: A systematic review. *BMC Public Health, 13*(1), 82.

Gilboa, S., Shirom, A., Fried, Y., & Cooper, C.L. (2008). A meta-analysis of work demand stressors and job performance: Examining main and moderating effects. *Personnel Psychology, 61*(2), 227–271.

Goodwin, L., Ben-Zion, I., Fear, N.T., Hotopf, M., Stansfeld, S.A., Wessely, S., & de Boer, A. (2013). Are reports of psychological stress higher in occupational studies? A systematic review across occupational and population based studies. *PLoS ONE, 8*(11), 1–22.

Greenberg, J. (1990). Organizational justice: Yesterday, today, and tomorrow. *Journal of Management, 16*(2), 399–432.

Guest, D.E., & Woodrow, C. (2012). Exploring the boundaries of human resource managers' responsibilities. *Journal of Business Ethics, 111*(1), 109–119.

Harms, P.D., Credé, M., Tynan, M., Leon, M., & Jeung, W. (2017). Leadership and stress: A meta-analytic review. *The Leadership Quarterly, 28*(1), 178–194.

He, W., Fehr, R., Yam, K.C., Long, L.-R., & Hao, P. (2017). Interactional justice, leader-member exchange, and employee performance: Examining the moderating role of justice differentiation. *Journal of Organizational Behavior, 38*(4), 537–557.

Her Majesty's Inspectorate of Prisons. (2019). *HM Chief Inspector of Prisons for England and Wales Annual Report 2018-19*. Her Majesty's Inspectorate of Prisons.

HM Chief Inspector of Prisons for England and Wales. (2020). *HM Chief Inspector of Prisons for England and Wales Annual Report 2019-20*. Stationary Office.

Holtz, B.C., & Harold, C.M. (2009). Fair today, fair tomorrow? A longitudinal investigation of overall justice perceptions. *Journal of Applied Psychology, 94*(5), 1185–1199.

Hu, L., & Bentler, P.M. (1998). Fit indices in covariance structure modeling: Sensitivity to underparameterized model misspecification. *Psychological Methods, 3*(4), 424–453.

Hu, L., & Bentler, P.M. (1999). Cutoff criteria for fit indexes in covariance structure analysis: Conventional criteria versus new alternatives. *Structural Equation Modeling: A Multidisciplinary Journal, 6*(1), 1–55.

Hu, Q., Schaufeli, W.B., & Taris, T.W. (2011). The Job Demands–Resources model: An analysis of additive and joint effects of demands and resources. *Journal of Vocational Behavior, 79*(1), 181–190.

Hu, Q., Schaufeli, W.B., & Taris, T.W. (2013). Does equity mediate the effects of job demands and job resources on work outcomes?: An extension of the job demands-resources model. *Career Development International, 18*(4), 357–376.

Hu, S., Wang, J.-N., Liu, L., Wu, H., Yang, X., Wang, Y., & Wang, L. (2015). The association between work-related characteristic and job burnout among Chinese correctional officers: A cross-sectional survey. *Public Health, 129*(9), 1172–1178.

Huang, J., Wang, Y., & You, X. (2016). The job demands-resources model and job burnout: The mediating role of personal resources. *Current Psychology, 35*(4), 562–569.

Iversen, A.C., Van Staden, Hughes, S.L., Greenberg, J.H., Hotopf, N., Rona, M., Thornicroft, R.J., … Fear, S. (2011). The stigma of mental health problems and other barriers to care in the UK Armed Forces. *BMC Health Services Research, 11*(1), 31.

James, L., & Todak, N. (2018). Prison employment and post-traumatic stress disorder: Risk and protective factors. *American Journal of Industrial Medicine, 61*(9), 725–732.

Johnson, S., Cooper, C., Cartwright, S., Donald, I., Taylor, P., & Millet, C. (2005). The experience of work-related stress across occupations. *Journal of Managerial Psychology, 20*(2), 178–187.

Jolly, P.M., Kong, D.T., & Kim, K.Y. (2021). Social support at work: An integrative review. *Journal of Organizational Behavior, 42*(2), 229–251.

Judge, T.A., & Colquitt, J.A. (2004). Organizational Justice and Stress: The Mediating Role of Work-Family Conflict. *Journal of Applied Psychology, 89*(3), 395–404.

Karam, E.P., Hu, J., Davison, R.B., Juravich, M., Nahrgang, J.D., Humphrey, S.E., & Scott Derue, D. (2019). Illuminating the 'Face' of Justice: A Meta-Analytic Examination of Leadership and Organizational Justice. *Journal of Management Studies, 56*(1), 134–171.

Kinman, G., Clements, A.J., & Hart, J. (2014). *POA members work-related stress and wellbeing survey*. London: POA.

Kinman, G., Clements, A.J., & Hart, J. (2017a). Job demands, resources and mental health in UK prison officers. *Occupational Medicine (Oxford, England), 67*(6), 456–460.

Kinman, G., Clements, A.J., & Hart, J. (2017b). Working conditions, work–life conflict, and well-being in u.k. Prison officers: The role of affective rumination and detachment. *Criminal Justice and Behavior, 44*(2), 226–239.

Kinnunen, U., Feldt, T., Siltaloppi, M., & Sonnentag, S. (2011). Job demands–resources model in the context of recovery: Testing recovery experiences as mediators. *European Journal of Work and Organizational Psychology, 20*(6), 805–832.

Klinoff, V.A., Van Hasselt, V.B., Black, R.A., Masias, E.V., & Couwels, J. (2018). The assessment of resilience and burnout in correctional officers. *Criminal Justice and Behavior, 45*(8), 1213–1233.

Koopman, J., Matta, F.K., Scott, B.A., & Conlon, D.E. (2015). Ingratiation and popularity as antecedents of justice: A social exchange and social capital perspective. *Organizational Behavior and Human Decision Processes, 131*, 132–148.

Kunst, M.J.J. (2011). Working in prisons: A critical review of stress in the occupation of correctional officers. In J. Langan-Fox, and C.L. Cooper (Eds.), *Handbook of stress in the occupations* (pp. 241–283). Cheltenham: Edward Elgar.

Lambert, E.G. Altheimer, I., & Hogan, N.L. (2010). Exploring the relationship between social support and job burnout among correctional staff. *Criminal Justice and Behavior, 37*(11), 1217–1236.

Lambert, E.G. Keena, L.D., Haynes, S.H., May, D., Ricciardelli, R., & Leone, M. (2019). Testing a path model of organizational justice and correctional staff job stress among Southern Correctional Staff. *Criminal Justice and Behavior, 46*(10), 1367–1384.

LaMontagne, A.D., Keegel, T., Louie, A.M., Ostry, A., & Landsbergis, P.A. (2007). Intervention evaluation literature, 1990–2005. *International Journal of Occupational and Environmental Health, 13*(3), 268–280.

Lazarus, R.S., & Folkman, S. (1984). *Stress, appraisal, and coping*. New York: Springer.

Le, H., Palmer Johnson, C., & Fujimoto, Y. (2021). Organizational justice and climate for inclusion. *Personnel Review, 50*(1), 1–20.

Lee, J., Henning, R., & Cherniack, M. (2019). Correction workers' burnout and outcomes: A Bayesian network approach. *International Journal of Environmental Research and Public Health, 16*(2), 1–14.

Lesener, T., Gusy, B., & Wolter, C. (2019). The job demands-resources model: A meta-analytic review of longitudinal studies. *Work and Stress, 33*(1), 76–103.

Lewis, R., Yarker, J., Donaldson-Feilder, E., Flaxman, P., & Munir, F. (2010). Using a competency-based approach to identify the management behaviours required to manage workplace stress in nursing: A critical incident study. *International Journal of Nursing Studies, 47*(3), 307–313.

Li, J., Zhang, M., Loerbroks, A., Angerer, P., & Siegrist, J. (2015). Work stress and the risk of recurrent coronary heart disease events: A systematic review and meta-analysis. *International Journal of Occupational Medicine and Environmental Health, 28*(1), 8–19.

Liu, S., Luksyte, A., Zhou, L., Shi, J., & Wang, M. (2015). Overqualification and counterproductive work behaviors: Examining a moderated mediation model. *Journal of Organizational Behavior, 36*(2), 250–271.

Martin, J.L., Lichtenstein, B., Jenkot, R.B., & Forde, D.R. (2012). "They can take us over any time they want": Correctional officers' responses to prison crowding. *Prison Journal, 92*(1), 88–105.

Maslach, C., Jackson, S.E., & Leiter, M.P. (1996). *Maslach Burnout Inventory manual* (3rd ed.). Palo Alto: Consulting Psychologists Press.

Maslach, C., Schaufeli, W.B., & Leiter, M.P. (2001). Job burnout. *Annual Review of Psychology, 52*(1), 397–422.

Ministry of Justice. (2021). *Her Majesty's Prison and Probation Service workforce quarterly: March 2021.* Accessed14 July 2021, https://www.gov.uk/government/statistics/her-majestys-prison-and-probation-service-workforce-quarterly-march-2021/her-majestys-prison-and-probation-service-workforce-quarterly-march-2021.

Misis, M., Kim, B., Cheeseman, K., Hogan, N.L., & Lambert, E.G. (2013). The impact of correctional officer perceptions of inmates on job stress. *SAGE Open, 3*(2), 1–13.

Nahrgang, J.D., Morgeson, F.P., & Hofmann, D.A. (2011). Safety at work: A meta-analytic investigation of the link between job demands, job resources, burnout, engagement, and safety outcomes. *Journal of Applied Psychology, 96*(1), 71–94.

Niehoff, B.P., & Moorman, R.H. (1993). Justice as a Mediator of the Relationship between Methods of Monitoring and Organizational Citizenship Behavior. *Academy of Managent Journal, 36*(3), 527–556.

Nielsen, K., & Miraglia, M. (2017). What works for whom in which circumstances? On the need to move beyond the 'what works?' question in organizational intervention research. *Human Relations, 70*(1), 40–62.

Penal Reform International. (2019). *Global prison trends 2019.* London: Penal Reform International.

Pérez-Rodríguez, V., Topa, G., & Beléndez, M. (2019). Organizational justice and work stress: The mediating role of negative, but not positive, emotions. *Personality and Individual Differences, 151* (April), 109392.

POA. (2021). *Welcome to the POA.* Accessed16 August 2021. https://www.poauk.org.uk/

Podsakoff, N.P., Lepine, J.A., & Lepine, M.A. (2007). Differential challenge stressor-hindrance stressor relationships with job attitudes, turnover intentions, turnover, and withdrawal behavior: A meta-analysis. *Journal of Applied Psychology, 92*(2), 438–454.

Poon, J.M.L. (2012). Distributive justice, procedural justice, affective commitment, and turnover intention: A mediation-moderation framework. *Journal of Applied Social Psychology, 42*(6), 1505–1532.

Renwick, D. (2003). HR managers: Guardians of employee wellbeing? *Personnel Review, 32*(3), 341–359.

Robertson, I.T., Cooper, C.L., Sarkar, M., & Curran, T. (2015). Resilience training in the workplace from 2003 to 2014: A systematic review. *Journal of Occupational and Organizational Psychology, 88*(3), 533–562.

Sallis, A., & Birkin, R. (2014). Experiences of work and sickness absence in employees with depression: An interpretative phenomenological analysis. *Journal of Occupational Rehabilitation, 24*(3), 469–483.

Schaufeli, W.B. (2015). Engaging leadership in the job demands-resources model. *Career Development International, 20*(5), 446–463.

Schiff, M., & Leip, L. (2019). The impact of job expectations, workload, and autonomy on work-related stress among prison wardens in the United States. *Criminal Justice and Behavior, 46*(1), 136–153.

Siegrist, J., & Li, J. (2016). Associations of extrinsic and intrinsic components of work stress with health: A systematic review of evidence on the effort-reward imbalance model. *International Journal of Environmental Research and Public Health, 13*(4), 1–15.

Soltis, S.M., Agneessens, F., Sasovova, Z., & Labianca, G. (2013). A social network perspective on turnover intentions: The role of distributive justice and social support. *Human Resource Management, 52*(4), 561–584.

Steiner, B., & Wooldredge, J. (2015). Individual and environmental sources of work stress among prison officers. *Criminal Justice and Behavior, 42*(8), 800–818.

Szucs, D., & Ioannidis, J.P.A. (2017). When null hypothesis significance testing is unsuitable for research: A reassessment. *Frontiers in Human Neuroscience, 11*, 1–21.

Taxman, F.S., & Gordon, J.A. (2009). Do fairness and equity matter?: An examination of organizational justice among correctional officers in adult prisons. *Criminal Justice and Behavior, 36*(7), 695–711.

Toderi, S., Gaggia, A., Balducci, C., & Sarchielli, G. (2015). Reducing psychosocial risks through supervisors' development: A contribution for a brief version of the "Stress Management Competency Indicator". *Science of the Total Environment, The, 518-519*, 345–351.

Van Selm, M., & Jankowski, N.W. (2006). Conducting online surveys. *Quality and Quantity, 40*(3), 435–456.

Vanhove, A.J., Herian, M.N., Perez, A.L.U., Harms, P.D., & Lester, P.B. (2016). Can resilience be developed at work? A meta-analytic review of resilience-building programme effectiveness. *Journal of Occupational and Organizational Psychology, 89*(2), 278–307.

White, L.M., Aalsma, M.C., Holloway, E.D., Adams, E.L., & Salyers, M.P. (2015). Job-related burnout among juvenile probation officers: Implications for mental health stigma and competency. *Psychological Services, 12*(3), 291–302.

Wright, L., Borrill, J., Teers, R., & Cassidy, T. (2006). The mental health consequences of dealing with self-inflicted death in custody. *Counselling Psychology Quarterly, 19*(2), 165–180.

AMStrength program in Canadian federal correctional services: correctional officers' views and interpretations

Rosemary Ricciardelli, Marcella Siqueira Cassiano, Michael Adorjan and Meghan M. Mitchell

ABSTRACT

Scholars and correctional officials have begun to recognize the association of correctional work with occupational stressors that deteriorate mental health and well-being. Yet, programs and policies to support prison staff as they navigate physical, emotional, and psychological challenges are limited, with scarce empirical evidence supporting their usefulness to employees. We examine the *Advanced Mental Strength and Conditioning* (AMStrength) program using semi-structured interviews with 70 correctional officers after they completed a year on the job. Among our findings, we highlight that 80% of participants have not used AMStrength since being their training during recruitment. However, AMStrength fulfills a vital role in promoting awareness, including self-awareness of mental health.

Introduction

Correctional work entails navigating a dangerous environment where exposure to stressful and potentially psychologically traumatic events is the rule rather than the exception (Oliphant, 2016). The dangerous and unpredictable nature of correctional work led researchers to identify and explore the factors underpinning the high-levels of occupational stress among correctional officers (COs) (Dowden & Tellier, 2004; Schaufeli & Peeters, 2000). Such factors include personal safety risks, role conflict, role strain, organizational stressors, and prison staff cultures. Personal safety risks refer to the fear of contracting infectious diseases (Alarid & Marquart, 2009; Hartley, Davila, Marquart, & Mullings, 2013) or being victimized by incarcerated persons (Gordon, Moriarty, & Grant, 2003; Gordon, Proulx, & Grant, 2013; Lai, Wang, & Kellar, 2012). Role conflict involves mainly the CO's inability to balance work and personal/family needs (Higgins, Swartz, & Roberts, 2021; May, Lambert, Leone, Keena, & Haynes, 2020), while role strain refers to the difficulties that COs experience in reconciling their custodial and rehabilitation job roles (Finn, 1998).

Institutional stressors include any organizational problem that can compromise job satisfaction such as poor leadership, co-worker conflict, and excessive workload (Kyonk et al., 2021,). Referring to values, norms, beliefs, and behavior patterns that circulate among employees of correctional institutions, prison staff culture is a powerful force shielding officers from stress by fostering group cohesion, solidarity, and reliability in the correctional work place (Higgins et al., 2021). However, prison staff culture, like any culture, often stigmatize and oppress ideas and behaviors that challenge the status quo, including rigid standards of masculinities that prevent both male and female officers from caring for their mental health (Ricciardelli, 2019). The high-stress levels that mark the correctional occupation also derive from the CO job role. COs also respond to assaults, self-harming situations, attempted or completed death by suicide, drug overdoses, and deaths regularly (Public Safety Canada, 2020).

The dangers and the stressors that outline correctional work translate into numerous mental health challenges, including Posttraumatic Stress Disorder (PTSD) and Major Depressive Disorder (MDD), which are explored in a growing body of literature (Carleton, 2021; Carleton et al., 2019, 2018; Carlson & Thomas, 2006; Gould, Watson, Price, & Valliant, 2013; Griffin, Hogan, Lambert, Tucker-Gail, & Baker, 2010; Oliphant, 2016; Regehr et al., 2021; Ricciardelli, 2019). Compared to the general population, COs are at a higher risk of experiencing psychological distress and depression, hypertension, and substance abuse (Kunst, Bogaerts, & Winkel, 2009; MacIvor, 2017; Regehr et al., 2021). Furthermore, the mental health challenges that COs experience negatively impact their families (Higgins et al., 2021) and the people they supervise (Ricciardelli & Power, 2020). Despite increasing attention directed at understanding the mental health needs of correctional workers, the field of correctional studies has paid limited attention to the programs and strategies available to support CO mental health and well-being, including those intended to reduce the potentially negative psychological effects of occupational stress injuries.

In this study, we analyze how COs view and perceive the *Advanced Mental Strength and Conditioning* (AMStrength) program, complementing the correctional scholarship on prison staff mental health by offering a glimpse into the problems of AMStrength from the officer's perspective (See Ricciardelli & Adorjan, 2021). To this end, we draw on semi-structured interviews with 70 COs. AMStrength is a psycho-educational training program specifically for COs geared to prevent negative psychological outcomes from correctional work and build prison employee resilience to occupational dangers (i.e. coping strategies geared to maintain personal well-being) (Trounson & Pfeifer, 2016). As such, AMStrength helps reinforce broader mandates for safety and security in the prison. We offer knowledge on how CO experiences on-site inform their reflections on mental health training and its relevance to their daily work. In the following sections, we outline relevant literatures produced thus far on the study topic, present our research methods and findings, and discuss the implications of our research results, including a subsequent discussion on implications and policy directions.

The literature on prison employee-oriented programs

Programs intended to promote the health and wellness of prison staff are still 'in their infancy' (Ferdik & Smith, 2017). Correctional agencies began to address the occupational health of prison staff in the 2000s. At the time, most mental health programs applied in correctional services were limited and designed for police officers, whose job is different from the job of a CO. While some authors compare police officers and COs in terms of the weapons they carry (Farkas & Manning, 1997) and the amount of dangers and pressures they experience (Brower, 2013), we believe that the main distinction between these two public safety personnel groups lies in their work environment and frequency of exposure to risks. In contrast with police officers, COs work in enclosed spaces and are continuously (as opposed to continually) exposed to risks during their shifts. Thus, the unique nature of correctional work raises questions about the applicability of police-oriented programs to COs. Regardless, empirical-based literatures on mental health support for prison employees are still limited. Literature on the topic tends to focus on Employment Assistance Programs (EAPs), critical incident debriefing (e.g. CISM), cognitive-based programs, and unstructured practices.

Although initiated by police departments in the United States (Sauter, 2001), EAPs have entered correctional services of most English speaking countries. EAPs usually provide in-person or over the phone counselling to prison employees to help them manage workplace problems, including those that are mental health-related (CSC, , 2008b; Lodewyk, 2011; Willemse, 2020). EAPs embody a reactive approach to mental health, as employees rely on it to solve existing problems. Cognizant that occupational stressors can impact family life, correctional agencies in Canada and the United States extend EAP to family members (Arredondo et al., 2002; CSC, , 2008b; Delprino, 2001). Based on research conducted in the United States and South Africa, the number of officers using such programs are relatively limited (Finn, 1998; Lodewyk, 2011). Among other problems, research conducted on EAPs in South Africa, Canada, and the United States report that such programs enjoy limited managerial support and awareness (Genest, Ricciardelli, & Carleton, 2021; Willemse, 2020), as well as trust from employees (Finn, 1998). Also, based on research conducted in South Africa, correctional institutions delivering EAP services do not always follow standardized practices, nor do they have adequate staffing to provide services (Bhoodram, 2010; Willemse, 2020), which can compromise the quality of the support delivered.

In addition to EAPs, correctional institutions also tend to provide post-incident debriefings to their employees. Debriefing programs are commonly known as 'Critical Incident Stress Debriefing,' 'Critical Incident Stress Management,' and 'Critical Incident Debriefs.' Despite their distinctive names, these programs share the same goal, which is to provide psychological first aid to help prevent the development of PTSD symptoms following involvement in a potentially psychologically traumatic event or critical incident. Like EAPs, debriefing programs also have a reactive nature. Overall, based on research conducted in Canada, the United States, and the United Kingdom, debriefings help COs to reduce stress levels (Gillan, 2001; Ruck, Bowes, & Tehrani, 2013; Wohlmuth, 2003), however, debriefings alone tend to be insufficient to relieve COs from the psychological burden of witnessing or participating in a critical event. Also, research based in the United States has shown that debriefing is associated with increased stress levels (Engelmann, 1997), leading correctional researchers to consider that debriefing is not inherently positive. For instance, scholarship on, among other occupations, emergency medical services personnel shows that structural and contextual factors, such debriefing timing, number of events, using judgmental communication, mandatory participation, and fear of stigmatization, may negatively affect employees' views of and experiences with debriefing (Swab, 2020). Based on research conducted in the United States, debriefings, like EAPs, would benefit from greater managerial support and increased professionalization (Gillan, 2001), which includes debriefings being conducted by trained professional debriefers, perhaps even persons with clinical or mental health training.

Adopted by several correctional agencies, cognitive-based support programs draw on cognitive behavioral and interpersonal theories to address mental health problems preventatively. Cognitive-based programs distinguish themselves from EAPs and debriefings primarily for their proactive approach to mental health. Practically, cognitive-based programs involve psychoeducation and the promotion of self-awareness. The most popular cognitive-based programs within law-enforcement agencies, including correctional services, are the 'Power to Change Performance Stress' (McCraty, Atkinson, Lipsenthal, & Arguelles, 2009), 'Stress Inoculation Training' (Backer, 1990), 'AMStrength' (Ricciardelli & Adorjan, 2021), 'Promoting Resilient Officers' (Shochet et al., 2011), 'Cognitive-Behavioral Stress Management' (Booth, 2009), and 'Road to Mental Readiness' (Mental Health Commission of Canada, 2014). Based on research conducted in Canada and Bosnia and Herzegovina, cognitive-based programs have positive effects in reducing stress and mental health stigma among officers (Bravo-Mehmedbasic et al., 2009; Fikretoglu, Beatty, & Lui, 2014; Ricciardelli & Adorjan, 2021). However, because cognitive-based programs tend to interfere with people's lifestyles and views of mental health, not every officer is willing to make the life changes that such programs recommend.

While some COs benefit from structured programs offered by their employer, others, based on research conducted in Canada and the United States, benefit from unstructured coping strategies (Finn & Kuck, 2005; Gould et al., 2013). These strategies include physical fitness, taking time off work, changing job positions, prison transfers, early retirement, religious activities, and support from co-workers and family members. Regular exercise is the most common coping strategy among law-enforcement personnel in England, the United States, and New Zealand (Finn & Kuck, 2005; Kielyl & Hodgson, 1990; Walmsley, 2015). The popularity of physical exercise results from its immediate nature, almost-guaranteed stress relief, low cost, and autonomous nature, that is, exercise does not require employer support.

Correctional researchers focused on prison staff mental health have provided numerous recommendations to improve the efficacy of the programs offered by correctional agencies. Most recommendations from research conducted in Canada and the United States entail improving the flexibility of those programs, allowing them to be adaptable to the needs of different individuals (Finn & Kuck, 2005; Ricciardelli & Adorjan, 2021). Research from South Africa also indicate a need for correctional managers to improve support to mental health programs (Willemse, 2020). Regardless of any recommendations, all researchers agree on the need for conducting more evaluation research on programs targeting the mental health of correctional employees. Understanding the programs available and identifying successful practices represents a crucial step in transforming correctional institutions into a safer and more effective work environment.

Correctional officer training and the AMStrength program

Correctional Services Canada (CSC), the agency managing federal prisons in Canada, provides three mental health programs to support prison employees, namely the EAPs (CSC, , 2008b), the *Critical Incident Stress Management* (CISM) (CSC, 2008a; Rosine, 1992), and AMStrength (Trounson & Pfeifer, 2016; Trounson, Pfeifer, & Ogloff, 2018), our study topic. While EAPs and CISM (i.e. debriefing) equip employees to respond to work-related problems, AMStrength provides employees a toolkit of knowledge and practices that help them develop the ability to self-manage their health.

CSC introduces AMStrength to COs during the Correctional Training Program (CTP), as they prepare to commence a career in the country's federal institutions (Adorjan, Ricciardelli, & Gacek, 2021). Organized in seven two-hour sessions, the AMStrength program is taught by staff trainers ranked CX3, that is individuals who have accumulated work experience as COs (CX1 and CX2). During the sessions, trainers emphasize the development of emotional self-awareness to facilitate understanding in relation to exposure to potentially psychologically traumatic events. Recruits learn to identify stress reactions and symptoms, as well as their response to adversity and how these responses relate to their well-being. Three of the sessions focus on specific states of well-being: the 'green zone' is the optimal state, i.e. the most mentally healthy zone, perceived through a sense of mental and physical balance; while 'amber' and 'red' zones indicate states of increasing risk, respectively, for mental health and well-being. Daily 'pulse checks' are encouraged, during these sessions, referring to a breathing technique geared to ascertaining one's state of mindfulness. Beyond learning about these 'zones', recruits are encouraged to develop personal 'action plans' if they find themselves in an amber or red zone; the objective is to return to a state of psychosomatic equilibrium in the green zone (Ricciardelli & Adorjan, 2021). Beyond providing lessons regarding mental well-being, workplace stressors, and mental fitness, AMStrength encourages recruits to relate lessons to personal experiences and practice the lessons learned through ongoing 'homework,' which includes numerous scenarios that mimic situations experienced in prisons. After learning about AMStrength during CTP, officers can take 'refresher' courses as part of their continued training.

Originally developed by Trounson and Pfeifer (2016)as a psycho-educational course targeted at COs, AMStrength essentially fuses a series of evidence-based frameworks, including cognitive behavior therapy, dialectical behavior therapy, and health psychology, to encourage individuals to stay aware of their mental health (Trounson & Pfeifer, 2017). The program assumes that mental health awareness (i.e. mindfulness) can lead to the gradual development of coping skills (Mongrain, 2019; Trounson et al., 2018) and help officers to prevent and address the unintended consequences of correctional work.

Methods

Our analysis draws on 70 interviews with COs employed in 19 of Canada's 43 federal prisons. We conducted these interviews as part of a multi-year mixed method study (2018–2028) that intends to map and analyze the structural and contextual factors that impact the occupational health of COs working federal prisons in Canada. Under this study, which is led by Ricciardelli, and referred to as Canadian Correctional Workers' Well-being, Organizations, Roles and Knowledge (CCWORK), we survey, clinically assess, and interview about 400 officers per year with several qualitative and quantitative instruments. Longitudinal in design, this multi-year study is used to collect data from officers during recruitment (i.e. baseline) and annually thereafter (i.e. follow-up waves). Semi-structured, the interviewers inquire into the officers' expectations, experiences, and perceptions of correctional work, including their occupational-related concerns (e.g.

stressors and challenges), views of prison, prisoners, and co-workers, work-life balance, exposure to potentially psychologically traumatic events, correctional policies, and health and wellness support received from correctional institutions (e.g. AMStrength, debriefing, and EAPs). CSC facilitated participant recruitment by allowing us to advertise our project to all CO recruits and conduct interviews during paid time, as well as providing a private space for the project team to conduct interviews in-person or over the phone (since the COVID-19 pandemic). Lasting between 45 and 90 minutes, the interviews were voice recorded and transcribed verbatim. Despite CSC's collaboration, participation in our project is voluntary, thus we study any CO recruit willing to contribute to the project. Also, according to our research agreement, CSC has no access to primary research data. All participant identifying information is anonymized; their names replaced with a participant identification number. The research's ethics protocols received approval from the Research Ethics Board of the Memorial University of Newfoundland (File No. 20,190,481).

The 70 interviews used in our analysis were conducted between October 2019 and May 2021, with COs who had completed their first year of occupational tenure (i.e. participants had been on the job for 15 months on average). Using NVivo software, we analyzed the interviews in a four-step coding process using a semi-grounded and constructionist approach (Charmaz, 2006; Glaser & Strauss, 1967; Ricciardelli, Clow, & White, 2010) that involved axial and open coding, as well as data quantification (numerical coding). The use of axial and open coding from a constructionist approach allowed us to analyze both expected and unexpected themes within the interviews.

Firstly, we axial-coded interview transcripts to identify and separate the section discussing AMStrength from the main interview, categorizing all AMStrength-relevant materials under a code titled 'AMStrength.' The excerpts categorized under 'AMStrength' derived from the following questions: Do you recall learning about AMStrength? Have you used the skills learned in AMStrength since CTP? Please share with me your thoughts on AMStrength. Have you done a pulse check? Do you have a plan if you were to enter an amber zone? Often, AMStrength content also resulted from probing questions made on the spot, which intended to fully capture if and how COs used AMStrength, as well as their views of the program. Secondly, also using axial-coding, we organized the excerpts under the code 'AMStrength' into sub-categories (i.e. codes) that reflected participant's (1) recollection of learning AMStrength, (2) program usability, separating discussions on pulse check and amber zone, and (3) opinions of the program. Thirdly, we used open coding to revise step 2 and code unexpected thematic patterns that emerged organically (without being asked) within the interviews. Such themes, which we organized under the codes 'deflection,' 'personal strategies to deal with mental health problems,' 'awareness of mental health,' 'culture,' and 'suggestions,' represent and structure our findings. Lastly, to gain a macro view of our data, we used the software IBM SPSS to code some of the textual answers into the following binary (yes or no) variables: AMStrength user; pulse check practitioners; and amber zone planner. We also used SPSS to code participant's comments on their personal strategies to deal with stress and mental health problems (only 52 participants mentioned their strategies) into activity categories. Using SPSS, we also coded and computed participant demographic information and ran Chi-Square tests of association to probe for any potential association between demographics and the variables we computed with SPSS.

Participants identified themselves as males (52.9%) and females (47.1%). Participants are aged 19–24 (27.2%), 25–34 (55.7%), 35–44 (11.4%), and 45–64 (5.7%). Approximately 90% of the sample is evenly split between individuals who had never married (45.6%) and individuals in a marital relationship (marriage or common-law, 45.6). Over three quarters of participants (75.4%) have a college or a university degree, while 18.8% have only a high-school certificate; the remaining have a technical diploma or a post-graduate degree. A quarter of participants (24.6%) have correctional experience in Canada's provincial/territorial prison system. We found no statistical association between demographics and participant's answers regarding AMStrength.

Findings

All 70 participants recalled learning AMStrength during CTP, but only 13 individuals (18.8%) reported using AMStrength at work. In other words, the largest majority or 81.2% of participants (56 individuals) have not used the program since they learned it in CTP. Among those 13 participants who used AMStrength, the majority remembered the three zones (69.2% or nine individuals) and pulse-checking (76.9% or 10 individuals). Beyond AMStrength, participants relied on the following strategies to manage their stress levels and mental health: extra-AMStrength mindfulness activities (30.8% or 16 individuals); communication with co-workers, including debriefing (30.8% or 16 individuals); physical exercises (21.2% or 11 individuals); family activities (5.8% or three individuals); religion (3.8% or 2 individuals); commuting time (3.8% or 2 individuals); psychological services (1.9% or one person); and drinking (1.9% or one individual). Most AMStrength users relied on mindful-based activities (50.0% or five individuals) and exercises to manage (20.0% or 2 individuals) their health, while most non-users relied on the following strategies: communication with co-workers (36.6% or 15 individuals); mindfulness activities (24.4% or 10 individuals); and exercises (22.0% or nine individuals). Essentially, about a quarter of AMStrength non-users still practiced mindfulness activities despite not using AMStrength.

Deflecting the utility of AMStrength in the correctional environment

Overwhelmingly, participants deflected the utility of AMStrength, often using a depreciative or dismissive tone to discuss AMStrength. For instance, some referred to the program as 'the psychological one' (P8), in a derogatory way, while others, sometimes laughing ironically, reported they only remembered it 'vaguely' (P2, P5, P30, P90, P149, and P90). There were also those participants who revealed having 'joked about it' with their 'buddies' (P18), those who used the word 'joke' to define the program, saying 'that was a joke' (P10), and those who bluntly described AMStrength as a 'stupid' course (P5 and P77).

Similar dismissive comments came in response to questions about whether COs had actively used the 'pulse check' technique learned during AMStrength training. When P18 was asked: 'Do you remember pulse checks?' he responded bluntly: 'Yeah, I – fuck, no one's doing pulse checks. The only time I've even done a pulse check is when an inmate was blue, I checked his pulse.' As he continued, he shared that he had never tried to find his pulse, suggesting that it was impractical in the correctional environment: 'That doesn't work .... [laughter]! It's – like – that's just hilarious and actually now that I'm thinking about that, they're [instructors] just kinda funny .... That [instructors] they even train us on that.' While some participants responded to AMStrength rather poorly, others viewed the program from a political standpoint: as a 'political response from CSC to the federal government's pressure to improve the mental health problems from this [correctional] job' (P18). P18's sentiment was quite negative, viewing AMStrength as CSC's strategy to reduce its responsibility for employee's mental health. P18 also complained about the quality of the mental health resources offered to COs in comparison to the resources offered to prisoners. He complained that COs, who were exposed to 'an inmate swinging from his fuckin' sprinkler, smoke detector thing in purple and blue and shades,' were sent to 'group class' [debriefing] afterwards. In addition to dismissing debriefing, which is widely adopted by CSC as part of its Critical Incident Stress Management (CSC, 2008a), P18 added that prisoners receive better mental health support than COs and 'cops' who 'shoot a perp on the street.'

Amid some critical and even derogatory allusions to AMStrength, participants objecting to the program argued that the program had no value for them because it did not fit their personal needs, or it was hard to practice in the correctional environment. In most cases, participants discussed the program's fitness to their personal needs in the context of correctional work, portraying AMStrength as unapplicable or unusable in correctional environments. For instance, when reflecting on AMStrength, P5 reported that AMStrength was not suitable for his 'personality,' viewing it as a 'waste of time.' P12 said it was 'easy to recognize' that she was 'in the red,' but it was 'a lot harder to put things into practice' when in the prison environment. With her comment, P12 dismissed the applicability of AMStrength to correctional work. In a similar fashion, P18 argued that AMStrength cannot provide the 'actual help' that officers need to deal with 'stressors' that include 'dealing with management and the way these institutions are ran.' P18's comments presents mental health problems as resulting from poor organizational management, suggesting that the solution for stress in correctional services lies beyond psychological interventions. However, the general dismissal of AMStrength on the basis of personal incompatibility that we found among participants did not mean a lack of support for the mental health cause. Instead, the dismissal meant only a deflection of the AMStrength program.

Personal strategies to ensure mental health

Beyond AMStrength, participants used two types of strategies to support their mental health: strategies that involved mindfulness (i.e. self-awareness), and therefore resembled AMStrength, and strategies that involved exercising or socializing with others. P22 reported employing a variant of AMStrength; not necessarily what she learned in CTP, but a strategy informed by AMStrength. She explained that although she did not use the expressions 'red zone' and 'yellow zone,' she still followed the process that AMStrength prescribes to calm herself. Similar AMStrength reappropriation strategies applied to conducting pulse checks. When asked if COs had completed a pulse check since learning the practice, most respondents redirected the conversation to speak of their personal ways of keeping their bodies in check and managing workplace stress. Alluding to challenges posed by the correctional environment, P119 first reported that she had a hard time practicing pulse checking: 'I just don't have them [abilities to do pulse checks] in me [laughter]. I try so hard to get on board, but if someone else is walking you through, I just can't walk myself through it.' Then, P119 said that she counts backwards from 10 to calm herself. Meanwhile, P4 felt he was 'able to get the same results by doing different things.' Also benefiting from AMStrength training, P2 started doing 'meditating stuff' after becoming an officer; he even bought an app to assist his endeavors. Some were already interested in meditation prior to CTP, considering the movement from learning AMStrength to engaging in meditation a 'natural transition' (P27). P113 also resorted to technology to assist her with mindfulness, reporting to have bought an Apple Watch that does the breathing techniques she learned in the AMStrength course.

While some participants discussed their appropriations of AMStrength, others mentioned exercises and interactions with family members and co-workers as their personal alternatives to manage their mental health. P7 explained that he goes to the gym after his shift, saying that 'working out' has always helped his mental health: 'I've worked out just for my own benefit and just keep my confidence high, my mental health, like control my anxiety stuff like that .... It's a nice stress reliever for me so I do that just for myself.' P90 also views exercise therapeutically, reporting that physical exercises make him more tolerant at work: 'I can take out whatever like aggression or whatever I'm feeling and just deal with it on the mats or in the gym.' Meanwhile, P18 cited 'hanging out with his daughter' in addition to going to the gym, to exemplify the notion of deflecting formal AMStrength practices for personal, informal ones. P18 reflected: 'Everyone has their own way of dealing with like their – when they're in that red zone. Everyone has their own – mine's my kid and my gym.' He explained that these two activities 'nullified' him 'completely' (i.e. recharged or refreshed him); that is, enjoying time with his daughter and going to the gym reset his mental state when he is in the 'most pissed off of moods.'

While P18 mentioned his daughter as a source of social support, others mentioned their co-workers. P228, after commenting on the 'mindful activities' that she practices, also emphasized the role that relationships play in keeping officers mentally healthy, especially her co-workers. She said that it is 'really important' to 'find your people' when she enters a zone that she 'should not be in.' Echoing several participants, P89 also illustrated the importance of co-workers in addressing mental health problems; she claimed that peers tend to know their co-workers well, as they work together regularly, becoming the first individuals to notice if something is wrong with their colleagues. Such a knowledge that employees have of each other facilitates the communication of feelings and discomfort: 'You work with them a lot. So, you know like if you're going through something, you can talk to that person about whatever you need.' For most COs, personal approaches to mental health management that included the practice of mindfulness, physical exercises or drawing from relationships with co-workers and family members usurped the need to follow the techniques learned in the AMStrength program.

AMStrength as a source of mental health awareness

Despite the COs' reservations about AMStrength, most participants indicated that AMStrength provided a space to start discussions on mental health and increase mental health awareness, including self-awareness. Despite not using AMStrength, P30 reported that AMStrength made her realize that 'mental health is important.' P149, another AMStrength non-user, appreciated the emphasis on mental health during the CTP, exclaiming 'that course was super it was really good! I think it's great that they put a focus on that at the beginning.' P119 felt that the strategies learned in AMStrength were especially applicable to officers, including herself, as they needed to be aware of their surroundings at all times: 'Just taking time and being aware of how you're feeling and what your surroundings are, and how to carry yourself.' When recalling AMStrength, P30, a non-user, explained that she learned the value of routine, describing the training as helpful because 'it brought awareness' to her work routine, stopping her from 'doing stuff' unconsciously, without realizing it. After alerting us that her opinion of AMStrength was biased because she had a 'personal interest in that kind of stuff anyways,' P158, who also did not use the program, reported that AMStrength was 'very helpful' for making her inquire into her mental state and how her mental health state can impact work situations: 'You know, like am I operating in the red zone right now?' She completed her comment suggesting that having a 'clear mind' improved her judgment of how her presence (i.e. 'calm' or 'agitated' state) 'affected' or 'tainted' a situation.

P35, another non-user, also felt that the 'course is valuable in making us you know aware that we have to pay attention to our mental health.' Applying AMStrength 'pretty religiously,' P115 recalled learning meditation as part of AMStrength and emphasized that the program 'made a big difference in how things have gone in these nine months [since he started on the job] just taking really good care of myself.' P134, an officer who has yet to employ the skills used from AMStrength, spoke of learning at CTP to be aware of her own mental health though the training: 'because of AMStrength, I know what to look for, stuff like that so if you're approaching the amber zone and you're getting to the red zone . . . .' Using the metaphor 'teering around the red zone' to signal the beginning of a decline in mental health, she concluded that AMStrength was a 'beneficial thing' that taught her when to 'seek help.' More succinct, P31 took from AMStrength the value of focusing on oneself, 'centering oneself when you're frazzled,' often using the program.

While some COs reported using AMStrength to improve self-awareness, others used AMStrength skills to build rapport with prisoners, as well as calm them. P387 described a situation where she used the skills learned in AMStrength to remain calm while dealing with an agitated prisoner in an observation cell. Despite 'getting anxiety,' feeling her shoulders starting to 'hunch,' and 'clenching' her fists, she managed to use AMStrength to remain calm and talk to the prisoner assertively. P387 also described how AMStrength led her to observe her mental state, calm herself, and help a prisoner 'bring himself down' by telling him 'I understand you're upset, right, can we talk about what happened?' These remarks and reflections suggest that, despite some overtly negative sentiments expressed regarding AMStrength, the vast majority of our participants nevertheless felt the program helped reinforce the value of mental well-being in correctional work, and drew from a variety of informal sources to support themselves.

Prison staff culture as a potential obstacle to AMStrength

The conversations about AMStrength also involved comments on the role that prison staff cultures played in the officer's decision to seek help for mental well-being. Prison staff cultures are influenced by, among other factors, management attitude, the officer's age (which is associated with job tenure), job role, and broader societal trends (Ricciardelli, 2019). Overall, our data showed that prison staff cultures create mixed dynamics in the correctional environment where mental health is both supported and stigmatized.

For some, mental health, and seeking help, is viewed positively in their correctional workplaces. P10 stated that mental health is actually quite openly discussed at his institution: 'I would say there are more people talking about mental health than I thought at work . . . the CO's [mental health]. We have one of our managers, he struggles with mental health, but he openly talks about it.' P10's words describes a progressive climate where staff openly discuss and share their mental health concerns. In P10's institution, managerial support facilitates such a progressive climate. In fact, several COs referred to the importance of management support in advancing mental health conversations. Reporting that his manager supported mental health care, P27 suggested that administrative support instills positive attitudes towards mental health and assistance seeking. Similarly, P12's comments on how her co-workers and managers are 'understanding' suggests that peer support determines courses of action involved with mental health recovery: 'If you're not doing well and you needed a break or you need whatever, people are really good . . . . Very supportive of each other.'

Some participants attributed the openness of mental health discussions in prisons to wider changes in society recognizing the legitimacy of seeking help for mental health. P13 described a 'wider societal shift to recognizing mental health.' He continued saying that 'crazy' were the people who did *not* address their mental health problems, not those who had someone to talk to, like a psychologist or a counsellor. Meanwhile, some COs suggested that positive views of mental health and seeking help are generational, that is more common among younger officers and staff. P49 described what she referred to as 'a shift' in institutional culture, but particularly among 'newer, younger officers' who are increasingly invested in mental health supports. P21, who had recently completed an AMStrength refresher course, offered a similar reflection. She said that, unlike the 'new officers,' the 'old officers' equate the need to be on stress leave with weakness. P21 outlined an organizational culture among 'older officers' that resisted mental health training, and considered users of supports as 'weak,' demonstrating that a culture that stigmatizes mental health concerns among correctional workers still exists within her institution. This persistent culture has negative impacts, especially for those more junior COs who may opt to not take a crucial leave of absence for fear of potential stigmatization. For these reasons, P21 suggested that mental health training is important for new recruits but may fall on deaf ears among more tenured staff, who tend to be older.

Occupational age, however, is not the only determinant of prejudice against mental health, as in some institutions the stigma against COs seeking mental health support comes from younger COs too. P27 reported that his 'fellow COs' view mental health as a 'point of weakness.' P27 explained that an 'old school mentality' persists at his institution regardless. P154 explained that some officers in her prison still experience stigma regarding mental health, as if officers had to 'suck it up' just because they were 'officers.' Meanwhile, other officers consider their mental health important, using their leave. A few participants explained the stigma that surrounds mental health, as well as the dismissal of AMStrength, by saying that some COs used mental health as an excuse to skip work, leaving others at work overloaded. P8 reported the case of an officer who was bullied by his co-workers for allegedly abusing stress leave. Although P8 never met this officer, he said that the officer was then 'pushing snow,' an expression for being ostracized: ' . . . .A snow removal guy for the institution, [while] making a guard's salary and everyone's always like "yeah, he wasn't even at the incident that caused the stress leave."' P8's reflection also indicates a hierarchy of credible reasons why one may take leave, assuming that if a CO is not directly involved in an incident, then the requested leave indicates fabricated trauma. One may argue that the stigma that P8 outlined does not target stress leave or mental health *per se* but the fact that some officers 'milk the system.' However, co-workers usually do not have enough information to judge how a person reacts to critical incidents. For instance, P8 had no direct knowledge regarding the CO who took leave, and his reflection suggested the significant role of hearsay and exaggeration. P8's views and interpretations resulted from prison cultures, or socially transmitted ideas and practices that officers use to deal with real-life problems, such as having to deal with the absence of a co-worker and the increased workload this absence generates.

Another factor influencing the degree COs feel support, or lack thereof, is the wider shift in Canadian correctional services towards considering the mental health needs of prisoners themselves. Some COs suggested that the priority given to prisoner's health is inadvertently acting to deemphasize a focus on CO well-being. P77 reflected on this topic saying the 'focus on inmate wellness,' despite being positive, lead to 'neglecting' and 'sacrificing' staff. Wider societal shifts in attitudes towards seeking help for mental health and trauma are no doubt influencing officer cultures within Canadian prisons.

Recommendations from COs

Several COs offered suggestions for improving the program. They grounded their recommendations in making AMStrength more relevant for the realities of prison work. Some suggested AMStrength instructors could do more to emphasize the relevance of the program to correctional work, for instance by emphasizing work-based scenarios and examples. Also desiring AMStrength to be more relevant to correctional services, P36 recommended the eight hours of mental health training delivered by his institution via on-the-job training over the content learned in CTP. P36 stated that the content taught at his institution was 'more interesting and like realistic ... than what they did in CTP because it has a lot of real examples real situations and how people dealt with them.' Arguing that AMStrength at CTP was 'dry' (P36) and 'monotone' (P387), some officers suggested changes in the course delivery format. P97 spoke about the need to 'revamp' the AMStrength course taught during CTP, which, according to him, should be customized to address the stressors of the correctional officer job. For P97, AMStrength should focus on teaching officers 'mental health well-being' and the 'stressors of the correctional environment,' instead of practices like the pulse check. Although P97 dissociated learning pulse checks from a focus on mental health, AMStrength prescribes pulse checks to be a regular way for individuals to self-manage their mental health state.

Discussion and conclusion

Among our findings, we highlight that over 80% of participants did not to use AMStrength, despite having received training on the program. Participants often deflected AMStrength by referring to it as a 'joke' or by simply disregarding the training as not applicable to their specific needs, including while performing their job role within the correctional environment. Participants who dismissed AMStrength, regardless of their tone or reason, still supported the need to care for mental health. Also, most participants viewed AMStrength as a reminder for them to remain vigilant about their mental health. Discussions of AMStrength usually resulted in participants commenting on the strategies they used to manage mental health, with a considerable number of AMStrength users (50%) and non-users (24.4%) reporting that they practiced mindfulness-based activities. In general, officers indicated a positive change in prison staff culture towards the importance of mental health, which seems to be largely generational, as well as contextualized in broader societal trends that value open discussions about mental health problems and solutions. However, many officers reported that prison staff cultures that legitimize stigma against mental health and mental health support (e.g. leave of absence) still exist within their workplaces. Some officers provided suggestions to improve the usability of AMStrength within correctional work, which included adjusting the program's practices to the prison environment and training details of how COs can apply the program in work situations. A few suggestions involved totally overhauling AMStrength to make it address the stressors that COs face daily. The findings we highlight have several implications.

Our finding regarding the AMStrength's lack of popularity echoes a previous study led by Ricciardelli and Adorjan (2021) on how CO recruits viewed AMStrength. Based on interviews with CO recruits during CTP training, their analysis demonstrates that recruits were positive about the AMStrength program's intentions but reserved about the usefulness or applicability of the program to their needs (Ricciardelli & Adorjan, 2021). AMStrength's unpopularity, however, does not necessarily mean that the program is a failure. On the contrary, AMStrength accomplishes its mission of promoting mental health awareness, especially self-awareness, among COs, including those who do not use the program. The incorporation of a program such as AMStrength into the training of CO recruits going to work in the country's federal prisons signifies a welcomed commitment from correctional services in Canada to raise awareness about the mental health of prison workers. The continued prioritization of prison staff mental health is vital to improving the prison experience of those who are federally incarcerated, as COs are charged with the supervision and security of prison populations – the care, custody, and control of prisoners – and preparing prisoners for community re-entry.

The percent of non-AMStrength users (24.4%) practicing mindfulness suggests that officers oppose AMStrength but not necessarily its cognitive approach, which can still be adopted by any AMStrength alternatives formulated in the future. Nonetheless, researchers and practitioners interested in developing cognitive-based mental health programs for COs should take into consideration that COs represent a unique group within public safety personnel due to their occupational characteristics. COs, unlike their peers in public safety, work in confined environments under great visibility and scrutiny, including from CCTV cameras. Thus, the proposition of programs that involve mediation and relaxation must accompany the creation of decompression rooms, and if possible, decompression rooms that are not monitored by cameras. On the flip side, unmonitored spaces within prison can potentially compromise security, including the officer's safety. Program developers also should account for the fact that it is simply impossible for officers to take a break during a shift to practice meditation if they are stressed or take their pulse using a pulse check during a tense encounter with prisoners. Meanwhile, programs must be flexible enough that officers can draw on the associated skills inside and outside of the workplace, as compromised mental health knows no boundaries – impacting personal and professional experiences. However, the impact of AMStrength-induced mental health awareness among COs' still needs to be clinically measured and assessed before further investing in cognitive-based programs.

Regarding the COs' reliance on communication with co-workers as an alternative strategy to mitigate stress and manage mental health, our finding confirms previous studies indicating that social support from colleagues and supervisors reduces stress (Cullen, Link, Cullen, & Wolfe, 1990; Cullen, Link, Wolfe, & Frank, 1985; Dollard & Winefield, 1995). Despite confirming previous studies on the positive role of peer support, we acknowledge the ambivalent role that co-workers play in the correctional workplace (or any workplace) also as a source of stress due to competition, gossip, disapproval, and even bullying in the worst cases (Schaufeli & Peeters, 2000). Although our study is not on stress and the factors that cause stress, our findings, particularly some of the recommendations COs made to 'revamp' AMStrength, suggest that acquiring clear knowledge of occupational stressors during recruitment, that is being provided a 'realistic job preview,' may improve job satisfaction and retention (Morgan & Smith, 2009). Conversely, a clear preview of the correctional work routine, including inherent risks, may also become a recruitment obstacle.

Our findings also demonstrate that prison staff cultures are diverse formations that evolve continuously, as opposed to monolithic, rigid structures that reproduce standards of masculinities and authority that completely exclude attention to feelings and emotions (Arnold, 2017; Arnold, Liebling, & Tait, 2012). Prison staff cultures within federal prisons in Canada still stigmatize officers struggling with burnout and other mental health problems, but those cultures, reflecting broader societal transformations, are clearly changing as new generations of officers join correctional work.

Researchers, we argue, must continue to examine the effectiveness of programs and create customized interventions geared toward improving CO mental health and well-being. With high levels of burnout, mental health disorders, and turnover within correctional work, the mental health load of staff needs to be recognized and supports put in place that alleviate strain and stress among officers. The AMStrength program is one attempt at doing so; more program development is necessary as well as greater supports.

Disclosure statement

No potential conflict of interest was reported by the author(s).

Funding

The research supporting this article received funding from the Canadian Institute of Health Research [grants No. 449140, 211387, 411385], Correctional Services Canada, and the Union of Canadian Correctional Officers (UCCO-SACC-CSN).

References

Adorjan, M., Ricciardelli, R., & Gacek, J. (2021). 'We're both here to do a job and that's all that matters': Cisgender correctional officer recruit reflections within an unsettled correctional prison culture. *The British Journal of Criminology, 61*(5), 1372–1389.

Alarid, L.F., & Marquart, J.W. (2009). Officer perceptions of risk of contracting HIV/AIDS in prison: A two-state comparison. *The Prison Journal, 89*(4), 440–459.

Arnold, H., Liebling, A., & Tait, S. (2012). Prison officers and prison culture. In Laurie A. Gould and John J. Brent., (Eds.), *Handbook on prisons* (pp. 501–525). New York, NY:Routledge. https://www-taylorfrancis-com.qe2a-proxy.mun.ca/chapters/edit/10.4324/9781315673073-21/psychological-emotional-effects-prison-prison-staff-helen-arnold?context=ubx&refId=46388052-7d3f-4e5c-b0bb-cef83017af2c

Arnold, H. (2017). The psychological and emotional effects of prison on prison staff. In *The Routledge International Handbook of Forensic Psychology in Secure Settings* (pp. 283-299). Routledge. doi:10.4324/9781315673073-21

Arredondo, R., Shumway, S.T., Kimball, T.G., Dersch, C.A., Morelock, N., & Bryan, L. (2002). Law enforcement and corrections family support: Development and Evaluation of a Stress Management Program for Officers and Their Spouses, Executive Summary (Report (Summary), Program/Project Evaluation No. 197899. April 24, 2019, https://nij.ojp.gov/library/publications/law-enforcement-and-corrections-family-support-development-and-evaluation

Backer, L.H. (1990). *The differential effectiveness of a stress inoculation training intervention as a function of coping style among correctional workers* [Ph.D., California School of Professional Psychology - San Diego].

Bhoodram, P.A. (2010). *An evaluation of the employee assistance programme in the department of correctional services benchmarked against the standards of the employee assistance professionals association of South Africa* [Ph.D., University of Pretoria].

Booth, B. (2009). *Cognitive-behavioral stress management program for correctional officers* [Ph.D., Nova Southeastern University].

Bravo-Mehmedbasic, A., Salcic, D., Kucukalic, A., Fadilpasic, S., Cakovic, L., Mehmedika-Suljic, E., & Masic, I. (2009). Impact of psychoeducation on professional stress reduction among prison guards. *Materia Socio Medica, 21*(1), 24–26.

Brower, J. (2013). *Correctional officer wellness and safety literature review*. April 24, 2019, https://nicic.gov/correctional-officer-wellness-and-safety-literature-review

Canada, P.S. (2020). *2019 corrections and conditional release statistical overview*. October 1, 2020, https://www.publicsafety.gc.ca/cnt/rsrcs/pblctns/ccrso-2019/ccrso-2019-en.pdf

Carleton, R.N., Afifi, T.O., Taillieu, T., Turner, S., Krakauer, R., Anderson, G.S., … McCreary, D.R. (2019). Exposures to potentially traumatic events among public safety personnel in Canada. *Canadian Journal of Behavioural Science/Revue Canadienne Des Sciences Du Comportement, 51*(1), 37–52.

Carleton, R.N., Afifi, T.O., Turner, S., Taillieu, T., Duranceau, S., LeBouthillier, D.M., … Asmundson, G.J. G. (2018). Mental disorder symptoms among public safety personnel in Canada. *The Canadian Journal of Psychiatry, 63*(1), 54–64.

Carleton, R.N. (2021). Collaborating to support the mental health of public safety personnel: The Canadian institute for public safety research and treatment. *Canadian Psychology/Psychologie Canadienne, 62*(2), 167–173.

Carlson, J.R., & Thomas, G. (2006). Burnout among prison caseworkers and corrections officers. *Journal of Offender Rehabilitation, 43*(3), 19–34.

Charmaz, K. (2006). *Constructing grounded theory*. Los Angeles, CA: Sage Publications Ltd.

CSC. (2008a). *Critical incident stress management (Guidelines No. 253–2)*. April 24, 2019, https://www.csc-scc.gc.ca/lois-et-reglements/253-2-gl-eng.shtml

CSC. (2008b). *Employee assistance program (Guideline 253-1)*. April 24, 2019, https://www.csc-scc.gc.ca/lois-et-reglements/253-1-gl-eng.shtml

Cullen, F.T., Link, B.G., Cullen, J.B., & Wolfe, N.T. (1990). How satisfying is prison work? *Journal of Offender Counseling Services Rehabilitation*, *14*(2), 89–108.

Cullen, F.T., Link, B.G., Wolfe, N.T., & Frank, J. (1985). The social dimensions of correctional officer stress. *Justice Quarterly*, *2*(4), 505–533.

Delprino, R.P. (2001). *Work and family support services for correctional officers and their family members: A national survey*. April 24, 2019, https://www.ojp.gov/pdffiles1/nij/grants/192292.pdf

Dollard, M.F., & Winefield, A.H. (1995). Trait anxiety, work demand, social support and psychological distress in correctional officers. *Anxiety Stress Coping*, *8*(1), 25–35.

Dowden, C., & Tellier, C. (2004). Predicting work-related stress in correctional officers: A meta-analysis. *Journal of Criminal Justice*, *32*(1), 31–47.

Engelmann, N.D. (1997). *The impact of critical incident stress debriefing on correctional officers* [M.A., Southern Connecticut State University].

Farkas, M.A., & Manning, P.K. (1997). The occupational culture of corrections and police officers. *Journal of Crime and Justice*, *20*(2), 51–68.

Ferdik, F.V., & Smith, H.P. (2017). *Correctional officer safety and wellness literature synthesis* (Trepidation among the "keepers": Gendered perceptions of fear and risk of victimization among corrections officers.

Fikretoglu, D., Beatty, E., & Lui, A. (2014). *Comparing different versions of road to mental readiness to determine optimal content: Testing instruction type, homework, and intelligence effects at two timepoints* [Scientific Report No. DRDC-RDDC-2014-R164]. April 24, 2019, https://apps.dtic.mil/sti/pdfs/AD1004306.pdf

Finn, P., & Kuck, S. (2005). *Stress among probation and parole officers and what can be done about it*. April 24, 2019, https://nij.ojp.gov/library/publications/stress-among-probation-and-parole-officers-and-what-can-be-done-about-it

Finn, P. (1998). Correctional officer stress: A cause for concern and additional help. *Federal Probation*, *62*(2), 65–74. November 2 2021, https://www.uscourts.gov/sites/default/files/62_2_9_0.pdf

Genest, C., Ricciardelli, R., & Carleton, R.N. (2021). Correctional work: Reflections regarding suicide. *International Journal of Environmental Research and Public Health*, *18*(8), 8.

Gillan, T. (2001). The correctional officer: One of law enforcement's toughest positions. *Corrections Today*, *63*(6), 112–115.

Glaser, B.G., & Strauss, A.L. (1967). *The discovery of grounded theory: Strategies for qualitative research*. Aldine Publishing Company. April 24, 2019, http://www.sxf.uevora.pt/wp-content/uploads/2013/03/Glaser_1967.pdf

Gordon, J.A., Moriarty, L.J., & Grant, P.H. (2003). Juvenile correctional officers' perceived fear and risk of victimization: Examining individual and collective levels of victimization in two juvenile correctional centers in Virginia. *Criminal Justice and Behavior*, *30*(1), 62–84.

Gordon, J.A., Proulx, B., & Grant, P.H. (2013). Trepidation among the "keepers": Gendered perceptions of fear and risk of victimization among corrections officers. *American Journal of Criminal Justice*, *38*(2), 245–265.

Gould, D.D., Watson, S.L., Price, S.R., & Valliant, P.M. (2013). The relationship between burnout and coping in adult and young offender center correctional officers: An exploratory investigation. *Psychological Services*, *10*(1), 37–47.

Griffin, M.L., Hogan, N.L., Lambert, E.G. Tucker-Gail, K.A., & Baker, D.N. (2010). Job involvement, job stress, job satisfaction, and organizational commitment and the burnout of correctional staff. *Criminal Justice and Behavior*, *37*(2), 239–255.

Hartley, D.J., Davila, M.A., Marquart, J.W., & Mullings, J.L. (2013). Fear is a disease: The impact of fear and exposure to infectious disease on correctional officer job stress and satisfaction. *American Journal of Criminal Justice*, *38*(2), 323–340.

Higgins, E.M., Swartz, K., & Roberts, A. (2021). How conflict 'bleeds over' for correctional staff: Exploring work-family conflict through correctional subculture. *Journal of Crime and Justice*, 1–16. doi:10.1080/0735648X.2020.1870526

Kielyl, J., & Hodgson, G. (1990). Stress in the prison service: The benefits of exercise programs. *Human Relations*, *43*(6), 551–572.

Konyk, K., Ricciardelli, R., Taillieu, T., Afifi, T., Groll, D., & Carleton, R.N. (2021, forthcoming). Identifying the relationship between relative stressors and mental disorders in correctional work. *International Journal of Environmental Research and Public Health*.

Kunst, M.J.J., Bogaerts, S., & Winkel, F.W. (2009). Peer and inmate aggression, type D-personality and post-traumatic stress among Dutch prison workers. *Stress and Health*, *25*(5), 387–395.

Lai, Y.-L., Wang, H.-M., & Kellar, M. (2012). Workplace violence in correctional institutions in Taiwan: A study of correctional officers' perceptions. *International Journal of Comparative and Applied Criminal Justice*, *36*(1), 1–23.

Lodewyk, L.B. (2011). *The official's perception of EAP services in the department of correctional services in the potchefstroom correctional centre* [Masters Thesis, Northwest University].

MacIvor, A. (2017). Number of prison workers suffering from PTSD much higher than official stats, union says. *CBC News*. April 8 2018, https://www.cbc.ca/news/canada/nova-scotia/canada-prisons-corrections-ptsd-first-responders-coverage-1.2735583

May, D.C., Lambert, E.G. Leone, M.C., Keena, L.D., & Haynes, S.H. (2020). Stress among correctional officers: An organizational justice approach. *American Journal of Criminal Justice*, *45*(3), 454–473.

McCraty, R., Atkinson, M., Lipsenthal, L., & Arguelles, L. (2009). New hope for correctional officers: An innovative program for reducing stress and health risks. *Applied Psychophysiology and Biofeedback*, *34*(4), 251.

Mental Health Commission of Canada. (2014). The Road to Mental Readiness (R2MR): Reduce stigma and increase resiliency in police employees.

Mongrain, S.J. (2019). Creating an impactful mental preparedness training at the correctional service of Canada: A consideration for pedagogy. *Asian and Pacific Conference of Correctional Administrators, Newsletter*, *47*, 12–16. April 24, 2019, https://apcca.org/uploads/47th_Edition_of_APCCA_2019_-_Sep_Issue.pdf

Morgan, M., & Smith, J.E. (2009, August). Hiring the right individual for your corrections staff. In *Corrections Today*. 22–26.

Oliphant, R. (2016). *Healthy minds, safe communities: Supporting our public safety officers through a national strategy for operational stress injuries*. April 24, 2019, https://www.ourcommons.ca/Content/Committee/421/SECU/Reports/RP8457704/securp05/securp05-e.pdf.

Regehr, C., Carey, M., Wagner, S., Alden, L.E., Buys, N., Corneil, W., . . . White, N. (2021). Prevalence of PTSD, depression and anxiety disorders in correctional officers: A systematic review. *Corrections*, *6* (3), 229–241.

Ricciardelli, R., & Adorjan, M. (2021). Correctional officer training: Opportunities and challenges of the AMstregnth program in Canada. *Journal of Forensic Psychology Research and Practice*, *21*(1), 40–60.

Ricciardelli, R., Clow, K.A., & White, P. (2010). Masculinity portrayals in men's lifestyle magazines. *Sex Roles: A Journal of Research*, *63*(1), 64–78.

Ricciardelli, R., & Power, N.G. (2020). How "Conditions of Confinement" impact "Conditions of Employment". *The Work-Related Well-Being of Provincial Correctional Officers in Atlantic Canada. Violence Vict*, *(1)*, 88–107.

Ricciardelli, R. (2019). *Also serving time: Canada's provincial and territorial correctional officers*. Toronto, ON, Canada: University of Toronto Press.

Rosine, L.P. (1992). *Exposure to critical incidents: What are the effects on Canadian correctional officers?* April 24, 2019, https://www.publicsafety.gc.ca/lbrr/archives/forum%204-1-1992%20e-eng.pdf

Ruck, S., Bowes, N., & Tehrani, N. (2013). Evaluating trauma debriefing within the UK prison service. *Journal of Forensic Practice*, *15*(4), 281–290.

Sauter, C. (2001). Health and wellness programs made available to Maryland correctional employees. *Corrections Today*, *63*(6), 110–115.

Schaufeli, W.B., & Peeters, M.C.W. (2000). Job stress and burnout among correctional officers: A literature review. *International Journal of Stress Management*, *7*(1), 19–48.

Shochet, I.M., Shakespeare-Finch, J., Craig, C., Roos, C., Wurfl, A., Hoge, R., . . . Brough, P. (2011). The development and implementation of the promoting resilient officers (PRO) program. *Traumatology*, *17*(4), 43–51.

Swab, J. (2020). Critical incident stress management: Perspectives on its history, frequency of use, efficacy, and success. *Crisis, Stress, and Human Resilience: An International Journal*, *4*, 2015–2226.

Trounson, J.S., Pfeifer, J.E., & Ogloff, J.R.P. (2018). *AMStrength participant workbook*. Ottawa, Ontario: Correctional Service Canada.

Trounson, J.S., & Pfeifer, J.E. (2016). *Advanced mental strength and conditioning (AMStrength)*. Melbourne, Australia: ForenSciTech Pty. Ltd.

Trounson, J.S., & Pfeifer, J.E. (2017). Correctional officers and workplace adversity. *Journal of Correctional Health Care*, *23*(4), 437–448.

Walmsley, A. (2015). Physical readiness assessment and staff resilience. *Practice: The New Zealand Corrections Journal*, *3*(1), 1–5. April 24, 2019, https://www.corrections.govt.nz/resources/research/journal/volume_3_issue_1_april_2015_desistance/physical_readiness_assessment_and_staff_resilience

Willemse, R. (2020). An investigation into the South African correctional officers' experiences of their work and the employee assistance programme. *South African Journal of Psychology*, 0081246320980312. doi:10.1177/0081246320980312

Wohlmuth, E.J. (2003). *The experiences of correctional workers to critical incident stress debriefings* [M. Ed., Acadia University, Canada].

A comparative perspective on officer wellness: American reflections from Norwegian prisons

Veronica L. Horowitz, Emily R. Greberman, Patrick E. Nolan, Jordan M. Hyatt, Chris Uggen, Synøve N. Andersen and Steven L. Chanenson

ABSTRACT

Correctional officers in the United States experience severe work-related stressors and are generally physically unwell compared to similar public employees. An innovative and new approach to improving American corrections that is starting to gain momentum stems from looking at the workplace dynamic in alternative international models, such as in Scandinavian prison systems, for models of workplace reform. This study examines the perspectives of staff and leaders from the Pennsylvania Department of Corrections who traveled to Scandinavia as part of a correctional exchange. Each day of the trip, correctional staff recorded their qualitative reflections and completed a basic survey about their observations and experiences. This article examines both forms of data to explore correctional officer wellness from the perspective of American correctional officers. Five key themes are discussed: morale, stress, danger, dynamic security, and communication. Survey results corroborate this pattern, as US correctional officers reported somewhat lower stress and more positive interactions during their time in Norway. Key takeaways and implications for policy are discussed.

Introduction

Just as the well-being of a society can be judged by the nature of its prisons, the well-being of prison staff is inextricably bound up with the well-being of those who are incarcerated (Churchill, 1910). There is much evidence that US prisons have become unhealthy places for both groups. This paper provides a unique vantage on officer wellness by examining the daily reflections of American correctional officers (COs) working in Scandinavia on a weeks-long correctional exchange. After briefly reviewing the foundational ideologies of Scandinavian and American prisons and their contrasting corrections systems we examine research on the key drivers of CO wellness and the costs of unwellness in US prisons. We then introduce the Scandinavian Prison Project (SPP) and the unique daily reflection data this paper analyzes. In these reflections, we find that the

American officers speak directly to the key challenges and opportunities surrounding officer wellness. These include discussion of morale, stress, danger, security, and communication. Finally, we conclude by noting the mutually reinforcing relationships between the social organization of prisons and the well-being of COs and incarcerated individuals.

Penal excess and penal exceptionalism: correctional officers and approaches to security

Prisons in the United States have long been recognized for their sheer capacity, large populations, austere environments, and the dehumanizing effect that these conditions can have on both incarcerated people and staff. Prisons in Scandinavia, on the other hand, are widely perceived as more humane and, in some cases, as 'exceptional' (Pratt, 2008a). The fundamental philosophical differences in prominence within these frameworks for incarceration – American retribution vs. Scandinavian rehabilitation – are reflected in myriad ways inside of their prisons (Hyatt, Andersen, & Chanenson, 2020). One of the most striking and salient distinctions, though difficult to observe and to quantify, is the nature of relationships between staff and incarcerated persons and how they impact each other's wellbeing.

Likewise, the contrary approaches to prison safety emphasized by these nations must have distinct impacts on the wellness of COs employing these methods. American prisons generally emphasize the need to control the carceral environment for practical and punitive reasons. This has translated to a strong and uniform emphasis on 'static' security. These means include the prototypical characteristics of a prison: locks, bars, and walls. The goals of the static security apparatus are to utilize barriers and power to enforce rules and regulations in a highly depersonalized way to limit disruptions to orderly and safe prison operation (Sykes, 1958). While static security measures are clearly present in Scandinavian prisons as well, those penal environments also emphasize another approach to security often lacking in the United States. 'Dynamic security,' an approach to security in which human relationships – especially those between staff and incarcerated people – is paramount in Scandinavian facilities (Høidal, 2018). Dynamic security emphasizes policies and practices based on continuous individualized, human interaction and adaptation of restrictions based on those relationships (Høidal, 2019; Pratt, 2008a). Dynamic security allows for the use of the least restrictive means necessary for security, the tailoring of responses, and ongoing engagement for staff and incarcerated people.

In Norway, the emphasis on rehabilitation and 'dynamic security,' though generally accepted today (Shammas, 2016), required effort to implement in Scandinavia. In the late 20th century, Scandinavian countries, including Norway, began reconsidering the purpose and operations of their prisons. Toward the end of the 1970s, Nordic countries had become increasingly critical of the reliance on 'outdated and overly severe criminal codes' and the 'excessive use of custodial sentencing' (Hinkkanen & Lappi-Seppälä, 2011; Lappi-Seppälä, 2007). During this period, Scandinavian countries began transitioning from a punishment-focused authoritarian model to a rehabilitative model (Hinkkanen & Lappi-Seppälä, 2011). The model that was implemented reflects the egalitarian nature of the Scandinavian welfare state and policies that are rooted in a humanist ethos (Pratt, 2008a, 2008b). The model was based, in part, on the idea that the most appropriate methods for in-prison rehabilitation were through the development of positive relationships and personal growth in an environment that reflects the community (Johnsen, Granheim, & Helgesen, 2011; Liebling, 2004; Norwegian Ministry of Justice and the Police, 2018). The extent to which Nordic nations live up to this aspirational ideal is a matter of some debate, as the state must exercise an overwhelming and paternalistic authority over those in custody (Barker, 2013; Smith & Ugelvik, 2017).

Although correctional ideologies, especially at the national level, can include elements from across the philosophical continuum (Morris, 1974), certain paradigms can become dominant. In the late 1960s and early 1970s, for example, rehabilitation was the preeminent approach in American corrections (see Menninger, 1968), though scholars challenged the role and applicability of rehabilitation through imprisonment (e.g. Von Hirch, 1976) in the decades following. Despite a relatively recent shift towards a stronger emphasis on a more rehabilitative agenda, American prisons still function primarily as a punitive environment for retributive, deterrent, and incapacitating purposes (Lambert, Hogan, & Jiang, 2010; Sykes, 1958). As Phelps (2011) points out, there remains a gap between the rhetoric regarding the intended treatment of incarcerated people and the realities in prisons. Simply put, many American prisons are overcrowded and understaffed (Gaes, 1985; Garland, 2001) making it difficult to ensure security and hindering correctional staff from developing positive relationships with incarcerated individuals.

Consistently, a recent study by Ferdik and Hills (2018) found that many COs believe rehabilitative programming within prisons was not worth the monetary investment. Historically, and despite movements toward a rehabilitative model of custody from a strictly retributive one, little focus has been put on correctional officer wellness and the potential impact of prosocial relationships in the penal environment. American CO attitudes about their role remains strongly rooted in maintaining the perception of control and security rather than engaging in the rehabilitation of incarcerated people (Cullen, Lutze, Link, & Wolfe, 1989; Ferdik & Hills, 2017; Liebling, 2011). This may place staff and incarcerated people in persistently distant, and occasionally adversarial, roles, which could contribute to an unhealthy and stressful work environment. This punitive attitude is further reinforced by institutional concerns about COs informally communicating with (often referred to as fraternizing) incarcerated people. Such constraints on positive relationships between staff and incarcerated people can result in aggression from incarcerated people and decreased CO tolerance for disruption (characterized by the excessive use of coercive and potentially illegitimate means of attaining control) (Ferdik, 2018; Lambert et al., 2010; Liebling, 2011). The absence of rapport reinforces how the use of different security practices and policies in prisons serve as a tool that can either build or burn alliances between incarcerated people and COs. The ongoing tension which develops may contribute to officer unwellness.

Contrasting correctional contexts: organization and population composition

The friction between COs and incarcerated persons in the US reflect American society more broadly which is rooted in hierarchical structures and varying levels of power. Thus, similar dynamics occur between COs and those in positions of greater authority in US prisons. Department of Corrections utilize a quasi-military structure, where rankings are intended to distinguish between those with authority and diminish their interpersonal relationships across these positions (Jermier & Berkes, 1979). This structure provides strict organization; relying on a clear chain of command which heavily diminishes the staff's ability to form personal and positive relationships at work. This power structure also depersonalizes interactions between staff, making it harder to create positive relationships and disincentivizing connections (Jermier & Berkes, 1979).

In contrast, Norway's model, like the society more broadly, is rooted in egalitarianism (Pratt, 2008a, 2008b). The emphasis on dynamic security encourages open communication between correctional staff, those in their custody, and their superiors. Through interaction positive relationships with both trust and respect can form. Norwegian COs tend to emphasize individual-level relationships, both among staff and between staff and incarcerated people (Bruhn, Nylander & Johnsen, 2017). This may be driven by a system-wide emphasis on multiple forms of rehabilitation (see e.g. Hean Willumsen & Ødegård, 2017) and it is reinforced by a training program that emphasizes humanistic, as well as security, principles (Eide & Westrheim, 2020). When compared to their American counterparts, the Norwegian model of dynamic security encourages the exercise of discretion. Such relationships are paramount in shaping the climate within prisons (Crewe, 2011).

Alongside the contrast in correctional ideology and security emphasis another key point of difference between prisons in the US and Norway is the racial composition of prisons. In the US, racial minorities (especially black and brown men) constitute a dramatic overrepresentation of those in prison (Nellis, 2016) while those employed in correctional facilities are primarily white (DataUSA, 2014). Norway, conversely, is characterized by its great degree of racial homogeneity (Uggen, Stewart, & Horowitz, 2018). The shared characteristic of Whiteness within the Norway correctional system may help foster grater connections and personal relationships between correctional employees and those in custody while the discrepancy between staff and prison populations in the US may hinder the development of open, positive relationships. These differences may also influence institutional power-dynamics and the adaptability of Norwegian practices in the US.[1]

Correctional officer (un)wellness in the United States

Extant literature on CO experiences focuses almost exclusively on CO *un*wellness, and identifies problematic levels of stress, burnout, and mental health problems as an epidemic within the profession (Brower, 2013; Ferdik & Smith, 2017; Mack & Rhineberger-Dunn, 2021; Stack & Tsoudis, 1997). Like those they supervise, COs are exposed to the violent and abusive conditions of prisons. They are not passive witnesses; their work as COs occurs in close proximity to the individuals they oversee. Further, they are tasked with enforcing rules and regulations in varied contexts. This can create cognitive dissonance and role ambiguity (Cullen, Link, Wolfe, & Frank, 1985; Liebling, 2000). COs experience disproportionately higher levels of stress, mental health problems, physical injury, and ailments compared to the general public and law enforcement officers (Brower, 2013; Ferdik, 2018; Harrell, 2011; Lambert, Hogan, Paoline, & Clarke, 2005; Walters, 2020) and have fewer resources for addressing their stress (Ferdik & Smith, 2017). Studies have estimated their life expectancies at 62 ½ years (Parker, 2011) with other estimates even 59 years, 16 years lower than the national average (Cheek, 1984; New Jersey Police Suicide Task Force, 2009). Relatedly, research indicates the suicide rate of COs in New Jersey is twice that of police officers (New Jersey Police Suicide Task Force, 2009) and national estimates indicate their suicide rates are around forty percent higher than people of similar demographics in other professions (Stack & Tsoudis; 1997; Violanti, 2017).

CO stress has been linked to numerous factors: the degree of danger present and/or perceived within an institution, feeling unsupported by managers and supervisors, experiencing interactional problems with prisoners, feeling overworked, receiving inadequate compensation, struggling with role conflict and role ambiguity, and exhibiting a punitive orientation towards prisoners (Ferdik & Smith, 2017; Lambert, Hogan, & Barton, 2002; Liebling, 2011). COs must also navigate adherence to the rules of their institutions and deviations necessary to manage the environment. This inconsistency strains officers (Gilbert, 1997; Liebling, 2000). Role conflict or role ambiguity for correctional officers can lead to stress, burnout, and high rates of turnover (Leip & Stinchcomb, 2013; Matz, Wells, Minor, & Angel, 2013; Minor, Dawson-Edwards, Wells, Griffith, & Angel, 2009).

Stress is another major factor negatively impacting COs. Highly stressed officers are more likely to experience depersonalization, emotional exhaustion, and feelings of ineffectiveness (Ferdik, 2018; Griffin, Hogan, Lambert, Tucker-Gail, & Baker, 2009) and job stress also negatively impacts COs' commitment to work (Ferdik, 2018; Hogan, Lambert, Jenkins, & Wambold, 2006; Lambert et al., 2002). Stress and its consequences may lead to job burnout and work conflict. High turnover and absenteeism due to chronic occupational stress can result in understaffed and less secure facilities which have been linked to in-prison assaults (Ferdik, 2018; Lambert, 2004; Steiner, 2008). Thus, stress creates imbalances in the social dynamic of a prison which may result in situations that further erode correctional officer wellness.

Improving correctional officer wellness

Policy recommendations for improving CO wellness often emphasize the need for greater administrative support, such as creating open channels for communication from staff to incarcerated people, staff to staff, and among incarcerated people (Ferdik & Hills, 2018; Ferdik & Smith, 2017; Management and Training Corporation, 2011). Another suggested policy is to improve the intake process to better identify individuals who may pose particular threats to the institution upon arrival.[2]

Another set of recommendations for improving CO wellness focus on stress reduction. These have largely been instituted from the literature on policing, although Ferdik and Smith (2017) acknowledge a lack of evidence on efficacy. Other scholars found no evidence of benefit on stress-level outcomes after conducting a meta-analysis of programs (i.e. crisis intervention, stress management, exercise programs) intended to increase CO well-being (Evers, Ogloff, Trounson, & Pfeifer, 2020; Walters, 2020). An under-explored but promising opportunity for improving CO wellness revolves around the relationship between COs and those in custody (Steiner, 2009).

The formulation of positive relationships between COs and their superiors, peers, and with those in their custody holds great potential to improve prison culture and CO wellness. Open communication, if prioritized, can foster greater transparency leading to improved trust between COs and the incarcerated people they monitor. Norway provides a promising model to look to for facilitating positive relationships between COs and incarcerated people. While we noted several factors that currently inhibit the creation of positive relationships in US prisons, many of these could be mitigated by shifting towards greater emphasis on dynamic security practices and the removal or revision of policies prohibiting substantive communication between COs and people in custody.

Thus, we posit, applying Norwegian principles/practices in US prisons will likely improve the wellbeing of American COs. In line with this supposition, several American states have started to experiment with Norwegian (or more broadly, Scandinavian) principles in corrections, including California (Ahalt, Haney, Ekhaugen, & Williams, 2020); North Dakota (Hilliard, 2020), and Pennsylvania (Hyatt, Andersen, Chanenson, Horowitz, & Uggen, 2021) – the latter of which is the focus of the present study. This strategy has been descriptively linked to improved wellness of COs and improved job satisfaction (Ahalt et al., 2020). Our study builds on this small body of work.

Given the interdependence of CO wellness with the successes of other aspects of the prison system, our study adds to the current literature through first-person accounts of how COs in the US view aspects of officer wellness based on their observations and experiences in Norwegian prisons. Despite a growing body of research on COs and their (un)wellness, few studies seek to examine the perceptions of workplace safety and wellness from the perspective of COs (Ferdik & Smith, 2017). The present research will assist in developing a better understanding of CO perceptions and may aid in conceptualizing the adaptability of foreign penal policies intended to increase wellness of COs (as well as the wellness of those in custody) in the US.

Current study

This is a case study that examines correctional officer wellness from the first phase of a correctional initiative: the Scandinavian Prison Project (SPP). The SPP is a multi-phased international exchange and correctional reform program. The goal of this program was to provide American COs and leaders with the knowledge and experience to develop a housing unit in a Pennsylvania prison using principles and procedures adapted from Scandinavia. Of the 12 participants in the exchange, eight were COs and four were in leadership positions. In Phase 1 of the project a group of COs and the Pennsylvania Department of Corrections (PADOC) leaders traveled to Scandinavia to learn about, and work in, Scandinavian prisons. The correctional exchange was developed to provide the participants with a grounding in Scandinavian penal theory, applied correctional policy and, in the latter phases of the exchange, hands-on experience working in several Norwegian prisons. (See Chanenson et al., 2021; Hyatt et al., 2021for a more comprehensive summary of the history, challenges, objectives, and curricula from the program.)

In the first part of this phase, members of the group toured juvenile detention facilities, high security prisons, halfway houses, and other institutions in Norway (e.g. national headquarters, training academy), attended workshops, participated in weekly focus groups, and attended educational programs. During the second part, and in coordination with the Norwegian Correctional Service (NCS), the American COs were assigned to one of three Norwegian prisons, and each was given a Norwegian CO mentor with whom they worked daily. The American COs wore Norwegian uniforms and worked in the prisons in roles roughly equivalent to theirs in Pennsylvania. The research team accompanied the

American officers and leaders for all components of this exchange to conduct systematic observations and to facilitate the collection of contemporaneous data (including the narratives examined here).

Study participants

Of the 12 participants in the exchange, 8 were correctional officers and 4 were leaders. All 12 participants volunteered to be part of the exchange program and were then selected by the prison Superintendent. American officers were then paired with mentors in Norwegian prisons based on an assessment of who the warden of each Norwegian prison thought would be the best fit. Regarding race/ethnicity, 7 participants were Black, 2 were Hispanic, and 3 were white. Eight of the participants were female and 4 were male and their ages ranged from 23–63. Their tenure in the prison ranged from under 2 years to over five, and their educational attainment ranged from a high school diploma to a master's degree.

Data and methods

At the end of each day in Scandinavia, members of the research team collected two types of data from each American correctional employee: daily audio reflections and surveys. Audio reflections were recorded, in private, using a digital personal recorder. A semi-structured, optional guide was provided for the reflection (see Appendix B). Survey data were gathered using a paper-and pencil instrument that included several Likert-style items (anchored at strongly agree and strongly disagree) regarding their experiences and feelings at work that day. A single panel of interview and survey data was also collected prior to the beginning of the program and a follow-up survey administered on the last day in Norway.

During the program, recordings were immediately uploaded to secure cloud storage then deleted from the recorders which were returned to the corrections employees for the following day. Audio files were subsequently uploaded to Trint (transcription software), then cleaned by the research team. These transcripts were imported into NVivo for coding and analysis. A complete list of the codes used in this paper, the number of individual recording files that contain each code, and the number of times each code was referenced can be found in Appendix A.

The number and nature of recordings varied by participant. Some individuals recorded only one reflection per day, while others recorded many; time in Scandinavia also varied between two and three weeks. As a result, the number of reflections from each individual ranged from 13 to 79 with a mean of 35 reflections per individual, totaling 422 reflections analyzed in this paper. The survey data were collected both pre-trip (May 2019) and on the final day in Norway (June 2019). We compare Likert-scale responses from seven categories relevant to CO wellness (see Appendix C for survey questions).[3]

Findings

Coding the daily audio reflections in NVivo, we identified five wellness-focused themes: morale, stress, danger, dynamic security, and communication. These themes were not described in mutually exclusive ways by our participants, but for clarity we organize our findings by theme.

Morale

By drawing on the perceptions and observations of COs exposed to a wholly new context, our data and project provide a novel, and perhaps unique, vantage on correctional officer wellness. In line with the literature on the importance of workplace morale (Johnsrud & Rosser, 2002; Minor, Wells, Lambert, & Keller, 2014; Sudom, Dursun, & Flemming, 2006; Weakliem & Frenkel, 2006), we found that one of the most pervasive themes that emerged in US officer reflections was the high morale observed amongst officers in Norwegian prisons. For instance, on the third day of the trip Johnston noted:

> Everyone respects their coworker top to the bottom. Everyone speaks when you come in. Good morning. When you're leaving. Have a nice day. The simple things matter as far as staff morale and morale is very high around [this Norwegian prison].

This observation connects morale among Norwegian prison staff to mutual respect, both laterally amongst officers and hierarchically. The lack of hierarchical difference makes sense given the comparatively flat (less hierarchical) organization of Norwegian society (Pratt, 2008a) relative to the United States. Another major difference observed by the American officers was the quality and nutrition of the food. In Norway, unlike in the US, the COs and incarcerated persons ate dinner together sitting around a dining room table in their own unit. The meals consisted of fresh fruits, vegetables, and meats (without preservatives). As Steward stated:

> The food is like real food, it's just, it's just amazing. It was the reason why the jail has such high morale and a reason why things are so stress free and easy going.

American officers were acutely aware of a relationship between morale and stress on one side and the well-being of both themselves and incarcerated persons on the other. Many saw the SPP as an opportunity to improve the lives of both groups simultaneously. For instance, as Carroll emphasized:

> I just feel optimistic. I think that this is going to be a turn and a start of maybe a better corrections for everyone involved, not just staff, not just inmates, for everyone. I'm feeling hopeful and optimistic. I definitely think now more than ever is the right time for change. I feel hopeful. So, it looks like they're encouraging each other. Oh, they [Norwegians] said "There's hope for everyone." It's like their motto they stand by. It's definitely impressive, that slogan itself, it instills hope in the prisoners and hope in the community, it just makes ... everything is positive to promote a better feeling ....

A similar comparison was made by Newcomb who pointed out the difference between those who choose to work in corrections in Norway versus the US:

> They choose the profession mainly because they want to help people. Norway takes pride in the product that they produce. And both inmates and former inmates and their staff. In Pennsylvania, I think that employees come to work for the pay, and they see inmates as job security.

This observation was echoed by many Americans who were reminded throughout the trip that Norwegian officers received substantially greater education, training, salaries, and benefits than they did.

Identity and Uniforms: A subcomponent of morale unanticipated by the research team was the significance of the Norwegian prison uniform. When the American COs entered Norwegian prisons, they were given Norwegian correctional uniforms to wear during their shifts. These Norwegian uniforms were markedly different from the uniforms they were accustomed to wearing in the US; The American uniforms were gray and made of stiff material, resembling dress pants with a matching top, the Norwegian uniforms were dark blue and made from softer cotton-based fabric with cargo-style pants and a polo-style top. Upon receiving these uniforms and wearing them, their importance, and their role in the development of the morale of the American officers became apparent. In their reflections, American COs described an immediate shift in their appearance and confidence. As Newcomb's observation illustrates, the comfort of these new uniforms improved their demeanor and interactions with incarcerated persons.

> I really like the fact that the uniforms felt so comfortable, they felt so different. Having these [formal uniforms] and polos just gave it . . . gave us a different aura, gives a different outlook on what we are coming to work for. You know, the fact that we were initiating this helping process. The fact that we were comfortable and relaxed and that the inmates could view us in a more approachable way . . ..

Additionally, American COs noted that they would need to change their uniforms when returning to their own prisons in order to facilitate a shift in the way that those in custody perceived and interacted with them. As Johnston explained:

> The uniforms we currently have been the uniforms for forever. Inmates know these uniforms as the authority, the . . . those that have us in bondage, those that are the cops. They know these uniforms. Oppression.

Moreover, American COs believed that changing their uniforms in the US would provide them with a sense of pride and shared identity, boosting work morale and enthusiasm for the project. Upon first seeing the Americans in Norwegian attire, Raymond reflected:

> . . . It was rather impressive to see [American COs] in a uniform looking good. They expressed them, which they felt comfortable in those uniforms, felt less intimidating, less formal. They looked great. And it was somewhat emotional in that I felt a little tickle, you know, run through the body, a sense of pride, proud of them, happy for them.

Stress

Stress is a second theme that emerged as pertinent. The relationship between the comparative prison conditions in Norway and work-related stress was frequently observed by American officers, who offered varied explanations for their perception of reduced stress among Norwegian COs. For instance, Newcomb noted the impact of Norwegian vacation and break policies on officer stress:

> ... Today is maybe the first day a lot of officers will be going on holiday. And it is mandatory that they take three weeks during the summer, three weeks at the same time, consecutive three weeks. That is very different than what we do in Pennsylvania. You do get an allotted time for vacation, but you take it at will one day at a time if you would like to. But they have to take three weeks at the same time. I thought that was different. I think [time off] is very helpful. I think it reduces stress. We talked about the fact that during the day they get one and a half or two hours break. We talked about how beneficial that can be for an officer if they want to sleep, if they want to get on a computer, if they want to walk around the facility. How those are all stress relievers.

Raymond attributed the stress differences between Norwegian and American officers to structural features of the workplace environment.

> There is no way that I'm going to be [in corrections] 20 years. The stress of it would kill you. But he [the Norwegian officer] does not. There has to be a link between working in an environment like this, then not working an environment like I have. They have inner yards that ... evoke a sense of calmness and a sense of peace. So, I was shown that there is a place separate for the officers in where peace, quiet is really invoked, that they can then have their lunches here and it just allows them to be away from the hustle and bustle, as the gentleman says it can get very hectic and very loud.

Raymond similarly described the calming nature of Norwegian prisons and connected this feeling of tranquility to a feeling of safety:

> And they seem to be working hard and enjoying themselves. There's this sense of calm and peace here that doesn't feel like a prison. No one seems threatening. No one gives you the feeling that makes you feel uncomfortable. Very, very different. I felt calm, felt safe ....

The relative absence of stress among Norwegian COs was explained by Young as a result of CO interaction, both among prison staff and between COs and incarcerated people. This observation connects with both the themes of *dynamic security* and *communication* detailed in subsequent sections.

> ... Lack of stress. We noticed that here, in the Scandinavian project, was less stress. We are COs. We have come on your blocks at each of these prisons and we have duly noted how relaxed the atmosphere is, how cohesive the inmates and the staff get along.

Danger

The idea of safety, noted in Raymond's quote in the proceeding section, is interwoven with officers' perceptions of danger, which previous studies have identified as a key driver of poor health (Lambert & Paoline, 2008; Walters, 2020). American officers frequently highlighted the many items that people incarcerated in Norwegian prisons could potentially use as weapons, but also observed that despite this risk Norwegian officers and staff felt secure. For instance, Johnston noted:

> We are now at the visiting house unit for the inmates. And we do notice that cutlery is allowed. They have knives, scissors for cooking. Unlike prisons in the US. I was impressed with the fact that there was very little violence against their staff. And we're noticing a lot of the tools that they're using are unsecured, which is very different from what we're used to in the US. Even the tools and equipment is not tethered. So, you know, I'm feeling like they want to be there and they don't want to mess it up, it's that honor system. This is the way Scandinavians have grown up throughout their life, you know, treat each other fairly and properly. And it just overflows it to the Department of Corrections, like I said, they're on honor. There was shears everywhere, files, metal. That could be turned into weapons. And I spoke with the instructor and he said he's never felt unsafe. He's never been afraid. Likewise, the wood shop instructor said the same thing.

While the American officers were generally impressed by the high level of trust between Norwegian officers and those incarcerated, they also expressed apprehension and fear due to the potentially dangerous items that were readily available and the relative lack of weaponry at the Norwegian officers' disposal. As McPherson explained:

> I'm a little tense already because I know already, OK? Hey, I'm going in to this institution, what, 1,300 inmates? What's going to happen today? What can you know, do, or not do, to make sure we walk out in one piece? I'm just amazed how comfortable prison officers were in that environment. No. No. Oh, see? No handcuffs. Nothing to defend themselves but a pack. Yes, a pack. An alarm system, you just button hit something, you know? And then everybody rushes in and rescues you. They're looking at the inmates warning them if they got to pick it up and beat the crap out of me. They'll cut my head off or decapitate me. Beyond that, we discuss basic, you know, what our inmates do and how they deal with the equipment. You know, that trust factor is something else. I just still can't bypass that. But it's dangerous.

Graham also expressed misgivings about the potential danger Norwegian officers faced due to their trusting practices:

> Now the atmosphere is definitely more relaxed, but we still have to remember that they are inmates, we can't . . . I don't think you always have your back to 'em. That concerns me when I see a guard escorting an inmate and he's directly in front of them a few inches. And it's just like red flags going off in my head like that. You should not be in front of the inmate.

Dynamic security

Despite concerns about the potential for officer safety in Norwegian prisons as described in the section above, American officers had positive reactions to the Norwegian officers' heavy use of dynamic security strategies. For example, Steward stated:

> Their [Norwegian officers'] theories and their practices are basically conversation, conversation, pieces, conversation tools to mediate anything there needs to be solved is always to sit them down and talk to them or to try to calm them down through verbal communication versus hands on altercations. It is a different type of knowledge of the inmates, their relationship in their meaningful activities. They basically feel like they're that dynamic pieces. Their relation and individualism creates a more relaxed and better order present. So that's their goal is to create a relaxed atmosphere, to create an atmosphere that is you create in your next-door neighbor. You're creating the person that you want to live next to, because

> eventually they will get out because they do not have life sentences in Norway. These essential elements in dynamic security establish a positive relationship. They establish meaningful . . . they make them interact with meaningful activities.

When discussing dynamic security, another common observation American COs made was the recognition that American officers were already using this strategy, just not necessarily labeling it as such. As Jackson reflected:

> There was one thing that stood out to me when they mentioned dynamic security at first. You know, I jokingly said like, well, we've heard of the word dynamic, and we've heard of the word security, but we don't use it together. And that was actually false. After hearing what they referred to as dynamic security, just having a close knowledge of the inmates and relationship and getting them involved in meaningful activities, I do believe, at least in [my department], we do that. I can only speak for myself, but I spend about an hour to an hour and a half sometimes with inmates that have been incarcerated for more than 10 years . . .

However, American officers perceived barriers in implementing dynamic security principles at home due to the culture of corrections in their prison and the fraternization policy. Young's reflection described this contrast in culture:

> Now we're told not to be open with inmates. We're told not to be transparent. There's a culture of what we do. And we look at the idea of personal relationships really being a huge part of that process of reintegrating into somebody, somebody into society. You look at the way that we do it and you have a small amount of staff of the large amount inmates and everything's piecework . . . . . . And it's really the exact opposite of the way that you would want to foster relationships with people.

Clark likewise drew attention to the fraternization policy barrier to establishing meaningful relationships between officers and incarcerated persons:

> Another thing I saw today that differs from what we see in the P.A. prisons are the fact that we can sit down and have a meal with the inmates. At my prison, we can't sit down and have a meal with inmates. We can't talk to them for more than more than a five-minute span at any given time or it'll be considered fraternization.

The recognition that the fraternization policy required by their state corrections department was a barrier to fully implementing dynamic security was echoed by Jackson:

> But some of our policy and procedures do actually need to be changed. I was so happy and grateful that someone mentioned fraternization yesterday and how the definition how that policy has to be changed, because there's no way that our staff can engage and socialize and really get to know someone on that level that's expected under dynamic security in the current system the way it is. So, in the current system, we would be terminated for fraternization if we did utilize the Norwegian way immediately when we went back. If they tell us in paper or an e-mail or something that says that this is the new policy, then we can be truly engaging. Other than that, I don't see COs truly engaging with inmates with the current policies and procedures in place.

Communication

Another theme that emerged in the reflections of American COs was the lack of efficient communication with fellow staff in Pennsylvania. Participants reported that between each shift, the departing Scandinavian officers would relay information to the CO taking over regarding what occurred on the unit. American officers believed that this process both kept all officers up to date about current events and prepared them with greater knowledge of the type of environment they would be working in during their shift. This point was emphasized by Stevens:

> One thing that I take away that I appreciate it is the morning meeting and how both shifts meet all parties responsible for working in the area to actually sit down at a table and they review specific points from the log and anything that needs to be addressed …… Everything isn't communicated to the entire shift, to the entire staff. So, I believe their way of conducting the morning meeting would be more beneficial for us.

Study participants reported these meetings were transparent and that they facilitated a flow of information between prison staff. The result of this information sharing was reduced stress, as uncertainty about their workday diminished through this process. In addition to the between shift staff meetings, another opportunity for communication between staff occurred mid-workday in one prison during a 30-minute break. Carroll's reflection also provided insight into the varied types of staff meetings, indicating that even short meetings in which everyone gave quick check-ins and updates, were enough to make a difference in the social dynamic of staff.

> At 8:30 we had a staff meeting …… So that was the staff meeting. That was at a big group staff meeting. We were in the cafeteria and everyone from each block sort of just talked about what was going on on their unit, etc.

Survey results

Overall, these results affirm the contemporaneous observations reported in the audio reflections and the differential manner in which Norwegian prisons were experienced. These officers generally responded favorably to questions about their work experiences in both Pennsylvania and Norway, though they rated the Norwegian prisons somewhat more favorably on each question. Although our 5-point Likert items are ordinal rather

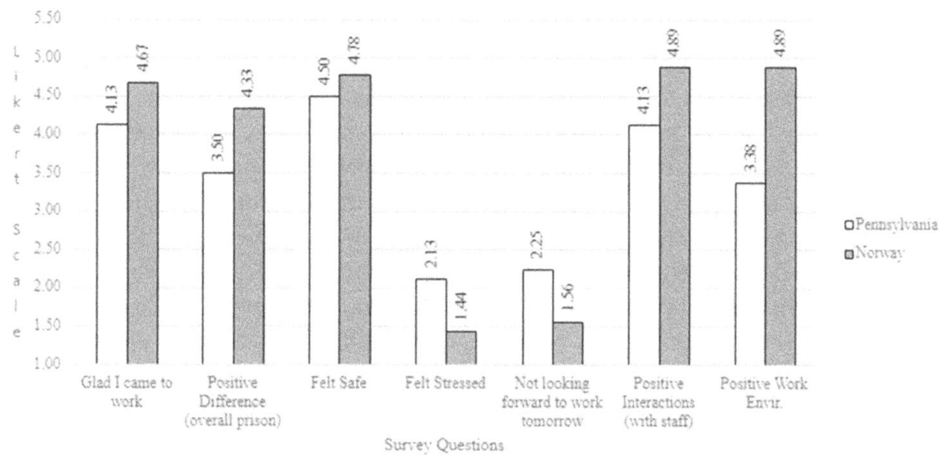

Figure 1. Co pre and post trip attitudes.

than interval-ratio measures, we present mean values for the simple comparisons shown in Figure 1 (with items coded 1 for strongly disagree, 2 for disagree, 3 for neutral, 4 for agree, and 5 for strongly agree), but note that we observe the same pattern of results when the variables are dichotomized to indicate either agreement or strong agreement.

Given our small sample of 9 COs, we do not present statistical tests of the differences between their experiences in Norway and Pennsylvania but show a descriptive comparison in (Figure 1.) The COs reported feeling somewhat less stressed and safer during their shifts in Norway than in Pennsylvania, though they generally agreed they felt safe in both settings. While in Norway, they were also more likely to say they were glad they came to work, that they made a positive difference in the overall prison environment, that they had positive interactions with staff, and that the prison provided a positive work environment. While in Norway fewer COs said they were not looking forward to coming to work the next day.

It is possible that the differences observed across the two settings (which ranged from .54 to 1.51 on our 5-point scale) reflect the excitement of international travel or the 'honeymoon' experience of a new setting. Nevertheless, the increase in positive attitudes and corresponding decrease in stress and negative outlooks corroborates the qualitative results, suggesting that Norway's prison system may be conducive to the wellness of COs.

Discussion, limitations and policy implications

Reflections from American COs throughout their trip served as a self-documenting, ethnographic recording of how prison culture and CO wellness in Norwegian prisons were perceived. In line with past research (i.e. Ferdik & Smith, 2017) these interview and survey data highlight the perceived relationship between the prison environment and job stress for COs. Comparing their experiences in Norway and in Pennsylvania, using both audio and survey data, illustrates the degree of differentiation within these two environments, with participants placing an emphasis on relationships, not on architectural or programming differences as might be expected. Though not establishing a causal relationship, the lower rates of stress and negative perceptions observed in Norway suggest that American prisons can reduce levels of stress – and the attendant harms – for COs by adapting some Norwegian policies by encouraging positive interactions between COs and those in custody; and through improving the conditions of employment for American COs (i.e. providing fresh healthy meals, frequent breaks, comfortable clothing), corroborating the suggestions in prior research on Norwegian corrections (e.g. Ahalt et al., 2020).

The SPP broadly, and the exchange more specifically, were intended to provide COs and corrections staff with the opportunity to reconceptualize their roles in prisons and consider the impact that changes could have on their own well-being and the well-being of incarcerated people under their supervision. As a 'bottom-up' reform effort, the COs in the exchange focused on their work and what they would be able to change on the SPP housing unit. Their reflections, as reported here, reinforce that focus. While possibly constrained by the resource limitations and policy restrictions within the PADOC, the work that followed the exchange would be an effort to demonstrate the adaptability and transplantability of the Scandinavian approaches on a hyper-local level. Additional expansion of these efforts would require buy-in from a range of stakeholders, including leadership at other prisons, agency leadership and, where additional fiscal resources and political support are needed, the legislature. The emphasis of the SPP, however, lies in these officers, their experiences, and the unit they will eventually oversee.

While this study contributes to the limited literature on CO well-being, its limitations should be acknowledged. First, the rich reflection data analyzed came from a small number of correctional employees (12) and as such, results should be interpreted with caution. Relatedly, the corrections staff that chose to participate in the SPP may be more receptive to adapting their perspective than corrections workers in the US as a whole. Similarly, these findings derived from COs in Pennsylvania may not be applicable to COs from other US states, and finally, the SPP is a unique project that will be difficult to replicate. That said, this study reveals several pertinent findings and future research should address the extent to which they are reproduced in other regions and correctional populations.

Notably, throughout these data, American COs emphasized the importance of trust among prison staff and with persons in their custody. This trust facilitated meaningful relationships which in turn were seen as improving officer security. In line with the goals of dynamic security, officers felt that deeper connections with incarcerated persons would help de-escalate conflict and reduce violence against staff. Over time, participating officers seemed to appreciate the benefits of reorienting staff-incarcerated people relationships in line with the new (to them) principles of dynamic security. While this would require modifying multiple rules in Pennsylvania, including the core definition of impermissible fraternization, these policies could radically reform the communication, behavioral and rehabilitative dynamic in those prisons. Fraternization policies act as a barrier to communication between COs and people in custody due to the fear of reprimand and penalty a CO can receive for interacting too personally with those who are incarcerated. Revising this harsh policy would allow an opportunity for open dialogue and communication – improving the quality of relationships between incarcerated people and prison staff. While power differentials and different life experiences between those in custody and those employed persist, improvements in positive relationships between these groups could help decrease emotional and situational distance and enhance the well-being of both populations.

Likewise, developing trust and transparency among staff could be beneficial. Frequent communication among prison staff may reduce stress, as it can improve the safe and smooth operations of facilities and alert staff to potential risks, ultimately improving safety. In support of this goal, participating officers suggested implementing a meeting between shifts, to both facilitate communication and to allow for relationships to develop. These changes would require reforms to the current organizational hierarchy of American prisons but could significantly improve the prison environment and the wellness of those within it.

Finally, the experience of American officers in Norway highlights fundamental differences in the priorities of corrections, visible both through contrasting emphases in prison security *and* shown by the conditions, amenities, and considerations of COs wellbeing. While it may be impossible to replicate the structure and benefits of the Norwegian prison environment and the larger welfare state, there are some simple lessons that can be learned. For example, our findings suggest that providing quality food to COs while at work, considering the comfort of their uniforms, and increasing the duration of at-work breaks for COs could improve both morale and reduce stress. This is consistent with past scholarship indicating that morale is crucial to workplace well-being (Minor et al., 2009, 2014; Sudom et al., 2006). In turn, these policy shifts are likely to help reduce levels of unwellness that are so pervasively documented among American COs today.

Conclusion

Comparative studies provide powerful leverage for informing both science and policy. Looking outward to Scandinavia, a region in which both incarcerated persons and COs fare better than in the US, provides a means to better understand and address US CO *unwellness*. In the SPP, the purpose of American COs shadowing their Norwegian counterparts was to identify, recognize, and adapt components of Scandinavian corrections that could improve American corrections. As we show, a number of key drivers of CO unwellness in the US are mediated through methods used in Scandinavian prisons. The relationships officers cultivate with fellow officers, as well as incarcerated individuals, are crucial to positive work-attitude and wellbeing and can reduce CO stress and improve health. Implementing new US communication protocols and expectations can promote a healthier and safer work environment for COs and incarcerated persons alike.

Notes

1. However, in our project we address this issue to some degree through our site selection. The prison from which the SPP officers were selected was chosen in part because it diverges from national trends and has the most racially diverse staff of prisons in the state.
2. Other recommendations include enhancing static security and even greater reliance on coercive measures, such as the use of solitary confinement to increase safety and thus officer wellbeing (Fredik & Smith, 2017). However, such static security practices have been shown to have negative effects (such as the well-known deleterious effects of solitary confinement (Smith, 2006).
3. Due to the relatively small number of DOC officials and COs who are involved in the SPP we do not differentiate between the types of correctional employees in our findings, nor do we identify their races or genders. We reference our participants using last-name pseudonyms.

Acknowledgement

The authors gratefully acknowledge support for this Article and the broader Scandinavian Prison Project from Arnold Ventures, the Norwegian Research Council for Criminology ("NSfK"), the Scandinavian-American Foundation, and Drexel University. This project would not have been possible without the support of the Norwegian Correctional Service, and the Pennsylvania Department of Corrections.

Disclosure statement

No potential conflict of interest was reported by the author(s).

ORCID

Steven L. Chanenson http://orcid.org/0000-0003-0744-9567

References

Ahalt, C., Haney, C., Ekhaugen, K., & Williams, B. (2020, January 1). Role of a US–Norway exchange in placing health and well-being at the center of US prison reform. *American Journal of Public Health*, 110(S1), S27–S29.

Barker, V. (2013). Nordic exceptionalism revisited: Explaining the paradox of a janus-faced penal regime. *Theoretical Criminology*, 17(1), 5–25.4.

Brower, J. (2013). Correctional officer wellness and safety literature review. US Department of Justice. Retrieved from http://www.middlesexsheriff.org/CorrectionalOfficerWellnessSafety%5fLitReview.pdf

Bruhn, A., Nylander, P.Å., & Johnsen, B. (2017). From prison guards to ... what? Occupational development of prison officers in Sweden and Norway. *Journal of Scandinavian Studies in Criminology and Crime Prevention*, 18(1), 68–83.

Chanenson, S. L., Andersen, S. N., Hyatt, J. M., Hoidal, A., Eason, K., & Connor-Council, P. (2021). " Ice in the Stomach": Reforming Prisons at Home and Abroad. *Am. Crim. L. Rev.*, 58, 1775.

Cheek, F.E. (1984). *Stress management for correctional officers and their families*. Alexandria, VA: American Correctional Association.

Churchill, W. (1910, July 20). Speech before the house of commons on the treatment of criminals. Retrieved from http://hansard.millbanksystems.com/commons/1910/jul/20/class-iii#S5CV0019P0_19100720_HOC_288

Crewe, B. (2011). Soft power in prison: Implications for staff–prisoner relationships, liberty and legitimacy. *European Journal of Criminology*, 8(6), 455–468.

Cullen, F.T., Link, B.G., Wolfe, N.T., & Frank, J. (1985). The social dimensions of correctional officer stress. *Justice Quarterly*, 2(4), 505–533.

Cullen, F.T., Lutze, F.E., Link, B.G., & Wolfe, N.T. (1989). The correctional orientation of prison guards: Do officers support rehabilitation?. *Federal Probation*, 53, 33–42.

DataUSA. (2014). Bailiffs, correctional workers, officers, jailers. Retrieved from https://datausa.io/profile/soc/bailiffs-correctional-officers-jailers

Eide, H.M.K., & Westrheim, K.G. (2020). Norwegian prison officers´ perspectives on professionalism and professional development opportunities in their occupation. *Journal of Prison Education and Reentry*, 6(3), 316–332.

Evers, T.J., Ogloff, J.R., Trounson, J.S., & Pfeifer, J.E. (2020). Well-being interventions for correctional officers in a prison setting: a review and meta-analysis. *Criminal Justice and Behavior*, 47(1), 3–21.

Ferdik, F.V., & Hills, P. (2018). Analyzing further predictors of correctional officer professional orientations: The role of turnover intentions. *International Journal of Offender Therapy and Comparative Criminology*, 62(6), 1668–1693.

Ferdik, F.V., & Smith, H. (2017). *Correctional officer safety and wellness literature synthesis*. Washington, DC: US Department of Justice, Office of Justice Programs, National Institute of Justice.

Ferdik, F.V. (2018). Correctional officer risk perceptions and professional orientations: Examining linkages between the two. *Criminal Justice and Behavior*, 45(2), 264–285.

Gaes, G.G. (1985). The effects of overcrowding in prison. *Crime and Justice*, 6, 95–146.

Garland, D., (Ed.). (2001). *Mass imprisonment: Social causes and consequences*. London: Sage.

Gilbert, M.J. (1997). The illusion of structure: A critique of the classical model of organization and the discretionary power of correctional officers. *Criminal Justice Review*, 22(1), 49–64.

Griffin, M.L., Hogan, N.L., Lambert, E., Tucker-Gail, K., & Baker, D.N. (2009). Job involvement, job stress, job satisfaction and organizational commitment and the burnout of correctional staff. *Criminal Justice and Behavior*, 37(2), 239–255.

Harrell, E. (2011). *Workplace violence, 1993-2009*. Washington, DC: U.S.Department of Justice, Office of Justice Programs, Bureau of Justice Statistics.

Hean, S., Willumsen, E., & Ødegård, A. (2017). Collaborative practices between correctional and mental health services in Norway: Expanding the roles and responsibility competence domain. *Journal of Interprofessional Care*, 31(1), 18–27.

Hilliard, T.E. (2020). *The impact of formal and informal controls on recidivism in Norway and the United States: The case of North Dakota prison experiment*. Greenville, NC: East Carolina University.

Hinkkanen, V., & Lappi-Seppälä, T. (2011). Sentencing theory, policy, and research in the Nordic countries. *Crime and Justice*, 40(1), 349–404.

Hogan, N.L., Lambert, E.G, Jenkins, M., & Wambold, S. (2006). The impact of occupational stressors on correctional staff organizational commitment: A preliminary study. *Journal of Contemporary Criminal Justice*, 22(1), 44–62.

Høidal, A. (2018). Normality behind the walls: Examples from halden prison. *Federal Sentencing Reporter*, 31(1), 58–66.

Høidal, A. (2019). Prisoners' association as an alternative to solitary confinement—lessons learned from a norwegian high-security *prison*. In *Solitary confinement: effects, practices, and pathways toward reform* (pp. 297). New York, NY: Oxford University Press.

Hyatt, J.M., Andersen, S.N., & Chanenson, S.L. (2020). Prison cells as a grounded embodiment of penal ideologies: A Norwegian-American comparison. In Turner J., Knight V. (eds),*The prison cell* (pp. 45–70). Cham: Palgrave Macmillan. https://doi.org/10.1007/978-3-030-39911-5_3

Hyatt, S.N., Andersen, S.L., Chanenson, S., Horowitz, V.L., & Uggen, C. (2021). 'We can actually do this': Adapting scandinavian correctional culture in Pennsylvania. *American Criminal Law Review*, 58(3), 1715–1746.

Jermier, J.M., & Berkes, L.J. (1979). Leader behavior in a police command bureaucracy: A closer look at the quasi-military model. *Administrative Science Quarterly*, 24(1), 1–23.

Johnsen, B., Granheim, P.K., & Helgesen, J. (2011). Exceptional prison conditions and the quality of prison life: Prison size and prison culture in Norwegian closed prisons. *European Journal of Criminology*, 8(6), 515–529.

Johnsrud, L.K., & Rosser, V.J. (2002). Faculty members' morale and their intention to leave: A multilevel explanation. *The Journal of Higher Education*, 73(4), 518–542.

Lambert, E.G. & Paoline, E.A. (2008). The influence of demographic characteristics, job characteristics, and organizational structure on correctional staff job stress, job satisfaction, and organizational commitment. *Criminal Justice Review*, 33(4), 541–564.

Lambert, E.G. (2004). The impact of job characteristics on correctional staff. *Prison Journal*, 84(2), 208–227.

Lambert, E.G, Hogan, N.L., & Barton, S.M. (2002). The impact of work-family conflict on correctional staff job satisfaction: An exploratory study. *American Journal of Criminal Justice*, 27(1), 35–52.

Lambert, E.G, Hogan, N.L., & Jiang, S. (2010). A preliminary examination of the relationship between organizational structure and emotional burnout among correctional staff. *The Howard Journal of Criminal Justice*, 49(2), 125–146.

Lambert, E.G, Hogan, N., Paoline, E.A., & Clarke, A. (2005). The impact of role stressors on job stress, job satisfaction and organizational commitment among private prison staff. *Security Journal*, 18 (4), 33–50.

Lappi-Seppälä, T. (2007). Penal policy in Scandinavia. *Crime and Justice*, 36(1), 217–295.l.

Leip, L.A., & Stinchcomb, J.B. (2013). Should I stay or should I go? Job satisfaction and turnover intent of jail staff throughout the United States. *Criminal Justice Review*, 38(2), 226–241.

Liebling, A., & Arnold, H. (2004). *Prisons and their moral performance: A study of values, quality, and prison life*. New York: Oxford University Press.

Liebling, A. (2000). Prison officers, policing and the use of discretion. *Theoretical Criminology*, 4(3), 333–357.

Liebling, A. (2011). Distinctions and distinctiveness in the work of prison officers: legitimacy and authority revisited. *European Journal of Criminology*, 8(6), 484–499.

Mack, K., & Rhineberger-Dunn, G. (2021). What matters most? Comparing the impact of individual, job, and organizational factors on job stress and job satisfaction among juvenile justice personnel. *Criminal Justice Studies*, 1–20. doi:10.1080/1478601X.2021.1929207

Management and Training Corporation. (2011). *Correctional officers: Strategies to improve retention.* Centerville, UT: Author.

Matz, A.K., Wells, J.B., Minor, K.I., & Angel, E. (2013). Predictors of turnover intention among staff in juvenile correctional facilities: the relevance of job satisfaction and organizational commitment. *Youth Violence and Juvenile Justice*, 11(2), 115–131.

Menninger, K. (1968). *The Crime of Punishment.* New York, NY: Viking Press.

Minor, K.I., Dawson-Edwards, C., Wells, J.B., Griffith, C., & Angel, E. (2009). Understanding staff perceptions of turnover in corrections. *Professional Issues in Criminal Justice*, 4, 43–57.

Minor, K.I., Wells, J.B., Lambert, E.G. & Keller, P. (2014). Increasing morale: personal and work environment antecedents of job morale among staff in juvenile corrections. *Criminal Justice and Behavior*, 41(11), 1308–1326.

Morris, N.(1974). *The Future of Imprisonment.* Chicago, IL: University of Chicago Press.

Nellis, A. (2016). The color of justice: Racial and ethnic disparity in state prisons.

New Jersey Police Suicide Task Force. (2009). *New Jersey Police Suicide Task Force Report.* Trenton, NJ: New Jersey Police Suicide Task Force. Retrieved from https://www.nj.gov/oag/library/NJPoliceSuicideTaskForceReport-January-30-2009-Final(r2.3.09).pdf

Norwegian Ministry of Justice and the Police. (2018). Punishment that works—less crime—a safe society: Report to the storting on the norwegian correctional services (english summary). *Federal Sentencing Reporter*, 31(1), 52–57.

Parker, J.R. (2011). Florida mortality study: Florida law enforcement and correctional officers compared to florida general population.

Phelps, M.S. (2011). Rehabilitation in the punitive era: The gap between rhetoric and reality in US prison programs. *Law & Society Review*, 45(1), 33–68.

Pratt, J. (2008a). Scandinavian exceptionalism in an era of penal excess part I: The nature and roots of Scandinavian exceptionalism. *The British Journal of Criminology*, 48(2), 119–137.

Pratt, J. (2008b). Scandinavian exceptionalism in an era of penal excess: part II: Does Scandinavian exceptionalism have a future? *The British Journal of Criminology*, 48(3), 275–292.

Shammas, V.L. (2016). The rise of a more punitive state: On the attenuation of Norwegian penal exceptionalism in an era of welfare state transformation. *Critical Criminology*, 24(1), 57–74.

Smith, P.S., & Ugelvik, T. (2017). *Punishment and welfare in Scandinavia.* In *Scandinavian penal history, culture and prison practice* (pp. 511–529). London: Palgrave Macmillan.

Smith, P.S. (2006). The effects of solitary confinement on prison inmates: A brief history and review of the literature. *Crime and Justice*, 34(1), 441–528.

Stack, S.J., & Tsoudis, O. (1997). Suicide risk among correctional officers: A logistic regression analysis. *Archives of Suicide Research*, 3(3), 183–186.

Steiner, B. (2008). *Maintaining prison order: Understanding causes of inmate misconduct within and across Ohio correctional institutions* (Doctoral dissertation). University of Cincinnati.

Steiner, B. (2009). Assessing static and dynamic influences on inmate violence levels. *Crime and Delinquency*, 55(1), 134–161.

Sudom, K., Dursun, S., & Flemming, S. (2006). *Perstempo in the canadian forces: The role of coping and cohesion in the relationship between job stress and morale.* Ontario: Department Of National Defence Ottawa.

Sykes, G. M.(1958). *The Society of Captives: A Study of a Maximum Security Prison.* Princeton, NY: Princeton University Press.

Uggen, C., Stewart, R., & Horowitz, V. (2018). Why not minnesota? Norway, justice reform, and 50-labs federalism. *Federal Sentencing Reporter*, 31(1), 5–13.

Violanti, J.M. (2017). Suicide behind the wall: A national analysis of corrections officer suicide. *Suicidology Online*, 8, 58–64.

Von Hirsch, A. (1976). *Doing Justice: The Choice of Punishments.* New York, NY: Hill & Wang.

Walters, G.D. (2020). Getting to the source: How inmates and other staff contribute to correctional officer stress. *Journal of Crime and Justice*, 1–14. doi:10.1080/0735648X.2020.1862696

Weakliem, D.L., & Frenkel, S.J. (2006). Morale and workplace performance. *Work and Occupations*, 33 (3), 335–361.

Appendices

Appendix A: Codebook.

Name	Description	Files	References
Danger	Any reference to danger	12	59
Direct Comparison International	Any direct international comparison.	12	208
Discipline-CO	Any reference to COs being disciplined	1	1
Discipline-Pris	Any reference to disciplining people in prison	11	51
Dynamic Security	Any mention of dynamic security	12	231
Exercise	Any mention of exercise	11	39
Food-Nutrition	Any discussion of food or nutrition	11	67
Fraternization	Any reference to the DOC's fraternization policy	8	62
Health depends on pris.	Any mention of how CO health depends on the wellbeing of incarcerated people.	10	25
Health-Mental	Any discussion of CO mental health	8	13
Health-Physical	Any discussion of CO physical health	10	15
Morale	Any discussion of correctional officer morale–positive or negative	12	116

Name	Description	Files	References
Staff-Prisoner ratio	Any discussion of staff-prisoner ratio	6	41
Stress	Any reference to work-related stress	11	47
Treatment by pris.	Any discussion of how incarcerated people treat COs/	11	66
Treatment by sup..	Any discussion of how COs are treated by their superiors	9	45
Uniforms	Any discussion of correctional officer uniforms	11	41
Weapons	Any discussion of weapons	8	25

Appendix B: Guide for Officer Daily Reflections

Correctional Officer Daily Diary Instructions

2019 PENNSYLVANIA CORRECTIONAL OFFICER DAILY DIARY

At the end of each day, use your recorder to answer the following questions: 15-45 min.

- Start by giving the date and time.
- Describe what you did during the day and where you were.
- What are the key things you learned?
- What, if anything, surprised you?
- How does what you saw today differ from what you see in Pennsylvania?
- What, if anything, stands out about the day?
- How do you feel about the day's experience?
- Record any other thoughts, feelings, or reflections you have about the day or your time in Scandinavian corrections to date.

Appendix C: Survey Instructions, Questions, Scoring

Survey Instructions:

For this section, think about your overall experience during this shift/day. Respond to each of the following statements indicating the extent to which you agree or disagree.

Exact Language of Questions Used in Figure:

(1) I am glad that I came to work today.
(2) I made a positive difference in prison life at least one inmate today.
(3) I felt safe during this shift/day.
(4) I felt stressed out during this shift/ day.
(5) I am not looking forward to coming to work tomorrow.
(6) I had positive interactions with other staff.
(7) This prison provides a positive working environment.

Survey Response Options and Scoring:

Each survey item is coded on a 5-point scale (1 = Strongly Disagree 2 = Disagree 3 = Neutral 4 = Agree 5 = Strongly Agree). The specific survey questions are as follows; (1) I am glad that I came to work today; (2) I made a positive difference in the overall prison environment today; (3) I felt safe during this shift/day; (4) I felt stressed out during this shift/day; (5) I am not looking forward to coming to work tomorrow; (6) I had positive interactions with other staff; (7) This prison provides a positive working environment.

Index

Italicized page refer to figures, those in **bold** refer to tables, and page numbers followed by "n" refer to notes.

www.ingramcontent.com/pod-product-compliance
Lightning Source LLC
LaVergne TN
LVHW080656011026
849160LV00014B/1450
* 9 7 8 1 0 3 2 4 0 7 0 9 8 *